D1571139

MARYLAND RENT ROLLS:

Baltimore and Anne Arundel Counties, 1700-1707, 1705-1724

A Consolidation of Articles from
the Maryland Historical Magazine

With a New Preface by Robert Barnes
and a Foreword by George B. Scriven

Reprinted with a New Index
By Anita Comtois

GENEALOGICAL PUBLISHING CO., INC.
BALTIMORE   1976

Excerpted from
the *Maryland Historical Magazine*,
1924-1931

Reprinted
with a New Preface,
Foreword, and Index
Genealogical Publishing Co., Inc.
Baltimore, 1976

Library of Congress Catalogue Card Number 76-1421
International Standard Book Number 0-8063-0716-1

Made in the United States of America

PREFACE

By Robert Barnes

The rent rolls in this volume were first published in the *Maryland Historical Magazine* from 1924 through 1931 and include the rent rolls for Baltimore and Anne Arundel Counties. The originals are part of the Calvert Papers now lodged in the manuscript division of the Maryland Historical Society. The Calvert Papers contain the rent rolls for several other Maryland counties and the collection is described more fully herein in the compiler's introduction. As the transcriber of these particular rolls points out, there were other rent rolls covering a later part of the colonial period. These rolls were deposited in the State Land Office but are now at the Hall of Records in Annapolis.

Rent rolls are of value to the genealogist in a number of ways. First, they help to establish an individual's date of arrival in Maryland. Dates of arrival are often difficult to ascertain since passenger lists for ships arriving in eighteenth-century Maryland have not survived in great numbers. The granting of land meant that the individual had arrived in Maryland by this time and—hopefully—was able to pay the taxes on the land.

Second, rent rolls often provide statements of vital genealogical significance. Not infrequently, remarriage of the widow of the original grantee can be traced, or the names of other heirs may be shown as later possessors of the tract. "Hooker's Chance" was surveyed for Thomas Hooker in 1678 in Anne Arundel County; a later owner was "Tho: Hooker the son, he lives in Balt. Co." Stephen Warman held 100 acres, part of "Townhill" (originally laid out for Edmund Townhill in 1659), in right of "his wife Hester the daughter of Nicholas Gassaway."

Finally, rent rolls may be helpful in supplying clues about the place of origin of a settler. "Ayno," surveyed in 1682 for Henry Hanslap, is the name of the English parish from which Hanslap came. Laurence Richardson named one of his surveys "Upper Tauton" [sic]. One must guard against the assumption, however, that a given tract name indicates an individual's place of origin. In 1663 Ferdinando Battee laid out a 300-acre tract called "Essex," but in 1677 he laid out another called "Suffolk."

These rolls may also be helpful to persons wishing to apply for membership in lineage societies such as the Daughters of American Colonists, who have as one of their entrance requirements proof of descent from an original grantee who received his land directly from the Crown or Proprietor of the colony.

Others besides the genealogist will find these rolls interesting. Students of local history and persons interested in the origin of place names will find interesting items in this volume. As the historian learns more and more of the tools and techniques of the genealogist, it may be that rent rolls such as these will prove helpful in studying patterns of land holding and sizes of plantations in early Maryland.

This book is one that will be of value to the genealogist, the historian, and the demographer. The Genealogical Publishing Company has made an important contribution to Maryland colonial history by making this material more accessible to the researcher.

FOREWORD

The Rent Rolls of Maryland

By George B. Scriven

The Rent Rolls were the private sets of manuscript books and pages which the Proprietors of Maryland had assembled at various times in the colonial period to keep account of the land grants in each county and of their owners from whom quit rent was due. A substantial number of these books have survived because it was customary to make duplicate copies. All of those in Maryland were confiscated by the new state government after the Revolution. Forty-nine volumes of them are at the Hall of Records at Annapolis, arranged, with few exceptions, under grant names, and usually within Hundreds. The Maryland Historical Society in Baltimore owns twenty-eight volumes of Rent Rolls which had been kept in England by the Calvert family and were purchased from the Calvert heirs in 1888.

Quit Rents came about in this way. In Colonial Maryland all land was first owned by the Proprietor, who had obtained it from the Crown before settlement began. He distributed land by gifts, in return for importing settlers and for other services, and by sale. In every instance the person who received the grant did not own it in the modern sense of the word, but held it under a medieval system "in common socage." In addition to whatever may have been paid in cash or services when the land was obtained, a semi-annual quit rent was due to the Proprietor forever after by the possessor of the land. These quit rents, though small in comparison with the land value, amounted in the aggregate to such a large figure that the Proprietors built up a system for keeping account of the debtors and collecting from them. Land might revert to the Proprietor for non-payment of quit rent and for certain other reasons such as treason, suicide, or lack of heirs. These quit rents, or their equivalent, were paid to the Proprietors throughout the colonial period, even during the time of the Royal Governors (1686-1715) when the Calverts did not have political control over Maryland.

From 1717 to 1733 when a tax of two shillings on each hogshead of tobacco replaced the quit rent, there was neglect in the keeping of the Rent Rolls. In 1734, when the rents were again paid to the Proprietor, new instructions were issued about collections, and thereafter additions of new grants and changes of possessors were made promptly in the Rent Rolls.

Rent Rolls, which continued to be made up to the Revolution, were supplemented by a series of Debt Books which began in 1733 and also continued to the Revolution. This series of books, consisting of annual books for each county, was organized under the names of land owners instead of the names of tracts of land.

Rent Rolls and Debt Books for Baltimore County for the whole colonial period (in addition to those at the Maryland Historical Society) are to be found at the Hall of Records at Annapolis where Libers 1, 2, 18, 19, 20, 21 and 22 in the Rent Roll series are concerned with Baltimore County, as are Libers 5 to 9 in the Debt Book series. For more information about these records see *Land Office and Prerogative Court Records of Colonial Maryland*, by Elisabeth Hartsook and Gust Skordas, (1948), reprinted Baltimore: Genealogical Publishing Co., Inc., 1968.

The Rent Roll of Baltimore County 1700

The portion of this volume dealing with Baltimore County is a reprint of a Baltimore County Rent Roll from the Calvert Papers which appeared in the *Maryland Historical Magazine* in various issues from December 1924 to December 1926. It lists the grants in the Baltimore County of that day (much larger than the present one) from the earliest grants to those of 1700, with later corrections to 1724. It thus provides much information about the settlers and the land grants of the seventeenth century, which is the basis upon which later history of the county was built.

All Maryland counties were divided into Hundreds, which were later replaced by electoral districts. The boundaries of Hundreds varied frequently, as did the limits of counties, most changes being due to growth in population. Within Baltimore County the names of the Hundreds and their boundaries were not always identical in the source documents for 1700.

The grants in this Rent Roll were divided into three Hundreds, namely, Spesutia, Gunpowder, and Patapsco. Each Hundred began at tidewater and went back into the woods, the outermost dwelling plantations in 1700 being about four miles from tidewater, though grants had been laid out about twice that far inland, especially in the stream valleys. It should be borne in mind that the Patapsco River was tidal in those days as far as Elkridge, where transoceanic ships landed. Spesutia Hundred lay between the Susquehanna River and Bush River, Gunpowder Hundred lay on both sides of Gunpowder River, extending from Bush River to Middle River, while Patapsco Hundred extended from Middle River to Anne Arundel County, thus placing within Baltimore County a strip of land a few miles wide on the south side of the Patapsco River.

As might be expected this Rent Roll fails to give some information which readers may hope to find, the most frustrating features being as follows:

1. The compilers did not always list grants in the Hundred in which the land was located.
2. Within Hundreds there is little apparent order in the sequence of listing.
3. Descriptions of locations are usually inadequate and sometimes in error.
4. Some entries are duplicated, and not all duplications are crossed out.
5. Grant names are not always given for some of the grants listed.
6. Some grants are listed which were taken away by older surveys. For example, within Spesutia Hundred "Ebeneezer's Lott" was wholly included within the bounds of "Mt. Yeo," though this fact was unknown to the compiler of the Rent Roll.

Certain of these inadequacies may be overcome by a comparison of this Rent Roll with the land owners mentioned in the ten-page "List of Taxables in Baltimore County, Anno. 1699" which was printed in the *Maryland Historical Magazine*, Vol. XII, No. 1 (March 1917). This list divides the Rent Roll's Gunpowder Hundred into the north and the south sides of Gunpowder River (the latter being called Middle River Hundred). It also divides Patapsco Hundred into Patapsco River North Side and Patapsco River South Side.

Great assistance in finding the location of grants may be obtained from the Plats of Land Grants in Baltimore County which are at the Maryland Historical Society. Other plats of individual grants and groups of grants are to be found in the courthouses of the areas which are now separated but were in Baltimore County in 1700, including Baltimore City. Many more plats are at the Hall of Records in Annapolis. Much information may be gleaned from the *Maryland Historical Magazine*, especially in the numerous articles by William B. Marye, which abound in information about specific grants within the original Baltimore County. Finally, if one persists in reading all of this printed information he may find more in the manuscript material to be searched in the Patent Series at the Hall of Records.

The Rent Roll of Anne Arundel County 1707

Reprinted in this volume there is also the 1707 Rent Roll of Anne Arundel County with some additions from the Rent Roll of 1705-1724. These Rent Rolls are also from the Calvert Papers and were originally printed in various issues of the *Maryland Historical Magazine* from

1927 to 1931. The Hundreds of the county mentioned are five: Herring Creek, West River, South River, Middle Neck, and a combined Broad and Town Neck Hundred. South River Hundred was then the most prosperous part of the county. Caleb Dorsey published "Original Land Grants of the South Side of Severn River," with a plat of the grants, in the *Maryland Historical Magazine*, Vol. 53, pp. 394-400 (Dec. 1958). See also his "Original Land Grants of Howard County, Maryland" in the same magazine, Vol. 64, pp. 287-294 (Fall 1969), for grants which were formerly in either Anne Arundel or Baltimore Counties.

Later Rent Rolls for this county are to be found in a volume for 1755 in the Calvert Papers and at the Hall of Records in the Rent Roll Series, Libers 1, 13, 14, 15, 16, and 17. See also in the Debt Book Series, Libers 1, 2, 3, 4 containing the Debt Book list for every year from 1753 to 1774, with the exception of the years 1772 and 1773.

MARYLAND RENT ROLLS.

The Maryland rent rolls are an invaluable source of information to students of the colonial history of the province. That so many have been preserved is doubtless due to the fact that the lord proprietary derived the greater part of his revenue from his annual quit-rents and from the alienation fees imposed whenever the ownership of land was transferred. From an early period he found it advisable to have duplicate copies of his rent rolls sent to him in England, probably both as a measure of safety in case of the loss of the copy preserved in the province, and as a means of checking up the zeal of his collectors of revenue there.

When the Maryland Historical Society in 1888 acquired from the heirs of the Calverts the priceless collection of manuscript material bearing upon the history of the province known now as the " Calvert Papers," among them were some twenty-eight rent rolls for the several counties compiled at various dates. In addition to the rent rolls among the " Calvert Papers," the Annapolis Land Office has a very complete series of rent rolls, numbering in all some forty-nine volumes, brought down to a later period than are those found in the " Calvert Papers."

In compiling the rent rolls, separate rolls were drawn up for each county and there was often a further subdivision of the county into hundreds. Each entry includes the name of the tract as given in the patent, the acreage, the date when the land was surveyed, the name of the original grantee, the location of the tract, the amount of the annual rent, and, usually, the name of the " possessor " of the tract at the time when the rent roll was compiled. The rent rolls for a given period thus form what is practically a complete list of all the landholders of the province, but do not usually include the names of lot owners in the various mushroom towns which existed largely on paper, nor do they include under the heading of " possessor " the names of those who may have actually occupied the lands but were simply lessees.

While owing to the diversity of dates a hard and fast grouping of the various rent rolls into definite series is difficult, for the purpose of reference some such classification must be attempted. This is made still more difficult because some of the rent rolls are not marked with the actual date of their compilation, and others have additional later entries in a different handwriting made several years after the original roll was compiled. The rent rolls of the various Maryland counties seem however in general to

1

fall into some five series, which for convenience of reference may be grouped as follows:

Series A. 1658-1659.

1658 Calvert County.	1659 St. Mary's County.
1659 Isle of Kent.	1659 Charles County.

These are unbound sheets and are probably the oldest original land records of the province.

Series B. 1700-1707.

1700 Baltimore County.	1707 Kent County.
1707 Anne Arundel County.	1707 St. Mary's County.
1707 Calvert County.	1707 Somerset County.
1707 Cecil County.	1707 Talbot County.
1707 Dorchester County.	

The rent roll for Baltimore County is made up of unbound sheets. Those for the remaining eight counties, all dated 1707, are small folios on rather thin paper in rough paper bindings.

Series C. Undated (about 1705-1724).

{Anne Arundel County.	{Somerset County.
{Baltimore County.	{Dorchester.
{Calvert County.	{Talbot County.
{Prince George's County.	{Queen Anne County.
{Kent County.	
{Cecil County.	

These are undated and it is difficult to fix the exact date, or rather dates, of their actual compilation. It would appear that the greater part of the entries, comprising about the first two-thirds of each book were largely based upon the 1707 series B rent roll, although there are a few differences in the names of the " possessors " of tracts, indicating that some later changes had been made. The latter third of each book is made up of a number of later entries, many in a different handwriting, bringing the lists down to about the year 1724. But it is to be noted that these later entries usually give only the names of the original patentees and do not give any changes in the names of the " possessors " which may have occurred since the patent was issued.

This series is in five large folio volumes on very heavy paper, two counties to each volume, and the volumes are substantially bound.

Series D. 1753-1762.

1755 Anne Arundel County.	1753 Charles County.
1753 Calvert County.	1762 Charles County.
1759 Calvert County.	

These are small folios bound in rough paper covers. It is to be noted that the only rent rolls for Charles County among the "Calvert Papers" are in this series.

Series E. The Land Office at Annapolis possesses a complete set of rent rolls for all the counties, but no description of these volumes need be made here.

It is proposed to print in the *Magazine* a rent roll for each of the counties, and Series B (1700-1707), where available, seems most suitable for this purpose. The first rent roll to appear will be that for Baltimore County. It will be noted that the Series B rent roll for this county runs down only to the year 1700. It therefore seems advisable also to make use of the rent roll for this county of Series C, bringing the roll down several years later. The Baltimore County rent roll, like others of Series C, is undated and seems to have been compiled at two different periods. The first two-thirds of the book is made up of a roll probably compiled about 1706 or 1707, and gives the names of the "possessors" of the tracts at this time; the remaining third of the book is made up of entries of tracts patented from about this date down to the year 1724, but in the case of these later entries, only the names of the original patentees are given, the names of the "possessors" not being entered at all. The two Baltimore rent rolls will be used to supplement each other. The 1700 rent roll will be first printed unchanged and in its entirety in Roman type, and where the later undated rent roll differs from that of 1700, the differences in the case of each tract entry will be added in italics. After all the entries in the Series B 1700 roll, thus annotated, and numbering in all about 600 have been printed, all entries appearing only in Series C will follow in later installments and will be printed in italics so as to distinguish them from the earlier roll.

It must be remembered that the bounds of Baltimore County at the time covered by these rent rolls were very different from its present limits. All of Harford County, a part of Carroll County, and that part of Anne Arundel County lying along the south side of the Patapsco River, from the bay westward to the highlands beyond Elkridge, were then parts of Baltimore County. The tracts of the 1700 rent roll are classified under the three hundreds into which the county was then divided, viz. Spesutia, Gunpowder, and Patapsco hundreds, while in the later roll there is no definite division under hundreds.

Baltimore County, 1700-1724.

Spesuty hunder[d]

Spesuty Island, 2300 acres surveyed the 25 July for Coll[l] Nathaniell Vtye and Island neare Western shore, neare the head

3

of the bay Called beare point granted by patten the 9th Day of August 1660 now in the " Ocupatio " of Jn⁰ Hall and Mark Richardson for the Orphans of George Vtye ℔ annum £2.. 6.. 0

C. Spesutie.

Carters Rest, 400 acres sur. the 25th July 1661 for Edward Carter on the South side of Musketo Creeke 130 acres part thereof sould to Edward Beedle and now in posetion of John Hall and Mark Richardson for the Orphant of George Vtye rent ℔ anum £—.. 2.. 7¼

C. In possession of John Hall, 130 a.; Anthony Drew, 180 a.; Samuel Jackson, 90 a.

Benjamins Choice, 400 acres sur. the 11th May 1678 of Coll George Wells at a bounded white oake by the Cranberry Swamp and sould to George Vtye and now in the posetion of John Hall and Mark Richardson for the Orphant of George Vtye Rent ℔ anum £—.. 16.. —

C. In pos. John Hall.

Vtyes Rumnye, 300 acres sur. the 15th July 1658 on the west side of Chesepeake bay neare rumley creeke posesed by Mark Richardson for the Orphant of the s^d Vtye, rent ℔ anum £—.. 6.. —

C. Rumney. [*Later known as Rumley and Romley.*] *In pos. John Hall.*

Vytes Adittion, 45 acres sur. the 19th May 1687 for George Vtye lying on the South side of Rumley creeke in posestion of Mark Richardson for the Orphan of George Vtye rent ℔ anum £—.. 1.. 9½

C. In pos. John Hall.

Beedles Reserve, 100 acres sur. Septem^r the 22nd 1680 for Edwd Beedle neare the head of Swan Creek at a bounded popelar by a small run belonging to the Orphan of George Vtye Rent ℔ annum £—.. 4.. —

C. In pos. John Hall.

Goldsmiths Enlargement, 90 acres sur. for George Goldsmith the 17th day of June 1663 on the west side of Spesuty Creeke and now in the posetion of Jn⁰ Hall for the Orphans of George Goldsmith rent ℔ annum £—.. —.. 5

C. 70 a. in pos. George Wells.

Stepney, 200 acres sur. the 3ᵈ of Octobʳ 1683 for John Miles on the East side of bush river on the Eastern branch of the sᵈ river, rent ℔ anum £—.. 8.. —

C. In pos. Archibald Buchanan.

Adition, 200 acres sur. the 6ᵗʰ of Octobʳ 1695 for John Miles called the adition on the north side of Eastern branch of back river beging at a bounded white oak neare a run on the south side, rent ℔ anum £—.. 8.. —

C. On Bush river.

Spryes Inheritance, 640 acres sur. the 12ᵗʰ febʳ 1668 for Oliver Spry on the East side of back river begingᵍ at a bounded red oak at the head of Rumley Creek, belonging to the Orphants of Cap. Henry Johnson it is supposed not halfe so much, rent ℔ anum £—.. 12.. —

C. On Bush river.

Hammond's Hope, 300 acres sur. the 13ᵗʰ May 1678 for James Hammond on the south side of Swan creek at a bounded red oake by a greate marsh and runing by the creek noe heires appear Hammond being dead, rent ℔ anum £—.. 12.. —
This Land is Lyeable To an Escheate

Planters Delight, 600 acres sur. the 15ᵗʰ July 1658 for John Hawkins and Tho. Goldsmith on the west side of Chesepeake bay respecting the mouth of Sasafras river and now in the posetion of the Orphans of Coll. Wells, rent ℔ anum £—.. 12.. —

C. 250 a. in pos. George Wells; 100 a. Thomas Frizbey; 250 a. Richard Smythers.

Colingham, 100 acres sur. the 4ᵗʰ Novemʳ 1658 for John Collet on the west side of Spesuty Creek sould to John Ireland being gone away is now in the posetion of Ralph Gilian rent ℔ annum £—.. 2.. —
This Land is Lyable to an Escheat

C. Colingham, now called Greenfields, in pos. of Thomas Greenfield's orphan.

5

Black Island, 100 acres Sur. the 12th May 1662 for John Collet on the south of the mouth of musketa Creek and posesed by the Orphants of Coll. Wells, rent ℔ anum £—.. 2.. —

    C. In pos. Thomas Frizby.

Goldsmith rest, 630 acres Sur. the 3rd July 1682 for George Goldsmith wth a south course for a bounded hickory tree wch is the first mentioned bounds in a patten &c and takeing in the orchard and some part of the plantation Containing noe more as ℔ certificate of resurvey returned into the office and now in the occupation of John Hall for the Orphant of George Goldsmith, rent ℔ anum £1.. 5.. 2½

    C. In pos. George Wells.

The Surveyor's point, 500 acres Sur. the 26 March 1666 for George Goldsmith on the northern branch of gunpowder river on the western side of the s^{d} branch and now in the posetion of John Hall for the Orphants of George Goldsmith rent ℔ anum £1.. —.. —

Relye, 200 acres Sur. the 9th August 1659 for James Robinson on the north side of Swan Creeke and now in the posetion of Mark Richardson Rent ℔ anum £—.. 4.. —

    C. Reylie, in pos. Thomas Wainwright.

Mattson Lot, 10 acres Sur. the 13th April 1682 for Andrew Mattson on the south side of Swan creeke at a bounded red oak the bounded tree and called reley and now in the posetion of Mark Richardson Rent ℔ anum £—.. —.. 5

    C. In pos. Thomas Wainwright.

Popular Neck, 1000 acres Sur. Septemb^{r} the 20th 1683 for Mark Richardson on the head of bush river on the south west branch of the s^{d} river at a bounded beach standing by a Valley by a run neare the afores^{d} branch rent ℔ anum £2.. —.. —

    C. Poplar Neck, in pos. William Nicholson.

Proctors Hall, 200 acres Sur. the 30th August 1659 for George Goldsmith and Nathaniell Proctor and now in the posetion of William Osburne for the Orphan of John Walsh rent ℔ anum £—.. 4.. —

    C. In pos. John Walston's orphan.

The Enlargment, 200 acres Sur. the 27th feb. 1665 for George Goldsmith lying in Swan creek on the south side joyning to the s^d proctors Hall and now in the posetion aforesaid for the aforesaid Orphants Rent ℈ anum £—.. 4.. —

C. Inlargement. In pos. of John Walston's orphan.

Holly Neck, 475 acres Sur. the 17th Novem^r 1664 for Richard Wells Senr on the south side of Middle river and now in the posetion of Orphant of Coll. Wells, rent ℈ anum £—.. 9.. 6 [1]

Colletts Point, 320 acres Sur. the 20th Novem^r 1668 for John Collett neare an Island Called the black Island formerly Sur. for John Collett posesed by the Orphant of Coll Wells rent ℈ anum £—.. 6.. 4

C. Pos. of George Wells. This land formerly called Wells Neck cont. 1100 a. resurv. and fo^d to contain no more y^n as above s^d.

C. In pos. Thomas Frizby.

Timber Proof, 200 acres Sur. the 22^d of decemb^r 1672 for George Wells in delph Creek at a marked gum upon the point of march at the head of the creek belonging to the Orphants of Coll. Wells rent ℈ anum £—.. 8.. —

C. In pos. George Wells, Jr.

Walston's Adition, 81 acres Sur. the 12th July 1678 for John Walston's in the woods at a bounded red oake by a pocoson of Coll. Wells his Land and now in the posetion of the Orphants of Coll. Wells rent ℈ anum £—.. 3.. 2

C. In pos. George Wells.

Goldsmiths Hall, 800 acres Sur. the 15th July 1658 for Sam^{ll} Goldsmith neare a joyning to the Land of John Hawkings upon the west side of Chesepeke bay belonging to the Orphans of Coll. Wells rent ℈ anum £—.. 16.. —

Porte Royall, 50 acres Sur. the 5th Jan^{ry} 1671 for John Disgarden in Rumley creeke at marked red oak wth in a point at

---

[1] In Gunpowder Hundred.

the side of a marsh and now in the posetion of Robert Gibson rent ⅌ anum £—.. 2.. —

C. In pos. Capt. Thomas Bale.

Porte Royall purchase, 100 acres Sur. the 13th Aprill 1680 for Miles Gibson to the norward of port royall at a bounded red oake and now in the poset of Robert Gibson rent ⅌ anum £—.. 4.. —

C. In pos. Capt. Thomas Bale.

Persimon point, 400 acr. Sur. 1st August 1659 for James Rigby on the north side of rumley creeke and now in the posetion of Robert Gibson rent ⅌ anum £—.. 8.. —

C. In pos. Capt. Thomas Bale.

Langleys Habitation, 300 acres Sur. the 30th of August 1659 for Thomas Overton on the west side of Spesuty creek and now in the posetion of John Kemball rent ⅌ anum £—.. 6.. —

C. In pos. John Hall.

Oakington, 800 acr. Sur. the 5th Septem^r 1659 for Coll. Nathall Vtye 500 them of sold to Edwd Beedle and now in posetion of Thomas Browne rent ⅌ anum £—.. 10..—

300 acr. Being the remaining part of oakington formerly surveyed for Coll. Vtye sold and in the posetion Garret Garretson rent ⅌ anum £—.. 6.. —

C. In pos. Thomas Browne, 500 a.; Garrett Garrettson, 300 a.

New Parke, 150 acr. Sur. Septemb^r the 25th 1683 for John Yeo near a place called the Levil in the woods begining at a marked red oake by a Swamp neare Calers rest bequethed by the s^d Yeo onto the afores^d Garrett Garrettson who poseseth the same rent ⅌ anum £—.. 6.. — [Rev. John Yeo]

Cranbury Hall, 1547 acr. Sur. the 14th Octob^r 94 for John Hall begining at a bounded popular stands by the mill spring runing south rent ⅌ anum £3.. 1.. 11

Aquilas Inheritance, 732 acr. Sur. decem^r the 19th 1699 for John Hall begining at a bounded popular standing in a fork of the branches deer creek and runing north 28 degrees Easterly, rent ⅌ anum £1.. 9.. 0

8

The fork, 150 acr. Sur. the 4th Septem^r 1683 for James Phillips on the East side of bush river at a bounded oake standing at the End of the west southwest side Line of Land Called Goodhope formerly sur. for James Baines and now in the posetion of Edward Welldy Rent ℔ anum £—.. 6.. —

The Stoop, 118 acr. Sur. the 24th March 1679 for George Yates between the lands of Capt Thomas Stockett at a bounded Chesnutt tree by a branch Called born branch posesed by Tho. Brown rent ℔ anum £—.. 4.. 8

C. In pos. John Brown.

Delph Island, 115 acr.. Sur. the 14th July 1662 for Henry Stockett on the northerly side of rumley Creek and now in the posestion of Robert Gibson, rent ℔ anum £—.. 2.. 4

C. In pos. Capt. Thomas Bale.

Gibsons Marsh, 200 acr. Sur. the 3rd Septemb^r 1683 for Miles Gibson joyning upon rumley Creek at the south point of an Island Called Delph Island and now In the posetion of Robert Gibson rent ℔ anum £—.. 8.. —

C. In pos. Capt. Thomas Bale.

Gibson Ridge, 500 acr. Sur. the 19th of Septem^r 1683 for Miles Gibson on the South west branch of bush river at a bounded popular on a ridge neare the affores^d branch and now In the posetion of Robert Gibson rent ℔ anum £1.. —.. —

C. In pos. Capt. Thomas Bale, 364 a.; Henry Rodes, 136 a.

Gibsons park, 800 acr. Sur. the 19th Septem^r 1683 for Miles Gibson on the South most branch of bush river at a bounded red oake standing neare the s^d branch and in the posetion of Robert Gibson, rent ℔ anum £1.. 12.. —

C. In pos. Anth. Bale, 500 a.; George Wells, 200 a.; Thos. Beale, 100 a.

North Yarmouth, 200 acr. Sur. the 14th Septemb^r 1683 for James Fugate upon the head of Swan Creek at a bounded Hickery standing by the head of the s^d Creek and now in the posetion of Robert Gibson rent ℔ anum £—.. 8.. —

C. In pos. Thos. Brown.

Halls ridge neck, 400 acr. Sur. the 19th of decemb^r 1699 for John Hall and Martha his wife beginging at a bounded black wallnut standing on a ridge near a branch of deer Creek, runing thence East west and be south rent ⅌ anum £—.. 16.. —

C. *Rich Neck.*

Hunting worth, 150 acres Sur. the 17th August 1659 for Abraham Holdman on the East side of bush river and now In posetion of Sam^{ll} Browne rent ⅌ anum £—.. 3.. —

C. *In pos. James Phillips, 100 a.; Samuel Brown, 50 a.*

Chilbery, 250 acr. Sur. the 2nd feb^{ry} for William Orchard lying on the East side of bush river and now In the posetion of Perygreen Brown of London Merchant, rent ⅌ anum £—.. 5.. —

The Adition, 400 acr. Sur. the 24th Octob^r 1668 for Walter Tucker on the East side of bush river on south ward of a creek posesed by the afores^d Browne, rent ⅌ anum £—.. 8.. —

Batchelors Hope, 400 acres Sur. the 28 Aprill 1668 for William Tomson on the East side of bush river on the west side of bush hunting creek branch and In the posetion of the afores^d Brown £—.. 8.. —

Batchelors Adition, 50 acr. Sur. the 28th Aprill 1673 for William Tomson on the north side of hunting Creeke the East side of bush river and now In the posetion of the afores^d Perigreen Brown all these aboves^d parcells of Land did formerly belong to one Walter Tucker and Company and since sould to the s^d Perigreen Brown, rent ⅌ anum £—.. 1.. —

French plantation, 100 acr. Sur. the 22nd Jan^{ry} 1673 for Peter Fewcate at the head of a little Creek Called Cathol Creeke at marked red oake nigh a pocoson and now in the posetion of Thomas Cord, rent ⅌ anum £—.. 2.. —

C. *Catthole Creeek.*

Collett point, 400 acr. Sur. the 30th Aprill 1668 for John Collet on the Eastward side of bush river between the north west branch and the midle branch Collet being dead and all his heires the Land In cultivated noe rent payd these 16 years it is lyable to an Escheat, rent ℔ anum £—.. 8.. —

   C. No rent paid these 20 years. [Note another tract of same name on the Chesapeake.]

Mascolls humor, 50 acr. Sur. the 6th Novemb^r 1673 for Andrew Bennet at the head of Musketo Creek at a Marked oake and In the posetion of Thomas Jackson, rent ℔ annum £—.. 1.. —

   C. Markoll's Humour in pos. John Hall.

Yorks hope, 200 acr. Sur. the 16 Novemb^r 1664 for William York on the northermost side of Gunpowder river John Yeo had a madamas upon the Land was granted him Yeo is since dead Left no heires here his relations live in the west of England rent not recev^d this 16 years the Land Cultivated, rent ℔ anum £—.. 4.. —

This Land Lyes Gunpowder hundred. This Land Charge after

The Grove, 250 acr. Sur. the 3rd Jan^{ry} 1671 for John Tarkinton at the Head of Musketa Creek at a marked white oake by the side of a branch of the said Creek Palmer dead and all his heires here the Land Cultivated and his Widdow holds it for right of her thirds the Land Lyes under an escheate, rent ℔ anum £—.. 5.. —

This Land Lyes under an Escheat

   C. Miles Hennis pays rent.

Clemmens Denn, 100 acr. Sur. the 16 of ———— 1664 for William Osburn in rumley Creek on the south side of the Creek and now in the posetion of John Savory, rent ℔ anum £—.. 2.. —

   C. In pos. William Prichard. [*St. Clement Danes?*]

Peter Adition, 100 acr. Sur. the 29th Novem^r 1685 for Peter Fewcate, rent per anum

   C. In pos. Thomas Cord.

Part of Carters Rest, 180 acr. Sur. W^{ch} was sume of the formerly sur. for Edward Carter the 25th of July 1661 wch was sold Ruthan Garrett and is now in the posetion of Anthony Drew, rent ℔ anum £—.. 3.. 7¼

90 acr. the residue of Carters rest wch was sold to Robert Jones and now in the posetion of Samuell Jackson, rent ℔ anum £—.. 1.. — [Not in *C.*]

Delph, 600 acre Sur. the 15th Aprill 1669 for Frances Stockett neare rumly marsh on the western side of a Tract of Land formerly taken up by Maj^r Goldsmith now belonging to the heires James Fendall but now in the posetion of Thomas Newsum, rent ℔ anum £—.. 12.. —

Delph's Neglect, 120 acr. Sur. the 13th March 1683 for Miles Gibson on the west side of Delph Creek at a Locust Stump the first bounded tree of delph and now to the heires of James Fendall in the Kingdome of England, rent ℔ anum £—.. 4.. —

Clement, 50 acr. Sur. the 15th Septemb^r 1666 for William Orchard in rumley Creek on the west side of the Creek and now in the posetion of John Savory, rent ℔ anum £—.. 1.. —
C. In pos. William Prichard.

Hunting Neck, 300 acr. Sur. the 25th Aprill 1668 for Thomas Cole and William Hollis on the East side of bush river at the head of hunting Creek and on the East side of the same Creek and now in the posetion of George Smith for the Orphans of Daniell Peverell, rent ℔ anum £—.. 6.. —
C. In pos. David Thomas for orphans of Daniel Peverill.

Mates Angle, 100 acr. Sur. the 12th Novemb^r 1668 for Wm Osburn and John Lee on the Eastern side of bush river at the norward bounds of Lamberts marsh and now in the posetion of George Smith, rent ℔ anum £—.. 2.. —
C. In pos. David Thomas for George Smith's orphans.

Palmers Forrest, 600 acr. Sur. the 9th of Septemb^r 1673 for Wm Palmer at a marked red oak upon a point in neck between 2 branches of the Cranbury Swamp Palmer being dead no heires here Land In cultivated noe rent payd these 16 years, rent ℔ anum £1.. 4.. 0
This Land is Lyable to an Escheat
C. No rent paid these 20 years.

Palmers point, 500 acr. Sur. the 23rd June 1675 for William Palmer on the west side of Swan Creek at a marked Locust upon the point of a marsh palmer being dead and noe heires here Land Cultivated noe rent payd these 16 years, rent ℔ anum £1.. —.. —

The Land is Lyable to an Escheat

Swan Harbour, 300 acr. Sur. the 5th August 1675 for Wm Palmer on the north East side of Swan Creeke the northermost tree of the Land Called oakington this Land Called as above, rent ℔ anum £—.. 12.. —

The Land is Lyable to an Escheat

Goodmans Adventure, 250 acr. Sur. the 13th May 1678 for Edward Goodman on Swan Creek beginging at a bounded wt oak and Runing south west and by south to a hickery Goodman being killed by the Indians no heires appear Land uncultivated, rent ℔ anum £—.. 10.. —

The Land is Lyable to an Escheat

Turky Hill, 200 acr. Sur. the 29th of June 1672 for John James in bush river in James Creek at a marked oak on the north side of a branch now posesed by Thomas Thurston, rent ℔ anum £—.. —.. —

C. In pos. John Devor.

Millend, 100 acr. Sur. the 5th July 1672 for Miles Gibson in rumley Creek on the East side of the northermost branch of the said Creek posesed by Roger Mathews, rent ℔ anum £—.. 4.. —

C. Mile End.

Wilson Range, 100 acr. Sur. the 18 Novemr 1686 for John Willson Lyeing in the north side of bush river and now in the posetion of Stephen Freeland, rent ℔ anum £—.. 4.. —

Pork Point, 100 acr. Sur. the 14th Aprill 1667 for James Phillips on the East side of bush river and posesed by the said James Phillips, rent ℔ anum £—.. 2.. —

Vper Eling, 100 acr. Sur. the 17th August 1659 for Thomas Sampson on the East side of bush river wch said Land was

Escheated and granted Petition unto James Phillips, rent ℔ anum £—.. 4.. —

Chelsey, 125 acr. Sur. the 10th March 1676 for James Phillips on the north side of bush river at the southermost bounds of the Land Called Crabhill 100 acr. part thereof sold and posesed by George Smith, rent ℔ anum £—.. 2.. —

The residue of Chelsey now in the posetion of James Phillips, rent ℔ anum £—.. —.. 6

C. Chelsea Resurveyed, In pos. David Thomas for George Smiths' orphans, 100 a.; James Phillips, 25 a.

Phillips Swamp, 100 acre Sur. the 15th July 1672 for James Phillips at the head rumley Creek at a marked Hickery in the woods at the west side of a pond, rent ℔ anum £—.. 4.. —

Pocoson, 100 acre Sur. the 20th Aprill 1673 for James Phillips at the head of rumley Creek at a marked wt oake in the woods, rent ℔ anum £—.. 4.. —

Lambarts Marsh, 100 acr. Sur. the 23rd March 1665 for William Orchard on the Eastern side of bush river and now In the posetion of James Phillips, rent ℔ anum £—.. 4.. —

C. 50 a. in pos. Thomas Hanson.

Crab Hill, 100 acr. Sur. the 23rd of March 1665 for John Lee on the East side of bush river at the Southermost bounds of a parcell of Land Uper Eling and now in the posetion of James Phillips, rent ℔ anum £—.. 2.. —

Rockford, 300 acr. Sur. the 10th June 1679 for Thomas Ford on the west side of Susquehanna at a bounded popular the northward bound of a Tract of Land Laid out for Edward Parish and now in the posetion of James Ford, Rent ℔ anum £—.. 12.. —

C. In pos. James Ford's orphans.

Eaton, 400 acr. Sur. the 14th June 1679 for John Larkins on the west side of Susquehanna river at a bounded Spanish oake and all one point by a small broock now in the posetion of James Phillips, rent ℔ anum £—.. 16.. —

Harmonds Swan Town, 200 acr. Sur. the 15th of Aprill 1658
for Godfrey Harmer and James Robertson neare Swan Creek
and now in the ocupation of James Phillips suposing to belong
to the orphan of Edward Boothbey, rent ℔ anum £—.. 4.. —

Martins Rest, 196 acr. Sur. for Lodwick Martin lying on the
west side of Chesepeeke bay neare the mouth of Susquehanna
river and now in the posetion of James Phillips for the Orphant
of Edward Boothbey, rent ℔ anum £—.. 7.. —

Chilberg Hall, 250 acr. Sur. the 15th June 1668 for John Lee
on the north side of bush river at a bounded oak at a point of
a marsh neare the head of the west branch 125 acres here of
posesed by Anthony Drew, rent ℔ anum £—.. 2.. 6
125 acres residue thereof noe heires here as yet Claimes any
Just title to same, rent ℔ anum
  C. Chilbury, in pos. Anthony Drew.

Friendship, 1000 acre Sur. the 15th June 1697 for Robert
Lockwood at a bounded Spanish oak on a point on the East side
of a branch of bush river Called the midle branch and now
in the posetion of John Wilson, rent ℔ anum £2.. —.. —
  C. In pos. heirs of John Wilson, of Ann Arundel co.

Moulds Sucses, 400 acre Sur. the 10th June 1681 for John
Mould on the west side of Swan Creek begining at a bounded
Locust tree standing on the south side of a deep Valley and now
In the posetion of Henry Borne, rent ℔ anum £—.. 16.. —
  C. 198 a. in pos. Lawrence Draper; 100 a, John Cotterel;
102 a. taken away by an elder survey.

Vincents Castles, 500 acr. Sur. the 13th July 1683 for Vincent
Low Esqr on the west side Susquehanna river begining at a
bounded Locust standing by the river side the bounded tree
of the Land Called Phillips hope formerly taken up by the s^d
Phillips & now belong^s to the Exec^r of the s^d Low, rent ℔
anum £1.. —.. —
  C. And belongs to exers of said Lowe, belongs to the heirs of
Coll. Burgess.

Mount Yeo, 400 acr. Sur. the 9th June 1683 for John Yeo on the west side of Susquehanna river beging^g at a bounded burch at the mouth of deer Creek runing along the river; Yeo dead Land uncultivated his heire in west of England noe rent made since it was first taken up rent set £—.. 16.. —

Phillips Purchase, 2000 acres Sur. the 15th July 1683 for James Phillips on the west side of Susquehanna river begining at a bounded Locust the bound tree of the Land Called Ann's Lott formerly taken up for Miles Gibson and now in the posetion of Thomas Tench Esqr, rent ℔ anum £4.. —.. —

Parker Chance, 550 acres Sur. the 15th June 1683 for George Parker on the west side of Susquehanna river beginging at a bounded red oak on the North side of deer Creek bounded tree of the Land Called Mount Yeo belonging to the Orphants of the s^d Parker, rent ℔ anum £1.. 2.. —

> C. In pos. Capt. Thomas Gray.

Elford Feilds, 500 acres Sur. the 10th June 1684 for Wm Blackinston at a bounded red oak standing upon a ridge neare to James run on the North East and by North Line of a parcell of Land Called Abbots forrest noe rent made here Blackinston gone the Land uncultivated, rent set £1.. —.. —

> C. Blackinston run away.

Langlyes Forrest, 356 acres Sur. the 10th March 1683 for Robert Langlyes in the woods above the head of Swan Creek Langlye dead noe heires here Land uncultivated noe mad since it was taken up first rent ℔ anum £—.. 14.. 3

Lines Tent, 1000 acres Sur. the 11th May 1684 for Phillip Lines on the west side of Susquehanna river at a bounded red oak and formerly sur. for Thomas Taylor, rent ℔ anum £2.. —.. —

Abotts Forrest, 1000 acre Sur. the 16th June 1684 for George Abott on the north side of the western branch of bush river at a bounded w^t oak standing by James run on the north East Line of Thomas Sterling Land belonging to the heires of Abott, rent ℔ anum £2.. —.. —

> C. In pos. Alexander Parran.

Friendship, 600 acres Sur. the 10th May 1684 for Wm Harris on the west side of Susquehanna river at a bounded red oak a bounded tree of the Land Called Canaan supose it belong to the Orphans of Wm Harris upon the Clift, rent ℔ anum £1..4.. —

Land of Promise, 2000 acres Sur. the 14th May 1684 for Coll. Thomas Taylor on the west side of Susquehanna river at a bounded oak stand on the decent of a hill near to a river standing at the west End of a parcell of Land taken up by Thomas Griffin, rent ℔ anum £4.. —.. —

Andrews Conquest, 780 acr. Sur. the 10th Septemb^r 1683 for Andrew Matson upon a Creek Called Swan Creek at a bounded red oak in the southwest and by south Line of Cooks Chance Matson dead the Land uncultivated noe rent mad of this since it was first taken up great p^{rt} of it taken a way by an Elder sur. noe heires appeare yet, rent set £1..11..2½
Q. Whether any heires or not,

Fewgates Fork, 300 acr. Sur. the 14th Septem^r 1683 for Fewgate in woods upon the branch of Swan Creek a bounded hickery standing by the main run of the afores^d Creek Fewgate run away Into Virginia noe heires appeare here as yet noe rent mad here as yet, rent set £—..12.. —

Benjamens Choice, 254 acres Sur. the 25th Septem^r 1683 for Thomas Hedge in the woods by the Cranbury Swamp at a bounded w^t oake a bounded tree of the Land of Coll. George Wells and now belong^g to the heires of Thomas Hedge, rent ℔ anum £—..10..2

Expectation, 350 acres Sur. the 25th September 1683 for Peter Ellis in the woods above the head of Musketa Creek at a bounded Spanish oak a bounded tree of Land Called the Grove belonging to John Ellises heires, rent ℔ anum £—..14.. —

C. 100 a. William Stevens; 200 a. Samuel Jackson; 50 a. Tobias Emerson.

Sisters Dowrey, 120 acres Sur. Anno Domini 1683 for Andrew

Matson near the head of Swan Creek at a bounded red oak standing by a Vally and now in the posetion of Emanuell Smith rent ℔ anum £—.. 4.. 4

    C. In pos. Emnanual Smith's orphan.

Robin Hoods Forrest, 150 acres Sur. the 8th Septemb[r] 1683 for Robert Jones near the head of Swan Creek in the woods at a bounded w[t] oak standing near the maine branch of the s[d] Creek and now In the posetion of John Hall, rent ℔ anum £—.. 6.. —

    C. In pos. John Hall, Sr.

Cookes Neck, 100 acres Sur. the 10th Sept. 1683 for John Cooke at a bounded red oake a bounded tree of the Land of Edward Beedle and belongs to the Orphants of John Cooke, rent ℔ anum £—.. 4.. —

    C. Cookes Rest, in pos. Thomas Coard.

Contest, 100 acre Sur. the 22[d] August 1683 for Samuell Brand on the head of Swan Creek at a bounded black oak by a marsh side and belonging to the Orphants of Capt. Henry Johnson, rent ℔ anum £—.. 4.. —

Beales Camp, 1000 acres Sur. the 22[d] Septemb[r] 1683 for Ninian Beale on the head bush river on the north side of the south west branch of the s[d] river at a bounded w[t] oak respecting to the Land of Mark Richardson, rent ℔ anum £2.. —.. —

    C. In pos. Archibald Edmondson.

Driesdale Habitation, 200 acre Sur. the 18 September 1683 for Robert Drisdale at a bounded red oak a bounded tree of Edward Beedles Land and in the posetion of John Fendall, rent ℔ anum £—.. 8.. —

    C. In pos. John Fendall; John Roberts claims.

100 acres Sur. the 22[d] Septemb[r] 1683 for Daniell Lawrence in the woods at the head of bush river at a bounded red oak Lawrence dead noe heire appears here Land uncultivated noe rent made since taken up, rent ℔ anum £—.. 4.. —
Q. Whether Lyable to an Escheate I am inform'd Thomas Lilefoot bought it if soe as the rest of Lilefoots Land.

Good hoope, 200 acres Sur. the 19th Septem^r 1683 for James Banister on the East side of bush river at a bounded oak a bounded tree of the Land Called East land wells formerly taken up for one Ogburn Banister dead his heires Carried out of this province 15 years agoe and not return'd the Land uncultivated noe made of this since the first takeing up rent set, £—.. 8.. —

Lynes Adition, 600 acres Sur. the 16th July 1684 for Phillip Lynes on the west side of Susquehanna river at a bounded red oak on a ridge at the End of the north and be west Line of another pcell of land formerly taken for the s^d Lynes, rent ℔ anum £1.. 4.. —

Contryvance, 200 acr. Sur. the 23rd August 1683 for James Phillips near the head of delph creek at a white oak by a swamp side and now In the posetion of John Carvell, rent ℔ anum £—.. 8.. —

C. In pos. Thomas Newsum.

Langleys Tents, 640 acr. Sur. the 4th Aprill 1684 for Robert Langley on the west side of Susquehanna river about two mile from the s^d river at a bounded Chesnut near a ridge neare a peice of Meddow ground Langley dead noe heires Land uncultivated noe rent made since it was taken up, rent set, £1.. 5.. 9

The Convenencye, 400 acre Sur. the 2nd Septem^r 1684 for Coll. Henry Darnell on the west Susquehanna river at a bounded red oak a mile up the river joyning to the Land Called Harmons Towne, rent ℔ anum £—.. 16.. —

Ebenezers Lott, 200 acre Sur. the 13 July 1684 for Ebenezer Blackston on the west side of Susquehanna river at a bounded gum a bounded tree Called the Land of Canaan, rent ℔ anum £—.. 8.. —

Parkington, 100 acre Sur. the 17th Novem^r 1683 for Richard Perkins on the head of Musketa Creek at a bounded tree in Swamp and now in the posestion of Thomas Edmonds, rent ℔ anum £—.. 4.. —

C. Sold to William Frisby.

The Reserve, 100 acres Sur. the 2ᵈ Oct. 1684 for Coll. Henry Darnall on the west side of Šusquehanna river at a bounded red oak a bounded tree of Langleys tent, rent ℔ anum £2.. —.. —

Johnston Bed, 268 acre Sur. the 16 Aprill 1684 for John Johnston in the woods on the branches of Swan Creek and now in the posestion of Thomas Freeborn, rent ℔ anum £—.. 10.. 9

Spring Garden, 200 acre Sur. the 8ᵗʰ Aprill 1685 for John Yeo in woods at bounded red oak in the Long Line between fewgates Land Yeo dead noe heires in England Land unculti-vated noe rent of this since it was first taken vp, rent set £0.. 8.. —

The Garden of Eden, 150 acre Sur. the 18 May 1685 for Adam Burchell on the head of delph Creek belonging to the Orphant of the sᵈ Burchell, rent ℔ anum £—.. 6.. —

Mount Surredoe, 550 acr. Sur. the 4ᵗʰ Novembʳ 1662 for Henry Ward on the west side of Susquehanna river at the northermost bounds of Stockets Chance belongs to the heires of the sᵈ Ward, rent ℔ anum £—.. 11.. —

Martins Rest, 196 acre Sur. the 15 July 1688 for Lockwick Martin Lying on the south side of Susquehanna river and now belonging to the Orphants of Edward Boothbey, rent ℔ anum £—.. 0.. — [Crossed out in original.]

Daniells Lott, 454 acre Sur. the 16 June 1688 for Daniel Pever-lye Lying on the East side of bush river and belonging to the Orphants of the sᵈ Peverlye, rent ℔ anum £—.. 18.. —

C. Peverell. In pos. Richard Ruff, who married the heiress of Peverill.

Dogwood Ridge, 99 acr. Sur. the 27 Decembʳ 1687 for Hugh Elbart Lying on the south side of Rumley Creek in woods and now In the posestion of John Paker, rent ℔ anum £—.. 3.. 11½

Thurstons Neighbor, 1000 acr. Sur. the 13ᵗʰ Octobʳ 1686 for Vincent Lowe of Talbot County Lying in Baltimore County on the East side of bush river and now belonging to the Executʳ of Coll. Lowe, rent ℔ anum £2.. —.. —

Edens Adition, 100 acre Sur. the 11th June 1685 for Adam Burchell Lying betwixt rumley Creek and Delph Creek belonging to the Orphants of the sd Burchell, rent ℔ anum £—.. 4.. —

C. In pos. Samuel Brown.

Hog Neck, 50 acre Sur. the 15th Novembr 1684 for Edward Reives on the west side of the west Line of rumley Creek and now in the posestion of John Savory, rent ℔ anum £—.. 2.. — This Land Taken a Way by an Ellder Survey.

Concord, 500 acre Sur. the 20th January 1686 for William Ayleward Lying on the East side of bush river Ayleward gone away the Land uncultivated noe rent reced heare, rent set £1.. —.. —

Aha at a venture, 200 acres Sur. the 7th May 1687 for John Hathaway Lying on the north side of bush river and now In the posestion of Humphry Jones, rent ℔ anum £—.. 8.. —

Hazard, 100 acres Sur. the 24 June 1681 for John Yeo on the western side of Swan Creek at a bounded Locust a bounded tree the Land of James Robison deceast this Land taken away by a write of resurvey and granted to Thomas Preble of Baltimore County and the rent will be Concluded a biger tract.

C. In pos. Mary Prebble for ye orphans of sd Prebble. Archibald Buchanan intermarried the widow.

Fannys Inheritance, 893 acre Sur. the 12 Janry 1695 for Edward Boothby Called Fannys Inheritance Lying on the west side of Swan Creek in Spesuty hundd begining at a bounded Maple in a branch of the Cranbury and now in posestion of the Orphants of Edward Boothby, rent ℔ anum £—.. 15.. 9

Paradice, 490 acre Sur. the 6th Aprill 1695 for Robert Mason Called paradice Lying on the branch of Swan Creek begining at a bounded red oak, rent ℔ anum £—.. 19.. 7½

C. In pos. John Mason of St. Mary's co.

Parkers Folly, 214 acre Sur. the 12th Septembr 1695 for John Parker Lying on the north side of bush river In the woods

21

Lying against Allyes Island marsh beginging at double Chesnut at the mouth of Jefferryes neck, rent ℔ anum £—.. 8.. —

C. In pos. orphans of s^d Parker.

Parkers Lott, 176 acre Sur. the 12 Septr 1695 for John Parker Lying on the north side of bush River begining at a Swamp neare Swamped point, rent ℔ anum £—.. 7.. 1

C. In pos. orphans of s^d Parker.

Hazard, 200 acre Sur. the 8th Novem^r 1693 for Thomas Greenfeild Lying up the branches of Swan Creek in woods begining at a bounded w^t oak on the north side of the maine run, rent ℔ anum £—.. 8.. —

C. In pos. orphans of s^d Greenfield.

Miles Hill, 100 acre Sur. the 11th Aprill 1695 for Thomas Newsum Lying above the head of bush river on the north East branch thereof in the woods begining a bound^d popular by a run, rent ℔ anum £—.. 4.. —

Harmonds Town, 200 acre Sur. the 19 July 1658 for Godfrey Harmond upon a point upon the south side of Susquehanna river and now in the posestion of William York for the Orphants of Jacob Lotton, rent ℔ anum £—.. 4..—

Eling, 100 acres Sur. the 17th August 1659 for Thomas Sampson on the East side of bush river this Land was Ex^d and granted to Wm Hollis and now In the posestion of his son William, rent ℔ anum £—.. 2.. —

C. In pos. Benj^a Smith for orphans of Hollis.

Hollye Hill, 50 acre Sur. the 18 August 1659 for William Hollis on the East side bush river near the Land of Thomas Sampson and now In the posestion of Wm Hollis, rent ℔ anum £—.. 1.. —

Owlets Nest, 50 acre Sur. the 20th of Octob^r 1668 for William Hollis on the East side of bush river on a Cove between 2 tracts of Land formerly Sur. for the s^d Hollis and now In the posestion of the s^d, rent ℔ anum £—.. 1.. —

C. In pos. Benj^a Smith for orphans of Hollis.

Hollis his Chance, 45 acre Sur. the 27 Octo^r 1679 for William Hollis on the East side bush river at a bounded black oak a bounded tree of a parcell of Land Called Holly hill in the posestion as above, rent ℔ anum £—.. 1.. 9½

Iselington, 22 acre Sur. the 27 Octob^r 1679 for Wm Hollis on the East side of bush river at a bounded stake standing by a marsh and runing north and be west posesed as afs^d, rent ℔ anum £—.. —.. 11

    C. In pos. Benj^a Smith for orphans of Hollis.

Planters Neglecte, 63 acre Sur. the 11th March 1680 for Wm Hollis on the East side of bush river at a bounded w^t oak in the north East side of Owlies Cove pos^d as above, rent ℔ anum £—.. 2.. —

Swampy point, 100 acres Sur. the 16 Novem^r 1664 for Wm Hollis Lyeing on the north side of bush river begining at a bounded Spanish oak of the Land Called Swampy point and now in the posestion of Wm Hollis, rent ℔ anum £—.. 2.. —

Hollis Refuse, 143 acre Sur. the 23 Septem^r 1695 for William Hollis Lyeing on the north side of bush river begining at a bounded Spanish oak of the Land Called Swampy point posesed as afores^d ℔ anum £—.. 5.. 9

    C. All these 8 tracts in pos. George Chancey who mar. one of ye orphans.

Broad Neck, 100 acre Sur. the 20th Septem^r 1664 for Wm Hollis on the south side of rumley Creek and now in the posestion of William Pridget, rent ℔ anum £—.. 2.. —

    C. In pos. William Prichett.

Hamsteds Marshall, 100 acre Sur. the 1st August 1659 for Godfrey Baylise to the southward of rumley marsh ajoyneing to the Land of George Vtye and now in the posestion of Anthony Drew, rent ℔ anum £—.. 2.. —

Gum Neck, 200 acre Sur. the 22 July 1662 for Thomas Overton on the western side of rumley Creek and posesed by Anthony Drew, rent ℔ anum £—.. 4.. —

The Narrow Neck, 100 acre Sur. granted to William Hollis by patan the second day of Octob[r] 1667 and the said patan Endorsed by Jeremiah White Sur[r] generall begining on the west side of rumley Creek at a bounded tree of broad neck a tract of Land formerly belonging to the s[d] and in the posetion of John Hall Jun[r], rent ℔ anum £—.. 2.. —

Mates Neck, 100 acres Sur. the 3[d] June 1667 for W[m] Osburn and John Lee on the side of rumley Creek and now in the posetion Henry Hedge, rent ℔ anum £—.. 2.. —

Common Garden, 450 acre Sur. the 3[d] June 1667 for W[m] Osborn and John Lee on bush river on the Eastern side begining at a point by the river side and granted to the said Osburn by a patan 1678; 100 acre thereof in posetion of James Phillips, rent ℔ anum £—.. 2.. —

100 acre part thereof sould to William Osburn Jun[r] and morgaged to the s[d] James Phillips, rent ℔ anum £—.. 2.. —

40 acre more thereof in the posetion of Henry Hedge, rent ℔ anum £—.. —.. 10¼

40 acre more thereof in the posetion of Henry Jackson, rent ℔ anum £—.. —.. 11

170 acre residue thereof in the posetion of William Osburn Sen[r], rent ℔ anum £—.. 3.. 5

C. Covent Garden. 150 a. in pos. Thomas Hanson; 50 a., James Phillips; 40 a. Henry Hedge; 40 a. John Roberts; 170 a., the remainder to y[e] orph. of William Osbourn.

Penny Cove Quick, 100 acre Sur. the 13th of Octob[r] 1665 for Thomas Overton in rumley Creek on the north side of the s[d] Creek and now in the posetion of Roger Matthews, rent ℔ anum £—.. 2.. —

C. Penny Come Quick.

Western frolick, 100 acre Sur. the 6th Septem[r] 1673 for James Ives on a small branch of a Creek Called Musketa Creek at a marked Live oak by a marsh In Troopers neck and now in the posetion of James Ives, rent ℔ anum £—.. 4.. —

C. Devised to Richard Smithers.

Beaver Neck, 200 acre Sur. the 28 of March 1663 for John Collet on the west side of a branch of Musketa Creek 125 acre p^t thereof in the posestion of James Ives, rent ℔ anum £—.. 2.. —

C. In pos. John Stokes, 125 a.; John Hall, 75 a.

Musketa Proofe, 250 acre Sur. the 22^d of decem^r 1672 for James Ives in Musketa Creek at a marked w^t oak by a marsh at the head of a Creek 200 acre p^t thereof in the posestion of James Ives, rent ℔ anum £—.. 8.. —
50 acre residue thereof sould to John Sheeles and now In the posestion of Elizth Sheeles his widdow, rent ℔ anum £—.. 2.. —

C. In pos. John Hall, Sr.

Cooks Chance, 158 acre Sur. the 13 May 1678 for John Cook on the south side of Swan Creek begining at a bounded oak by a marsh and runing north East up the Creek and now in the posestion of Wm Jeffs, rent ℔ anum £—.. 6.. —

C. In pos. Thomas Brown.

Gilbert Adventure, 150 acre Sur. the 7th August 1695 for Thomas Gilbert called Gilberts Adventure begining at a bounded Spanish Oak and popular, Rent ℔ anum £—.. 6.. —

C. In pos. Richard Simpson.

Simsons Choice, 53 acre Sur. the 15th July 1688 for Richard Simson Lying on the head of Swan Creek, Rent ℔ anum £0.. 2.. 1½

C. In pos. Emmanuel Smiths orphans.

Mates Affinitye, 200 acre Sur. the 1st March 1683 for Edward Douse and Emanuel Selye upon a Creek of gunpowder river Called Salt peter Creek near the head begining a bounded w^t oak a small fork of the s^d Creek belonging to Orphants of Edward Boothby, rent ℔ anum £—.. 8.. —

C. Edwd. Douce and Emmanuel Cealy, for Edward Booth-by's orphans.

Aitrop, 500 acre Sur. the 29th of decemb^r 1664 for Mr Thomas Griffith on the west side of Susquehanna river beginging at a marked Spanish oake standing at a Low point by a small brook or Valley and given by the s^d Griffith to one Henry Hazallwood who was his copartner or mate and sould by the Execut^rs of the s^d Hazallwood to Richard Perkin and William Loftin and now in there posestion, rent ℔ anum £—.. 10.. —

C. In pos. Richard Perkins, 468 a.; Dan Johnson, 32 a.

Strawbery Hill, 200 acre Sur. the 18 May 1684 for Thomas Thurston on the East side of Susquehanna river at a bounded w^t oak at the mouth of James branch a bounded tree of turky hill and now in the posestion of Thomas Thurston, rent ℔ anum £—.. 8.. —

C. In pos. John Deavor.

Elberton, 1000 acre Sur. the 15th August 1683 for Thomas Thurston on the west side of Susquehanna river at a bounded hickry by the river side a bounded tree of mount Yeo and now in the posestion as aforesd, rent ℔ anum £2.. —.. —

C. In pos. James Empson, 500 a.; Thomas Manning, 500 a.

Addition Lott to Levyes Tribe, 50 acre Sur. the 14 Aprill 1681 for John Durham Lyeing on the west side of bush river and on the north side of a Creek Called Swan Creek begining at a bounded w^t oak and now in the posestion of Samuel Durham, rent ℔ anum £—.. 2.. — Gunpowder hundred

C. In pos. John Durham.

Anns Lott, 500 acre Sur. the 8th June 1683 for Miles Gibson on the west side of Susquehanna river begining at a bounded Locust by the river side and now In the posestion of Thomas Thurston, rent ℔ anum £1.. —.. —

C. In pos. Fran Smith. Sold to Thos. Edmonds who died without heirs.

Jones Adition, 100 acre Sur. the 20th July 1696 for Humphry Jones Lying neare the head of bush river begun at a bounded w^t oake £—.. 4.. —

Peirsons Park, 300 acre Sur the 24 August 1698 for Simon Peirson Lying above the head of bush river begun at a bounded w^t oak, rent ℔ anum £—.. 12.. —

In the posestion of Henry Wriothsley

Thomas Ann Desire, 107 acre Sur. the 25 Oct[r] 1697 for Thomas Ann Depost begun at a bounded red oak standing on the south side of Church Roade, rent ℔ anum £—.. 4.. 3½

C. Last line reads: " Spesutie Church Road."

Denis Choice, 300 acre Sur. the 5 feb[ry] 1698 for James Denis Lying above the head of bush river begun at a bounded Spanish oak, rent ℔ anum £—.. 12.. —

C. 100 a. in pos. Jeremy Hakes.

Battsons Fellowship, 150 acre Sur. the 6th Jan. 1698 for Edward Battson Lyeing above the head of bush river beyond a bounded red oak, rent ℔ anum £—.. 6.. —

C. Land sold but I know not to whom; supposed taken away by older survey.

Good Neighborhood, 699 acre Sur. the 19th decem[r] 1699 for Samuell Young begun at a bounded Hickery, rent ℔ anum £1.. 7.. 11½

Spring Garden, 127 acre Sur. the 22 Sept[r] 1697 for Samuell Baker Lyeing betwixt rumley & delph Creek begun at a bounded sweet gum, rent ℔ anum £—.. 5.. 1
This Land Lyes und[r] an Escheat

C. Baker dead. No heirs.

Brotherly Love, 100 acres Sur. the 28th August 1697 for Richard Perkins and W[m] Lofton Lyeing on the south side of Susquehanna river begun at Spanish oak, rent ℔ anum £—.. 4.. —

C. In pos. William Loftons orphans.

Parkers Choice, 224 acre Sur. the 10 August 1698 for W[m] and John Parker Lyeing on the East side of bush river begun at a bounded oak in the posestion of John Parker, rent ℔ anum £—.. 8.. 11½

Chapmans Fellowship, 150 acre Sur. the 6 Jan[ry] 1698 for John Chapman Lying above the head of bush river begun at a bounded red oak, rent ℔ anum £—.. 6.. —

Billingate, 79 acre Sur. the 14th Octr 1694 for Francis White-
head Lyeing in Spesuty hundred on the head of a creek called
Swan creek begining at a bounded red oak of James Fewgates
Land Called north Yaremouth, rent ℔ anum £—.. 3.. 2

Peters Addition, 100 acre Sur. the 29th of decem^r 1685 for
Peter Fugat Lyeing on the west side of Swan creek in the
woods begining, at a red oak of a pcell of Land the french
plantation runing East and by north and now in the posestion
of Thomas Cord, rent ℔ anum £—.. 4.. —
  C. Reads: " west side of Spesutia Creek."

Johnson Rest, 150 acre Sur. the 10 Sepr 1662 for John Johnson
in the woods above the head of Swan Creek at a bounded black
oak on a Ridge 100 acre p^t thereof in the posestion of William
Lofton & Rich. Perkins, rent ℔ anum £—.. 4.. —
50 acre residue thereof In posestion of Thomas Freeborne of
Ann Arundell County, rent ℔ anum £—.. 2.. —
  *C. Date of survey given as 1683. 100 a. in pos. orphans of
William Lofton.*

The Rich Levell, 800 acre Sur. the 24 March 1679 for George
Yates at the End of the west Line of Henry Stockett at a
bounded Chesnut by bourn branch now in posestion of Thomas
Plummer In Prince Georges County, rent ℔ anum £1.. 12. —
  C. In pos. Coll Henry Darnall of Pr. Geo. co.

Levell Addition, 118 acre Sur. the 15th decemb^r 1686 for George
Yates Lyeing on the west side of Susquehanna river posesed
by Thomas Plummer In Prince Georges County, rent ℔ anum
£—.. 4.. 9

Harwood Retirement, 50 acre Sur. the 24th Aprill 1675 for
Henry Harwood on the north side of Spesuty Creek at a point
of a marsh at the mouth of Collett back Creek now posesed by
Ralph Gellum under an Escheate, rent ℔ anum £—.. 2.. —
  C. In pos. Thos. Greenfields orphans.

Ebenezars Park, 200 acre Sur. the 16 Aprill 1684 for Ebenezar

Blackeston upon the head of Salt peter Creek at a bounded red
£—.. 8.. —

This is In gunpowder hundred
oak of Mates Affenity by the s^d Creek side, Rent ⅌ anum

Gods Speed, 200 acre Sur. the 21 Septem^r 1685 for Lawrence
Taylor in the woods begining at a bounded red oak stånding
in a Swamp in the northermost Line of George Goldsmith in
the ocupation of his son Lawrence, rent ⅌ anum £—.. 8.. —
[Not in C.]

Gunnells devotion, 60 acr. Sur. the 12 Aprill 1680 for George
Gunnill standing by Chesepeak bay side nigh the mouth of
rumly creek it appeares to be noe such Land Gunnell dead see
Void
[Not in C.]

James Parke, 1175 acre Sur. the 23 Aprill 1681 for James
Phillips on the East side of bush river at a bounded red oak
of a Tract of Land Called hunting neck, rent ⅌ anum £2.. 7.. —

Paradice, 1000 acre Sur. the 8th June 1687 for Thomas
Litefoot on the west side of Susquehano river at a bounded
Locust by the river side this land under the same denomination
of the rest, rent ⅌ anum £2.. —.. —

The Good Indeavor, 500 acre Sur. the 15th Oct. 1686 for
Robert Gelly Lyeing on the East side of bush river, rent ⅌
anum £1.. —.. —

MARYLAND RENT ROLLS.

Gunpowder hundred

Bush Wood, 150 acre Sur the 15th August 1659 for Abraham Holdman on the west side of Bush river near the Land of Oliver Sprye and posesed by John Hall, rent ℔ anum £—.. 3.. —

Galliers Bay, 100 acr. Sur. the 24 March 1665 for Joseph Gallion on the south side of bush river In Erbie Creek sould to Edward Gunell who Left it to his brother George who sould the same to James Milles who sould the same to James Phillips and now sold and in the posestion of John Hall, rent ℔ anum —.. 2.. —

Yorks Hope, 200 acre Sur the 16 November 1664 for Wm York on the northermost side of gunpowder river John Yeo had a mandamus upon wch the s^d Land was granted him Yoe is since

30

dead Left noe heires his relations Live In the West of England rent not received these 16 yeares the Land Cultivated, rent p^r anum 1.. 4.. —

Jones Addition, 79 acres Sur the 11 of July 1676 for Thomas Jones on the north side of gunpowder river this Land granted to Yoe as above rent ℔ anum 1.. 2.. 10

The Fooles Refuse, 100 acre Sur. the 26 March 1663 for John Collier on the west side of bush river a little wth in ye river and in the posestion of John Hall for the heires of the s^d Collier, rent ℔ an —.. 2.. —

   C. In poss^n Jon^a Marsey.

Colliers Meddow, 150 acr Sur. the 24 March 1665 for John Collier at the mouth of bush river being the nethermost point of the s^d river and posesed as aforesd (In Spesuty hundred), rent ℔ anum —.. 3.. —

Olivers Addition, 200 acr Sur the 6th Aprill 1667 for John Collier on the western side of bush river at a marked Spanish oak a point by the river side posesed as aforesd, rent ℔ an. —.. 4.. —

   C. Poss^n Jon^a Marsey. This formerly call^d Upper Ollives for Oliver Sprye but resur. & made as above.

Phillips Choice, 100 acr Sur the 20 Sepr 1667 for John Collier in bush river on the south side of the south west branch belonging to the Orphant of John Wood, rent ℔ anum —.. 2.. —

   C. Phils choice.

Colliers Neglect, 300 acr. Sur the 19 August 1677 for George Holland on the north side of gunpowder river at a marked popular in a Line of the Land formerly Laid out for Edward Reeves and Lodwick Williams, rent ℔ anum —.. 6.. —
150 acr. part thereof posesed by John Rawlins
150 acr. residue thereof posesed by John Armstrong, rent ℔ anum —.. 6.. —

   C. Collets neglect . . . Poss^{rs} 191 a. Jno Rawlins 78 a. Abra Taylor who resur. ye Same and found no more.

William Ridge, 200 acre Sur. the 3^d July 1672 for Lodweck Williams in the woods on the south side of bush river at a marked w^t oak neigh the head of bow Creek posesed by Aquila Picka, rent ꝑ anum —.. 8.. —

C. *Poss^r Aquila Paca.*

Prosperity, 140 acre Sur. the 20 Sepr 1664 for Thomas Lytfoot on the west side of bush river at a point at the mouth of the midle branch of the s^d river and now in the posestion of Aquila Packa, rent ꝑ anum —.. 5.. 7

C. *Poss^r Aquila Paca.*

The Island, 150 acr Sur the 15 Novem^r 1664 for John Lee upon Gunpowder river right opesight to the river mouth and now in the posestion of John Carvell, rent ꝑ anum —.. 3.. —

C. *Poss^r John Carwell.*

Phillips Addition, 200 Acre Sur. the 24 Octr 1669 for James Phillips in gunpowder river on the west side of Lees Island and now in the posestion of John Carvell, rent ꝑ anum —.. 4.. —

C. *1668. Poss^r Jno Carwell.*

Little Marlye, 200 acr Sur the 27 Sepr 1684 for Miles Judd in a neck between bush river and Gunpowder river and sold to John Hathaway who bequeathed the same by will to George Smith, rent ꝑ anum —.. 8.. 0

C. *Little Marly. Surv. for Mich^{ll} Judd.*

Locust Neck, 100 acre Sur the 4 March 1668 for James Phillips on the west side of bush river And on the north side of possum Creek posesed by Evan Miles, rent ꝑ anum 0.. 2.. 0

C. *Poss^r Corn. Herrinton for Evan Miles orp^{ns}*

Palmers Forrest, 600 acre Sur. the 9th Sepr 1673 for Wm Palmer at a marked red oak vpon a point In a neck between 2 branches of the Cranbury Swamp Palmer being dead noe heires here Land vncultivated noe rent payd these 16 yeares, rent ꝑ anum £1.. 4.. 0 (Crossed out in the original)

C. *[Page 112.] No rent p^d these 20 years.*

Palmers Point, 500 acre Sur. the 23 June 1675 for William Palmer on the west side of Swan Creek at a marked Locust vpon a point of a marsh Palmer being dead noe heires here Land vncultivated noe rent payd the 16 yeares, rent set £1.. 0.. 0   0.. 0.. — (Crossed out in the original)

Holmwood, 100 acre Sur the 17th August 1659 for Abrah Hollman on the East side of the north branch of gunpowder river posesed by Robert Jackson, rent ℔ anum —.. 2.. —

C. Abra Holdman.

Halls Ridge, 218 acre Sur the 30 Janry 1687 for John Hall Lyeing on the west side of bush river in the woods in a line of Olivers Addition begining at a Spanish oak and now in the posestion of Robt Jackson, rent ℔ anum —.. 8.. 9

C. [Page 112.]

Wilsons Range, 100 acre Sur the 18 Novemr 1686 for John Wilson Lyeing in the north side of bush river and now in the posestion of Stephen Freeland   Charg'd in Spesuty hundred rent ℔ anum —.. 4.. — (Crossed out in the original)

Wansworth, 200 acre Sur. the 15 Sepr 1666 for William Orchard in bush river on the west side of the river at the northermost bounds of Abraham Hollman soe thereof posesed by Abraham Taylor, rent ℔ anum —.. 2.. —
100 acr of the abovesaid Land In the posestion of John Debrulor, rent ℔ anum —.. 2.. —

C. Abrah Holdman.. Possrs 100 a.   Abra Taylor 100 a. Francis Dellahyde.

Ayres Addition, 100 acre Sur the 28 Aprill 1668 for Edward Ayres on the west side of bush river at the head of a Cave now posesed by Abraham Taylor, rent ℔ anum —.. 2.. —

Warington, 650 acre Sur the 9th of febry 1664 for Natl Stiles at a point of a marsh being the Southermost side of bush river posesed by William Hill, rent ℔ anum —.. 13.. —

C. Warrington.   Nath Sheilds.   This land formerly called Powdersbey.

Eastland Wills, 100 acre Sur. the 9th June 1672 for William Ogburn in bush river at a marked Chestnut on a point of the mouth of the north east branch on the South of the s^{d} branch Land vncultivated Ogburn being dead noe heires noe rent pay^{d} these 20 years, Rent ℔ anum £0.. 4.. 0 —.. 4.. —
Charg'd in Spesuty hundred

C. Ogbourn. No rent paid these 24 y^{rs}

Samuells Hill, 150 acr Sur the 3rd July 1672 for Samuell Hill on the south side west branch of bush river at a marked tree in the Valley Hill being dead or run away and noe heire here Land vncultivated noe rent payd these 20 yeares £0.. 6.. 0 —.. 6.. — This Land Lyable to an Escheate.

C. No rent paid these 24 y^{rs}

Betty's Choice, 480 acr. Sur. the 20 July 1678 for George Yates at a bounded gum a bounded tree at the Land Called Benjamins Choice and now In the posestion of Benjamin Burges, rent ℔ anum —.. 19.. 2 In Spesuty hundred.

C. [Page 113.] Poss^{rs} John Watkins orp^{ns}.

Pole cat Ridge, 150 acr. Sur. the 29th Octob^{r} 1679 for James Phillips between bush river and gunpowder river at a bounded w^{t} oak near the road by Elkneck Creek, rent ℔ anum —.. 6.. —

C. What is clear bel. to Jno Gallion Supposed not above 50 a.

Rangers Lodge, 500 acr Sur the 15 June 1682 for David Jones at the head of bush river between the middle branch at a bounded w^{t} oak on the north East side by the main run and now in posestion of James Phillips, rent ℔ anum £1.. —.. —

Sedgley, 200 acre Sur. the 4th Sepr 1683 for James Phillips on a run Called Bynums run at a bounded w^{t} oak of rangers Lodge, rent ℔ anum —.. 8.. — In Spesuty hundred

C. Poss^{r} John Webster.

Planters Paradise, 829 acre Sur the 29 Novem^{r} 1679 for William Cornwallis on the west side of the northwest branch of back river the s^{d} Cornwallis is dead noe heires here noe

Cultivation noe rent for this 16 yeares, rent ℔ anum £1.. 13.. 0
1.. 13.. — posesed by Steven Bently

Fryes Plaines, 400 acre Sur the 7ᵗʰ Sepʳ 1678 for David Frye
on the south side of gunpowder river in the woods at a bounded
tree of the Land of Robert Gudgeon Suppose it belongs to the
Orphant of Edward Frye, rent ℔ anum —.. 16.. —

    C. Robᵗ Couthen.

The Three Sisters, 1000 acre Sur. the 6 Octoʳ 1679 for Majʳ
John Welch on the south side of the great falls of Gunpowder
river at bounded popular by the river side nigh an Island belongs to the Orphant of the sᵈ Welch, rent ℔ anum 2.. —.. —

    C. Possʳˢ Tho. Stockett 250 a. Dan Richardson 250 a.
John Giles 250 a. Joseph Twogood 250 a.

Tomsons Choice, 1000 acr. Sur the 12 March 1679 for James
Tomson on the ridge of gunpowder river at the wester most
bounds of the Land of Maj Sewall 800 thereof belonging to
Arthur Tomson his Brother, rent ℔ anum 1.. 12.. —

    C. [Page 228.] Thomsons choice. Possʳ 800 a. Arthur
Thomson 200 a. Geo. Parker.

Charleses Purchase, 300 acre Sur the 15 March 1676 for
Nicolas Gassoway on the north side of gunpowder river at a
bounded running East wᵗʰ the Line of the Land of Arthur
Taylor Called georges hill belonging to the orphant of John
Gassoway, rent ℔ anum —.. 12.. —

    C. [Page 228.]

Taylors Choice, 300 acre Sur. the 28 July 1667 for John
Taylor on the north side of Eastern branch of gunpᵈ river
posesed by Stephen Johnston, rent ℔ an. —.. 6.. —

    C. [Page 228.] Possʳˢ 150 a. Moses Groom. 150 a. Col.
Maxwell. Interlined " & now possᵗ by Ann Phelks."

Forsbery Neck, 180 acres Sur the 10 July 1676 for Wᵐ Ebden
on the South side of gunpowder river in a fork of salt peter

Creek at a bounded w^t oak and now in posestion of Francis Dolarhide, rent ℔ anum —.. 7.. 2

C. [*Page 228.*] *Forberry Neck.* *Poss^r Tho. Frisby, Cecil Co^y*

Daniells Neck, 150 acre Sur. the 8th of Aprill 1663 for Thomas ODaniell on the Eastern side of Gunpowder river at a bounded w^t oak belonging to the orphants of Wm Westbury, rent ℔ anum —.. 1.. —

C. [*Page 228.*] *Poss^r Fran. Dallehyde, belonging to ye orp^ns of Wm Westbury.*

Chestnut Neck, 150 acre Sur. the 4th May 1678 for William Westbury at the south side of gunpowder river at a bounded w^t oak belonging to the Orphants of William Westbury, rent ℔ anum —.. 6.. —

C. [*Page 229.*] *Poss^r Simon Pierson.*

Hornisham, 50 acre Sur the 18 June 1681 for William Horn on the East side of gunpowder river ajacent to the Land Called daniells Neck belonging to the orphants of William Wesbury, rent ℔ anum —.. 2.. —

C. [*Page 229.*] *Poss^r Fra Dallahyde.*

Waterton, 200 acre Sur the 3 August 1667 for John Waterton on the East side of Gunpowder river near the mouth of Holmans Creek soe the record says but supposed not to be so an belonging to Thomas Read and Thomas Ridge in the Ile of white In the Kingdom of England to whom the s^d Waterton bequeathed by Will the record says, rent ℔ anum —.. 4.. —

Daniellston, 150 acre Sur the 20 Sepr 1667 for John Waterton on the west side of gunpowder river near a point Called Colletts point this Land belongs as afores^d to Thomas Reed and Thomas Ridge, rent ℔ an. —.. 3.. —

C. Poss^r Geo Grover.

Waterton, 50 acr Sur the 4th of Novemb^r 1679 for John

Waterton on the west side gunpowder river at a bounded tree of Land of danielston posesed by Thomas Reed and Thomas Ridge as afores^d, rent ℔ anum —.. 2.. —

C. Poss^r Geo Grover.

Watertons Angle, 31 acr Sur the 26 decem^r 1679 for John Waterton on the north side of gunpowder river at a bounded oak by a Creek Cave at the head of a branch Creek posesed as afores^d, rent ℔ anum —.. 1.. 3

C. Poss^r Robt. Jackson.

Olives, 100 acre Sur. the 15 August 1659 for Oliver Spry on the north branch of Gunpowder river now in posestion of James Maxwell, rent ℔ anum —.. 2.. —

Sampsons, 140 acre Sur. the 16 August 1659 for Thomas Sampson on the East side of gunp^r river and now in the posestion of James Maxwell, rent ℔ anum —.. 2.. 9

Midle Olives, 100 acr Sur the 15 August 1659 for Oliver Spry aboute 2 miles vp gunpowder river posesed by James Maxwell, rent ℔ anum —.. 2.. —

Hopewell, 50 acr Sur. the 20 July 1662 for Oliver Spry between two tracts formerly taken vp by this Sprye Called Olives and O midle Olives posesed by James Maxwell, rent ℔ anum —.. 1.. —

Chestnutt neck, 150 acr Sur the 20 July 1662 Oliver Sprye on the north side of the Land Called Olives joyning vpon the Long Line of the s^d Olives posesed by James Maxwell, rent ℔ anum —.. 3.. —

Hopwell Marsh, 50 acr Sur. the 11th June 1667 for Oliver Spry adjoyning to the south side of sd. Spryes plantation and now In posestion of James Maxwell, rent ℔ anum —.. 1.. —

Harmon Addition, 100 acr Sur the 11th June 1667 for Godfrey Harmon on the Eastern side of gunpowder river posesed by James Maxwell, rent ℔ anum —.. 2.. —

Marys Blanks, 58 acr Sur. the 25 Novemb^r 1673 for Godfrey

Harman on the north side of gunpowder river at a marked tree a bounded tree of Harmons Choice pos^d by Ja Maxwell, rent 𝕡 an. —.. 2.. 4

C. Mary's Banks.

Halls Hope, 45 acr. Sur 18 July 1684 for John Hall on the north side of gunpowder river and now in posestion of James Maxwell, rent 𝕡 an. —.. 1.. 9½

Island Point, 100 acr Sur the decemb^r 1688 for Mary Stansby at the mouth of gunpowder river on the East side thereof at the East north East end of a point of Land by a marsh at the bay side now in posestion of James Maxwell, rent 𝕡 anum —.. 4.. —

Maj^{rs} Choice, 553 acr Sur the 13 of Aprill 1695 for James Maxwell Lyeing above the head of bush river on a branch thereof Called Bynums branch beginging at a bounded popular by the s^d branch, Rent 𝕡 anum 1.. 2.. 1½

James Chance, 47 acr Sur the 13 of Aprill 1695 for James Maxwell Lyeing in Baltimore County begin^g at a bounded Hickory, rent 𝕡 anum —.. 1.. 11

Chilbury Hall, 250 acr. Sur. the 15 June 1668 for John Lee on the north side of bush river at a bounded oak at a point of a marsh neare the head of the west branch 125 acr hereof possesed By Anthony Drew, rent 𝕡 anum —.. 5.. 0 In Spesuty hundred

Swan Harbour, 200 acr Sur. the 27 of feb^{ry} 1668 for Oliver Sprye on the south side of bush river on the south of the north west branch posesed by Charles Jones, rent 𝕡 anum —.. 4.. —

C. Poss^r Ew^d Smith for ye orp^{ns} of Cha. Jones.

Hews Island, 50 acr. Sur. 29 of June 1672 for Thomas Heath on the south side of bush river on the south side of a greate marsh being the northermost bounds of the Lands of Joseph Hews, rent 𝕡 anum And In posestion of Henry Mathews —.. 2.. —

C. Poss^r Hen. Mathews.

Cadwallader, 100 acr. the 8 of Septem^r 1683 for Thomas Jones vpon bush river at a bounded w^t oak standing by a small pocoson now in the posesh^n of Charles Jones, rent ℔ anum —.. 4.. —

    C. Poss^r Ed^w Smith for ye orp^{ns} of Cha. Jones.

St Jones, 100 acr Sur the 4 of July 1672 for Thomas Jones on the southermost side of the south west branch of bush river at a marked red oak in a point by a Cave and in the posestion of Charles Jones, rent ℔ anum —.. 4.. —

    C. Poss^r Ed^w Smith a af^d

Blocksedge, 50 acr Sur the June 1680 for Thomas Heath and now in the posestion of Henry Mathews granted by pattan the 10th day of August 1684, rent ℔ anum —.. 2.. —

Hollands Lott, 400 acr Sur the 16 of August 1678 for George Holland and assigned to Thomas Francis at a bounded oak a bounded tree of the Lands formerly Laid out for George Gates Called Bettye Choice and now in the posestion of Samuel Younge, rent ℔ anum —.. 16.. — In Spesuty hundred

The Adventure, 1000 acr. Sur. the 16 June 1681 for George Lingan on the south side of the great falls of gunpowder at a bounded popular, rent ℔ anum 2.. —.. —

    C. Poss^{rs} 500 a. Hen. Butler. 500 a. Josiah Wilson.

Buck Range, 750 acr Sur the 19 of Octr 1611 for John Fanning at a bounded Hickory on the west side of a branch of back river over against the Land Called paradise the Land vncultivated Faning being dead noe heires appear it is set £1.. s10.. d0   1.. 10.. —

    C. [Page 203.] " Buck Range. Sur 6 Feb: 1687 for John Fuller at ye head of Back River. Poss^r Jno Anderson"; & at page 161, " Buck Rayn, Sur 3 Nov 1701 for Mathew Hawkins, in ye Drafts of Potapsco, at a bo^d Black Oak."

475 acr Sur the 20th Novemb^r 1673 for Thomas Long on the south side of midle river at a bounded wt oak on the north side

of a Creek 100 acre thereof in the posestion of the Orphants
of Thomas Pearth, rent ℔ anum —.. 4.. —
300 acr part thereof sold to Thomas Gibson and now in the
posestion of John Kingsbury, rent ℔ anum —.. 12.. —
75 acr residue thereof rep^r away by Wm Cornwallis

    C. 400 a. Poss^{rs} 100 a. ye orp^{ns} of Tho Peart. 300 a.
Jno. Kingbury.

Pole cat Neck, 100 acr Sur the 6 July 1676 for Henry Poules
on the north side of Gunpowder river at a bounded Locust on
a point of the north side of the river and in the posestion of
Francis Lefe, rent ℔ anum —.. 4.. —

    Poss^r Patrick Dew.

Richardsons Levill, 207 acr Sur the 10 of July 1676 for
Thomas Richardson on the south side of Gunpowder river on a
branch of Salt Peter Creek and belongs to the orphants of John
Rochhold, rent ℔ anum —.. 8.. —

MARYLAND RENT ROLLS.

Gunpowder hundred

Boughtons Forrest, 575 acr Sur. the 29 August 1677 for
Richard Boughton on the head of the western branch of gunpowder river at a bounded w^t oak 400 acr part thereof in
posestion of Edward Smith rent ℔ anum —.. 16.. —
175 acr resident thereof belongs to the Orphants of Joseph
Peek rent ℔ anum —.. 7.. —

    C. Poss^{rs} 400a Ed Smith 175a. Jos Peak's orp^{ns}

375 acr Sur the 10 of July 1678 for Richard Boughton between
the falls of Gunpowder river in the woods at a bounded oak
running West rent ℔ anum —.. 15.. —

Shewels Fancyes, 1000 acr Sur. the 30 of May 1679 for Maj Nicolas Shewel at the head of gunpowder river upon a ridge at a bounded oak betweene the two falls of the river rent ℔ anum 2.. —.. —

    C. Sewalls Fancy. Maj^r Nich. Sewall.

Hathcoat Cottage 500 acr Sur. the 22 march 1678 for Nathaniell Hathcoat between the two great falls of gunpowder river at a bounded popular at the head of the thurd branch and as I can find it belongs to the orphants of Joseph Hathcoat who are the next heires that appear here rent ℔ anum 1.. —.. —

    C. Heathcots. Cottage. As far as can find belongs to the orp^{ns} of Jos. Heathcoat. Supposed to belong to Wm Pickett who marry'^d ye heiress.

Cullens Lott. 300 acr Sur. the 17 June 1683 for James Cullens at the head of gunpowder river on the north side of the south branch on the said river begining at a bounded red oak the bounded tree of the Land Called Trumans Aquitance. Rent ℔ anum —.. 12.. —

    C. Poss^r Wm Bladen, Esqr.

Barklingham, 525 acr. Sur. the 6 Novemb^r 1682 for George Lingam on the north side of river Called back river begining at a bounded Spanish oak Standing at the mouth of a small Cove on the south side thereof Rent ℔ anum 1.. 1.. —

    C. Back Lingan 450a. Poss^r. Edwd Butler.

Trumans Aquitance 500 acr Sur. the 15 May 1682 for Maj^r Thomas Truman on the north side of the south branch of gunpowder river begining at a bounded w^t oak standing by the s^d branch and now in the posestion of Coll Thomas Greenfield rent ℔ anum 1.. —.. —

    C. Trumans acquaintance.

Haphazard, 100 acr Sur. the 11 May 1682 for John Bevan on the south side of gunpowder river at a bounded Chestnut a bounded tree of the Land Called Harrods Lyon formerly taken up for Capt Harrod thurty acr. thereof in the posetion of the s^d Harrod rent ℔ anum —.. 1.. 3

70 acr residue thereof in the posetion of Edward Jones rent ℔ anum —.. —.. 9

C. . . ye Land called Herod's Line Poss^r 64a Ed^w Jones. 36 poss^r R^d Harwood.

Johns Interest, 150 acr Sur the 12th May 1683 for Micall Judd on the west side of bush river begining at a mouth of a Creek Called bone Creek at a bounded w^t oak a bounded tree of the Land formerly taken up formerly Wm Tompson and Lodwick Williams and now in the ocup. of Elizth Ebden for the orphants of Wm Ebden Rent ℔ anum —.. 6.. —

C. Poss^r Jno Nicholson's orp^n

Darnells Camp, 1000 acr Sur the 7 June 1683 for John Darnell Esqr on the south branch of gunpowder river begining at a bounded tree of adventures. Addition formerly taken up for George Lingan belonging to Execu^{rs} of the s^d Darnell Coll Henry Lowe being one of them Rent ℔ anum 2.. —.. —

C. Darnalls Camp. Poss^r Coll. Hen. Lowe.

Ebinezars Park, 200 acr Sur. the 16 aprill 1684 for Ebinezar Blackiston at the head of Salt Peter Creek at a bounded red oak of mates affinity by the s^d Creek side rent ℔ anum —.. 8. —
Taskars Camp, 500 acr Sur. the 17 May 1684 for Thomas Tasker upon the head of gunpowder river on the north side of the south branch at a bounded tree standing at the End of the north East Line of Trewmans Aquitance to Taskers heires rent ℔ anum 1.. —.. —

C. Poss^r Jno Addison. P. G. Co.

New Yeares Purchase, 500 acr sur the 25 Feb^r 1684 for Richard Tydeing on the head of Gunpowder river at a bounded red oak on the south side of the north branch of the s^d river at bounded tree of James Park belonging to the heires of Richard Tydeings Rent ℔ anum 1.. —.. —

Symes Choice, 150 acr. Sur the 28 of Novem^r 1683 for Richard Symes on the north side of gunpowder river neare the head of the river at the northermost bounds of the Land Called Swampton 50 acr thereof in the posestion of Micall Judd 100 acr residue thereof belonging to Enoch Spink rent ₱ anum —.. 4.. —

C. Sims Choice. Sur 1673 for R^d Sims . . . Land called Swanson. Poss^r Dr Gideon Skates.

Windlyes Forrest, 100 acr Sur. the 22 of August 1667 for Richard Windly on the north East branch of gunpow^r river on the north side of a Creek posesed by Miles Judd Junr rent ₱ anum —.. 2.. —

C. Windleys Forest. Pos^t by Jno Taillor & Dr Skates as I suppose.

Affinity, 1500 acr Sur the 4th Septem^r 1683 for John Darnel Esqr upon the head of gunpowder on the south branch thereof at a bounded w^t oak a bounded tree of the Land Called rent set ₱ anum £3.. 0.. 0

C. Poss^r Col. Hen. Lowe.

Hills Forrest, 1000 acr Sur the 4th Septem^r 1683 for Richard Hill in the woods above the head of Gunpowder river on the south side of the north branch of the s^d river at a bounded red oak standing at the head of the north Line of James Tompsons Land belonging to the heires of the s^d Hill rent ₱ anum 2.. —.. —

C. Poss^r Joseph Hill.

2000 acr Sur the 14th Septem^r 1683 for Nicolas Shewell Esqr upon the head of gunp^r river upon the north side of the south branch of the s^d river at a bounded white Wallnut Standing By the s^d branch Rent ₱ anum 4.. —.. —

C. Maj^r Nich. Sewall.

Hollands Park 150 acr Sur the 14 Octr 1683 for George Holland in the woods above the head of gunp^r river at a bounded tree standing at the End of a pece of Land Called Hills forrest the northermost bounded tree thereof rent ℀ anum —.. 6.. —

C. Poss^r John Ford.

The Vally of Jehosaphet 2500 acr Sur the 27 Sepr 1683 for Capt Richard Smith upon the head of gunp^r river on the north side of the south branch at a bounded white Walnut at a bounded tree of Maj^r Shewells Marsh rent ℀ anum 5.. —.. —

Hills Camp, 1000 acr Sur. the 10th March 1683 for Clement Hill in the woods above the head of gunpowder river between the fork of the s^d river at a bounded popular in the south west Line of his Lordship Man^r Rent ℀ anum 2.. —.. —

Land of Promise, 2000 acr Sur. the 5th Octr 1683 for Coll Henry Darnell upon the head of gunpowder river on the north side of the south west branch of the s^r river at a bounded red oak standing by the s^d branch rent ℀ anum 4.. —.. —

Cullens Addition, 500 acr Sur the 25 Septr 1683 for James Cullens assigned to Thomas Grunin at the head of gunpowder river at the East End of north East Line of Cullens Lott rent ℀ anum 1.. —.. —

C. Poss^r Wm Bladen.

Clarksons Hope, 600 acr Sur. the 28 of Septem^r 1683 for Robert Clarkson at the head of gunpowder river on the south side of north branch of the s^d river at the End of the West Line of Capt Thomas Francis and now belonging to the heires of Robert Clarkson, rent ℀ anum 1.. 4.. —

C. Claxons hope. Sur. for Robt Claxon. Poss^r Ed^w Reynolds.

Jones inheritance, 1000 acr Sur. the 28 Sep 1683 for Robert Jones on the head of gunpowder river at a bounded black oak on the north Line of Tompsons Choice Jones dead I know noe heires Land uncultivated noe rent made this Rent set £1.. 0.. 0

The Grove, 1150 acr Sur. the Sepr 1683 for Richard Jones

on the south west branch of bush river at a bounded w^t oak on the south side of the s^d branch opesit to first bounded tree of popular neck, Rent ꝑ anum 2.. 6.. —

 C. The Groves sur. for R^d Johns.

Gassaways Addition, 280 acr. Sur. the 24 Sepr 1683 for Nicolas Gassoway at the head of gunpowder river at a marked Chestnutt at the End of the west Line of Gassaways ridge belonging to the heires of the s^d Gasoway rent ꝑ anum —.. 11.. 2

Darnills Silvania, 500 acr Sur. the 28 Sepr 1683 for John Darnell on the head of gunpowder river on the South side of the south branch of the s^d river at a bounded popular at the End of the west and the north Line of Darnells Camp and now In the posestion of Coll Henry Lowe and his Execu^r rent ꝑ anum 1.. —.. —

 C. Darnalls Silvania.

Dunkeele, 500 acr Sur. the 22^d of Septr 1683 for John Scot on the head of bush river on the south west branch of the s^d river at a bounded tree of Gibsons ridge and now posesed by Gilbert Scott rent ꝑ anum 1.. —.. —

 [*Later written Dunkiel.*]

Crycrafts Purchase, 300 acr. Sur. the 5 of feb^{ry} 1683 for John Crycraft on the head of gunpowder river at a marked red oak on a ridge in the north west Line of my Lords man^r belonging to Crycrafts heires rent ꝑ anum —.. 12.. —

 C. Craycrofts purchase . . . for John Craycrofts. Poss^r Ignatius Craycroft.

Clerksons Purchase, 600 acr Sur. 24 of Sepr 1683 for Robert Clerkson on the southside of the southwest branch of bush river at a bounded white oak In a Vallye belongs to the heires of Robert Clarkson rent ꝑ anum 1.. 4.. —

 C. Claxons purchase . . . Robt Claxon Poss^{rs} 400a Hen. Wright 200a. Jno Bowen.

Plasterers Hall, 100 acr Sur. the 17th of July 1683 for John Nicolson on the East side of bush river on the west side of bynums branch at a bounded popular standing near the run Rent ℔ anum —.. 4.. —

  C. Poss^r Henry Carter.

Samuells Delight, 150 acr Sur. the 13 Sepr 1683 for Samuell Sicklemore on the head of gunpowder river on the East side of the north branch of the s^d river at a bounded oak in a Vallye by a run side and in the posestion of John Taylor and John Lowe, Rent ℔ anum —.. 6.. —

Novascotia, 1500 acr Sur. the 9th of June 1684 for Thomas Sterling on the north side of the midle branch of bush river at a bounded oak of Robert Lockwoods the greatest part of this Land taken away by an Elder survey and now belongs to Younge Sterling rent ℔ anum 3.. —.. —

  C. Poss^rs 1000a Tho Sterling 500a. Wm Derumple.

Osburns Lott, 500 acr Sur. the 15 July 1684 for William Osburn on the East side of bush river on the west side of bynums run at a bounded gum Close by the run neare the Land Called Anns Lott Rent ℔ anum 1.. —.. —

  C. Poss^r Joseph Willson.

Harrises Trust, 300 acr Sur. the 5 August 1684 for William Harris on the East side of bush on the west side of a branch Called bynums branch at a bounded red oak and now In the posestion of Peter Bond rent ℔ anum —.. 12.. —

  C. Poss^rs 100a Jno Bond 100a Wm Bond 100a Tho. Bond.

Anns Dowry, 200 acr Sur. the 22 Septr 1683 for Ann Grove on the north side of the western branch of bush river at a bounded w^t oak standing on a bank on the west side of Bynums run, rent ℔ anum —.. 8.. —

  C. Sur. for Ann Gross.

Oglesbyes Chance, 200 acr Sur. the 5th August 1684 for George Oglesbye on the head of the main branch of Midle river at a bounded red oak standing In a Levill near the s^d branch rent ℔ anum —.. 8.. —

C. *Oglebys chance. Poss^r Fra^s Whitehead.*

Goodwill, 200 acr Sur. the 5 august 1684 for George Burges upon the head of bush river on the East side of the southwest branch at a bounded red oak in the East north East Line of Gibsons park rent ℔ anum —.. 8.. —

C. *Poss^r Hen. Roades.*

Adventure Addition, 300 acr Sur. the 11th July 1683 for George Lingan on the head of gunpowder on the south side of the south west branch of the river at a bounded black oak at the end of the south west Line of a pcell of Land Called Lingan Called the Adventure rent ℔ anum —.. 12.. —

C. *Addicōn.*

St Dennis, 500 acr Sur. the 18 Septem^r 1684 for Edward Dennis on the head of gunpowder river on the south side of the south west branch at a bounded popular Standing by the said branch Dennis dead noe heires appeare here Land uncultivated noe rent made of this since the first taking up rent set £1.. 0.. 0

C. *St. Denis als Edmondsbury. Edmond Dennis Poss^r Tho Jameson.*

Sargents Hall, 500 acr Sur. the 14 of Sept. 1684 for seath Sargent on the head of gunpowder run on the South side of the south west branch at a bounded popular a bounded tree of St Dennis; Seargent dead I know noe heire Land uncultivated noe rent made of this since the first taking up rent set £1.. 0.. 0

C. *Sergants Hall. Sur for Seth Sergant.*

Christophers Camp, 1000 acr Sur. the 5th of July 1684 for Christop^r Beans on the East side of bush river between James branch and bynums branch at a bounded Chestnutt Standing on a ridge belong^g to the orphants of the s^d Beans rent ℔ anum 2.. —.. —

C. *Christopher Baynes . . . poss^r his son Christopher.*

Brooms Bloome, 1000 acr Sur. the 5 August 1684 for John Broom on the East side of bush river betwixt bynums branch and James branch at a bound Chestnut a bounded tree of Chris Camp belongs to the Orphants of the s^d broom Rent ₱ anum 2.. —.. —

Burges Camp, 1000 acr Sur. the 21 of Septem^r 1683 for George Burges on the head of bush river on the south west branch of the s^d river at a bounded white oak by the s^d branch in the north East Line of Burgess Parke rent ₱ anum 2.. —.. —

C. Burgess Camp . . . Poss^r Cha Carroll.

Meritons Lott, 500 acr Sur. the 18 Octr 1684 for John Meryton on the East side of bush river on the west side of bynums branch at a bounded red oak by the s^d branch rent ₱ anum 1.. —.. —

C. Merryton's Lott, Poss^r John Selman.

Abells Lott, 300 acr Sur. the 15 July 1684 for Abell Brown on the East side of bush river on the west side of bynums branch at a bounded oak on a bank 8 perches from the said branch belonging to the Orphants of the s^d Brown rent ₱ anum —.. 12.. —

C. Abel's Lott . . . Poss^r Robert Brown.

Gillingham, 400 acr Sur. the 6th of August 1684 for Coll Henry Jowles on the East side of bush river on the west side of bynums branch and now In the posestion of Amos Garrett Rent ₱ anum —.. 16.. —

Gates Close, 30 acr Sur. the 5 June 1684 for Thomas Richardson on the East side of the south west branch of gunpowder river and now In the posestion of John Fuller rent ₱ anum —.. 1.. 2

C. Poss^r Cha Hewett. Taken away by an old^r Survey.

James Parke, 500 acr Sur. the 28 Septem^r 1683 for James Ellis on the head of Gunpowder river on the north side of the

south west branch belonging to the Orphants of the s^d Ellis
rent ℔ anum 1.. —.. — ....

C. Poss^r Mary Ellis.

My Lords Gift, 500 acr Sur. the 5 of August 1684 for Bazwell
Brook on the East side of bush river on the East side of bynums
branch rent ℔ anum 1.. —.. —

C. Basil Brookes.

Richardsons Prospect, 100 acr Sur. the 7 of Octr 1684 for
Thomas Richardson on the south side of a branch of gunpowder
river Called back river and now In the posestion of Walter
Bayly Rent ℔ anum —.. 4.. —

C. Poss^r Walter Bosley.

Clegates Forrest, 1000 acr Sur. the 4 of August 1684 for
Capt Thomas Clegate on the south side of the main branch
of bush river Called the south west branch rent ℔ anum
2.. —.. —

C. Clegat's Forest. Poss^r sd. Clegat's widow.

Keytons Range, 500 acr Sur. the 26 of August 1684 for Thomas
Keyton on the East side of bush river on the west side of
bynums run I know not the man the Land uncultivated noe
rent made of this since the first takeing up rent ℔ anum
£1.. 0.. 0

*C. Keytin's Range . . . Thomas Keyting. Keytin dead.
No heir. Land uncultivated.*

Brook Cross, 1500 acr Sur. the 23 Septem^r 1684 for Roger
Brook on the head of Gunpowder river at a bounded red oak
on a ridge at the End of the north East Line of my Lords Man^r
rent p^r anum 3.. —.. —

*C. Brook's Cross. Poss^{rs} 1000a John Brooke 500a Basil
Brooke.*

Hopwell Marsh, 55 acr Sur. the 16 July 1684 for John Hall
on the north side of gunpowder river and now In the posestion
of Wm Lenox rent ℔ an. —.. 2.. 2½

Gresham Colledge, 500 acr Sur. the 27th of Oct 1684 for John Gresham on the south west branch of bush river rent ℔ anum 1.. —.. —

St Georges, 400 acr Sur. the 13 Jan^{ry} 1684 for George Tompson on the East side of bush river between bynums branch and James branch rent ℔ anum —.. 16.. —

   C. St. George . . . Geo. Thomson.

Tompsons Lott, 600 acr Sur. the 26 of Octr 1685 for George Tompson on the head of gunpowder river on the south side of the south west branch Rent ℔ anum 1.. 4.. —

Bonners Camp, 1000 acr Sur. the 29 of Octr 1684 for Henry Bonnar in James branch on the East side of bush river rent p^r anum 2.. —.. —

   C. Poss^r s^d Bonn^{rs} widow.

Hathaways Trust, 150 acr Sur. the 28 of March 1685 for John Hathaway on the East side of the south west branch of bush river now in the posestion of Mark Rifle rent ℔ anum —.. 6.. —

   C. Poss^r Jno Gresham.

Constant Friendship, 1000 acre Sur. the 2^d Novem^r 1685 for Robert Dians on the head of bush river on the East side of south west branch of the s^d river belonging to the Orphants of the s^d Dyans, Rent ℔ anum 2.. —.. —

   C. Poss^r Wm Hutchens.

Bonners Purchase, 500 acre Sur. the 12 of Octr 1685 for Henry Bonner on the East side of bynums branch In bush river 200 acr thereof posesed by Nicolas Waterman, rent ℔ anum —.. 8.. —

300 acres residue thereof In posestion of the s^d Bonnar rent ℔ anum —.. 12.. —

   C. Poss^{rs} 200a Nich Waterman; 300a Tho Bale.

Collinborn, 200 acre Sur. the 6 of June 1669 from Henry

Howard on the midle branch of gunpowder river on the south side of the main run and now In the posestion of Sarah Blackwell to whom the same was bequeathed to her by the said Howard rent ℔ anum —.. 4.. —

C. Collingborn.

Pooles Island, 200 acre Sur. the 27 of July 1659 for Capt Thomas Morris neare the west side of Chesapeak bay the s^d Morris being dead he left the same to a man In New York Land uncultivated noe rent made here this 20 yeares rent set £0.. 4.. 0

C. Pool's Island. Poss^r John Carvell, Cecil County.

The Lyon, 300 acr. Sur. the 19th Novem^r 1669 for Capt. Thomas Herod on the nothermost branch of gunpow^r river on the west side of the s^d river and In the posestion of Richard Herod rent ℔ an. —.. 6.. —

C. Thomas Harwood. Poss Ric'd Harwood in Ann Arundle County.

Elk Neck, 600 acre Sur. the 20th 8^{ber} 1667 for John Collet Junr in gunpowder river on the East side of the river near delph Creek Collett dead bequeathed this Land to one Mathew Gouldsmith and In case he dyed wth out heires to goe to some relations in England none can be heard of it is now In the posestion of Samuel Standifer Who payes rent ℔ anum —.. 12.. —

Winters Runn, 200 acr Sur. the 5th June 1668 for John Lee on the head of bush river in the western branch thereof a little up the mouth of the fresh and In the posestion of Phillip Greenslat noe rent p^d this 16 yeares Greenslet in England noe distress rent set £0.. 4.. 0.

C. Bel. to Phil Greensted in England.

Stocktylemoe, 550 acr Sur. the 5th Septem^r 1669 for Vincent Elliott on the western branch of bush river of the main run of the s^d river on the north side thereof this Land given by the s^d Elliott towards the maintainance of a protestant Minister this Land as new surv^d does not make a hund^d acr thereof rent set £0.. 11.. 0

C. Stocktilemore.

Williams Fortune, 150 acr Sur. the 15 August 1670 for Lodwick Williams on the west side of back river on a branch of bone Creek at a bounded tree of the Land Called Tompstons fortune Lockwick Williams run away twenty years agoe Into the Southward noe rent made of this soe Long Rent set £0.. 3.. 0

Laurance his Claime, 10 acr Sur. the 13 August 1688 for Henry Larance on the west side of gunpowder river Larance run away noe heires nor noe distress here Rent set £0.. 0.. 5

Oglesby his mount, 45 acr Sur. the 23 of July 1688 for George Oglesby Lying upon gunpowder river and now In the posestion of John Hall for the Orphant of George Gouldsmith rent ℀ anum —.. 1.. 9½

C. Ogleby's mount.

Cuny Hill, 25 acr Sur the 24 of July 1688 for Henry Larance Lying on the south side of Gunpowder river Lawrance run away noe heirs noe distress here rent set £0.. 1.. 0

C. Canny Hill.

Watertons Neglect 6¼ acr sur the first of August for Micall Judd Lying on the north side of the fork of gunpowder river rent ℀ anum —.. —.. 3¼

C. Possr. Willm Peckett.

Morefields, 164 acr Sur the 22^d of February 1688 for Thomas Stayley Lying in the woods between bush river and gunpowder river neare to a pcell of Land Called Lockwicks Ridge and now in posestion of James Durham rent ℀ anum —.. 7.. 6

C. Moorfields. Possrs. Robert Shaw & John Armstrong.

Andersons Lott, 400 acr Sur the 15th of Octr 1685 for John

Anderson of Sumerset County Lying upon the head of bush river rent ⅌ anum —.. 16.. —

C.   Poss^r Howard's Orpⁿ

Edwards Lott, 300 acr Sur the 9 of July 1686 for William York Lying upon bynums branch and now in the posession of Mark Swift Rent ⅌ anum —.. 12.. —

Grooms Chance, 300 acr Sur the 28th Aprill 1687 for Moses Groom Lying on the north East side of the falls of gunpowder river rent ⅌ anum —.. 12.. —

Rangers Range, 200 acr Sur the 18 May 1687 for Charles Rangers Lying between gunpowder river and bush river by the Little falls Ranger dead his brother has Children in Anarundel County rent set £0.. 8.. 0

Jerusalem 318 acr Sur 29 May 1687 for Nicolas Hemsted and John Valley on the north side of the Little falls of gunpowder river and now In the posession of Enock Spinks rent ⅌ an —.. 12.. 9

C.   John Walley. Poss^r Henry Wriothsley.

Aha the Cow pasture, 194 acr Sur the 3 of May 1687 for Jno Hathway Lyeing on the north side of bush river on the western branch and now in the posession of John Webster and Wm Howard Rent ⅌ anum —.. 7.. 9

C.   Hathoway. Poss^r Christoph^r Cox.

Hopewell, 204 acr Sur the 4th June 1687 for William Standifer Lying on Sinika ridge and now In the posession of the Executor of Edward Boothby rent ⅌ anum —.. 8.. 2

Morgans Lott, 200 acr Sur the 25 May 1687 for Wm Morgan Lyeing on the south side of bush river on the south side of the western branch Morgan gone to Wales the Land uncultivated noe rent made since first taken up rent set £0.. 8.. 0

Dandy Hill, 171 acr. Sur the 10 Aprill 1695 for George

Burges called dandy Hill Lyeing on the head of gunpowder river begining at a bound red oak neare Winslyes branch Rent ℔ anum —.. 7.. ½

C. Windly's branch. Poss^r John Bayly.

Tapley Neck, 306 acr Sur the 11 Aprill 1695 for George Burgess called Taply Hill Lyeing on the south side of bush river begining at a bounded white oak by Waltons Creek, Rent ℔ anum —.. 12.. 3

C. Poss^r Geoge Parker of Calvert Co.

Mount Hayes, 317 acr Sur the 2^d July 1694 for John Hayes Called mount Hayes Lyeing on the north side of back river begining at a bounded w^t oak on the west side of the double run below the near road (In Patapsco hundred) Rent ℔ anum —.. 12.. 8½

Beare Neck, 500 acr Sur the 10 of Octob^r 1697 for Walter. Smith called bear neck Lyeing on the south side of gunpowd^r falls begining at a bounded w^t oake at the side of a high Hill near the place Caled Newport rent ℔ anum 1.. —.. —

Cub Hill, 500 acr Sur 1 of Octr 1695 for William Burges Called Cub hill Lyeing on the south side of the mainfalls of gunp^r River begining at two bounded w^t oaks on the south side of a greate branch belonging to Benjamin Burges Rent ℔ anum 1.. —.. —

Franceses Freedom, 1000 acr Sur the 27 Sepr 1682 for Samuell Young called Franceses Freedom Lyeing In Baltimore County on the north branch of the head of Gunpowder river begining at a bounded popular in a Valley by a peice of Meddow ground rent ℔ anum 2.. —.. —

C. France's Freedom.

Back Lingan, 450 acr Sur the 30 March 1696 for George Lingan

Lyeing on the north side of back river begining at a bounded Spanish oak by the river side rent ℔ anum —.. 18.. —

C. Poss^r Edward Butler.

Scotts Grove, 500 acr Sur the 6 Novemb^r 1695 for Daniell Scott Called Scotts Grove Lyeing above the head of bush river between bynums run and winters run begining at a bounded beach by a small run rent ℔ anum 1.. —.. —

Chevy Chase, 400 acre Sur the 26 of July 1695 for John Thomas Chase in the woods begining at a bounded w^t oak of Edward Folkes Land Rent ℔ anum —.. 16.. —

C. Chivy Chase. Poss^{rs} 100a, Elisha Sedgewick, 100a Joshua Sedgewick, 200a Seborn Tucker.

Sisters Hope, 200 acr Sur the 12th Novem^r 1695 for Frances Watkins Called Sisters Hope Lyeing the side of back river on duck Creek begining at a bounded pine of paradice, rent ℔ anum —.. 8.. —

C. Poss^r ye orpn of sd Watkins. Tho Bedeson.

The Narrows, 77 acr Sur the 11th Septem^r 1695 for James Maxwell Lyeing on the north side of Gunp^r river near the mouth begining at a bounded w^t oak near the s^d river rent ℔ an —.. 3.. 1

C. Narrow. [Author tract called The Narrows is described on page 148 of C].

Good Endeavor, 139 acr Sur the 29 of July 1695 for James Dennis Lyeing above the head of gunp^r river in the woods on the East side of the little falls begining at a bounded w^t oak on the south side of the s^d branch rent ℔ anum —.. 5.. 7

C. Poss^r Wm Noble.

Friendship, 400 acr Sur the 7 of May 1685 for Micall Judd on the north side of gunpowder river begining at a bounded red oak by a small branch and now In the posestion of Wm Hicks rent ℔ anum —.. 16.. —

Warram, 75 acr Sur the 8 of decem[r] 1685 for Robert Owlis on the north side of gunpowder river begining at a bounded Spanish oak by a marsh rent ℔ anum —.. 1.. 6

C. Norram 37a. 8 xber 1694.

Smith Begining, 100 acr Sur the 18 of March 1688 for Thomas Smith Lyeing on gunpowder river begining at a bounded red oak upon a point on the south side of the mouth of Rogers Hills Creek rent ℔ anum —.. 4.. —

C. Poss[n] of the orp[n] of sd Thos Smith. Qr. If any Land.

Evells Chase, 230 acr Sur the 30 of May 1696 for Thomas Norris Lyeing in the woods on bush river branch on the East side of the bald fryar on the north side of the Sweat house branch begining at a bounded white oak on a pocoson rent ℔ anum —.. 9.. 2½

C. Evil Chace.

Leafe Jun[r], 252 acr Sur the 14 of June for Frances Leafe Lyeing on the north side of bush river in the woods begining at a bounded Hickery wth a Chestnut tree growing out of the root, rent ℔ anum —.. 10.. 1

C. Leafe's Forest & Leafs Chance, neither of which agree with this description.

MARYLAND RENT ROLLS.

Baltimore County.

Inlargment to Jehosaphet 500 acr. Sur the 2 of Septemb^r 1695 for Richard Smith Lyeing vp the falls of gunpowder river beginning at a bounded w^t walnut on the north side of the falls a bounded tree of Jehosaphet rent ⅌ anum 1..—..—

Lawrances Pasture, 150 acr. Sur the 28 of Septemb^r 1683 for Larance Richardson on the south of a branch of gunpowder river Commonly called back river at a bounded Chestnut standing by the side of Windleys branch rent ⅌ anum —..6..—

Windleys Rest 200 acr Sur the 7 of July 1686 for Richard Windley on the south side of back river at a bounded Chesnut tree on the west side of Windleys branch and now in the posestion of Francis Dallerhide rent ℔ an —..8..—

C. Poss^r Wm Slade..

Taylors Mount, 200 acr Sur the 28 of July 1661 for John Taylor on the South side of the Eastern branch of gunpowder river and 200 acr in the posestion of Thomas Richardson rent ℔ an —..4..—

50 acr residue thereof in posestion of Thomas Marley rent ℔ anum —..1..—

C. 250 a Poss^r Wm Adams.

Long Point 150 acr Sur the 1 of Septemb^r 1687 for Thomas Richardson on the south side of gunpowder river at a bounded w^t oak of the Land Called Taylors Mount And now In the posestion of John Richardson rent ℔ anum —..6..—

C. Poss^r James Crooke.

Love Point, 100 acr Sur the 10 of July 1672 for Richard Symes on the north side of the westerne branch of gunp^r river at a marked oak on a point by the side of the said branch posesed by Lawrence Richardson rent ℔ anum —..4..—

C. For R^d Lines.

Tall Hill 100 acr Sur the 22 of August 1669 for Arthur Taylor in the North East branch of gunpow^r river on the South Side of the branch 50 acr thereof in the posestion of Mary Litton for the orphants of Thomas Litton rent ℔ anum —..1..—

50 acr residue thereof posesed by Robert West rent ℔ anum —..1..—

C. 1667. Poss^r 50a Walter Morrow.

Tracys Levill, 200 acr Sur the 9 of March 1670 for Samuell Tracye at the head of gunpowder river at the head of one of the branches of the s^d river Called back river and the head of

Light woods Creek, and now In the posestion of Lawrence Richardson rent ℔ anum —..8..—

C. *Traceys Level.*

Dixsons Chance, 300 acr Sur the 8th of June 1667 for John Dixon in gunpowder river on the southward side of the river and now In the posestion of John Richardson rent ℔ anum —..6..—

C. *Dixons Chance. Poss^r Wm Adams.*

Mates Affinity, 200 acr Sur the 1 March 1683 for Edward Douse and Emanuel Selye vpon a Creek of gunpowder river Called Salt peter Creek near the head begining at a bounded w^t oak a small fork of the s^d Creek belonging to the Orphants of Edward Boothbye rent ℔ anum —..8..—

S. *Edward Douce & Emanuel Cealy.*

The Range, 200 acr Sur the 11th of Novem^r 1686 for Edward Donse and Emanuel Selye Lyeing on the head of Salt peter Creek and now In the posestion of William Dane in Kent County rent ℔ anum —..8..—

C. *Douce & Cealy.*

Gassaway Ridge 500 acr Sur the 11 of May 1678 for Nicolas Gassaway between the falls of gunpowder river next a Joyning to Leafes Chance rent ℔ anum 1..—..—

C. *Poss^r S^d Gassoways orp^n.*

Littleton, 600 acr Sur the 14 of May 1684 for Thomas Thurston on the East side of bush river and on the west side of bynums run at a bounded Ash by the run side 452 acr part thereof In the posestion of Robert Love ℔ anum —..18..1

180 acr residue thereof in the posestion of Stepton Gill rent ℔ anum —..7..2½

C. *632a. Poss^rs 180a. Stephen Gill, 452a John Israel.*

William the Conqueror, 200 acr Sur the 24 May 1685 for William Ramsey on the head of qunpowder river 150 acr part thereof in the posestion of Nicolas Day rent ℔ anum —..6..—

100 acr residue thereof in the posestion Wm Lenox rent ₱ anum —..2..—

C.   Poss^r 150a Nich^o Day.   50 Wm Lennox.

Come by Chance, 200 acr Sur the 9th June 1671 for James Bynum on James branch on bush River at a marked red oak by the s^d branch and granted to Thomas Thurston by vertue of a madamas In the yeare 1684.   167 acr part thereof in the posestion of the s^d Thomas Thurston rent ₱ anum —..6..—

33 acr the residue in the posestion of Robert Love rent ₱ anum —..1..—

C.   Record incomplete.

Joyce Tripass, 150 acr Sur the 5th Octr 1674 for William Joyce on bush river at a marked red oak on the south side of the river the westernmost bounds of Christopher Topley and Levy Warfe posesed by John Durham and now In the posestion of John Boone rent ₱ anum —..6..—

C.   Joyce Stripes.   Poss^r Mathew Green.   [Interlined] " Poss^r 87a Jno Boone.   63a Jno Durham."

Levyes Tribe, 100 acr Sur the 4th July 1672 for Christopher Topley and Levy Wharfe on the south side of bush river at a marked white oak by a Marsh at the side of the said river and now In the posestion of Samuell Durham rent ₱ an. —..4..—

C.   Leaveys Tribe.   Poss^r Mathew Green [Interlined] " by Jno Durham."

Addition to Levyes Tribe, 50 acr. Sur the 14 of Aprill 1681 for John Durham Lyeing on the west side of bush river and on the north side of a Creek Called Swan Creek begining at a bounded white oake and now in the posestion of Samuell Durham rent ₱ anum —..2..—

C.   Poss^r John Durham.

Georges Hill 150 acr Sur the 20th of Octob^r 1667 for George Collet on gunpowder river on the East side of the river near Fosters Creek 20 acr part thereof in the posestion of Thomas Preston rent ₱ anum —..—..5

130 acr residue thereof belonging to the Orphants of William Lewis rent ꝑ anum —..2..7

The Chance, 43 acr Sur the 12 of July 1676 for Edward Reives on the north side of gunpowder river at a red oake abounded tree posesed by Thomas Preston rent ꝑ anum —..1..8¼

    C. Edwd Reeves.

Lodwicks Refuse, 50 acr Sur the 7th of Decemb^r 1667 for Thomas Preston on the north side of gunpowder river at a red oak a bounded red oak a bounded tree of Edward Reeves Land rent ꝑ anum —..2..—

    C. 1676.

Hog Point, 40 acr Sur the 7 of decem^r 1676 for Thomas Preston on the north side of gunpd^r river at a marked w^t oak Standing by a ꝑcell of Land formerly laid out for Arthur Taylor rent ꝑ anum —..1..8

Hopewell, 60 acr Sur the 7 of decemb^r 1676 for Thomas Preston on the north side of gunpowder river on the north side of a Creek rent ꝑ anum —..2..7

    C. Poss^r 41a John Rawlins, ye rest Abra Tyler.

The Vnity Friendship, 350 acr Sur the 12 of July 1676 for Edward Reeves and Lodwick Williams on the north side of gunpowder river at a bounded w^t oak near a pocoson, near the head of Middle Creek 175 acr part thereof in the posestion of Thomas Preston rent ꝑ anum —..7..—

175 acr residue thereof belonging to William Burne who has Left this province 16 yeares agoe noe rent rent set £ 0..7..0

    C. The United Friendship. Poss^{rs} 175a Tho. Preston, 175a Wm Burn who left this province 20 years ago. Preston claimes the whole.

Prestons Luck, 50 acr Sur noe time When for Thomas Preston in a small Creek on the East side of gunpowder River Called Cookes creek at a bounded Spanish oak Stump posesed as afores^d rent ꝑ anum —..2..—

Chance, 150 acr Sur the 10 of August 1669 for Joseph Herves on bush river on the west side of the river and on the north side of a marsh near Hog neck and now in the posestion of Thomas Preston, rent ℔ anum —..3..—

Who marryed the heires of the s^d Herves

Judds Addition, 28 acr Sur the 28th of feb^r 1688 for Michaell Judd Lyeing between gunpowder and bush river and now In the posestion of Thomas Preston rent ℔ anum —..1..1½

Pitchcraft, 112 acr Sur the 29 of Decemb^r 1694 for Thomas Preston Lying on the north side of bush river begining at a bounded red oak near Tilliers Creek rent ℔ anum —..4..6

   C. Gilliers Creek. Poss^r Robt Shaw.

Everly Hill, 394 acr Sur the 29 of decemb^r 1694 for Thomas Preston Lyeing in the woods above the head of bush river begining at a bounded red oak on the East side of Winters run Rent ℔ anum —..15..9½

Brodwell Hill, 288 acr Sur the 16th Oct 1695 for Thomas Preston Lyeing on the south side of bush river begining at a bounded white oak by Sam's Cove rent ℔ anum —..11..6½

   C. Broadwell hill.

Richardsons Out Let, 808 acr Sur the 12 of March 1686/7 for Thomas Richardson Lying on the south side of gunp^r river 100 acr part thereof in the posestion of Walter Marrow rent ℔ anum —..4..—

230 acr part thereof in the posestion of Thomas Sterling in Talbot County rent ℔ an —..9..2

478 acr residue thereof in the posestion of James Richardson rent ℔ anum —..19..1¼

Leaf's Chance, 375 acr Sur the 10 July 1678 for Francis Leafe between the fall of gunpowder river at a bounded Hickory on the ridge between the falls 125 acr p^t thereof in the posestion of Wm Lenox rent ℔ —..5..—

100 acr part thereof in the posestion of John Boone rent ℔ anum —..4..—

150 acr residue thereof in poses. of Charles Hewit rent ℔ anum —..6..—

C. Poss^{rs} 125a Wm Lenox, 100a Tho. Hutchins, 150a Edward Selby.

Sarah's Delight 80 acr Sur the 14 of July 1676 for John Tilliard on the south most side of bush river at a bounded tree of the Land formerly laid out for Francis Trippass Called bridewell Dock rent ℔ anum —..3..3

God's Providence, 200 acr Sur the 14 July 1676 for John Tilliard formerly Called puddle wharfe on the south west side of bush river at a bounded w^t oak of the Land formerly Laid out for Francis Stripass Called bridewell dock these 2 ℔ cells of Land Sur into one 160 acr part thereof In the posestion of Charles Adams rent ℔ an. —..6..5

140 acr rescidue thereof in the posestion of Richard Tilliard rent ℔ anum —..4..10

C. Sarahs Delight & God's providence. The two tracts are included in one entry. 280a rent 0, 11, 3, Poss^{rs} 160a Tho. Chamberlain, 120a R^d Tilyard.

Bridewell dock, 100 acr Sur the 5 Aprill 1667 for Francis Tripass on the west side of bush river on the northward side of the Land Called Tripilo suposed not to be above twenty acr rent Set £ 0..2..0

C. Francis Stripas. Land call^d Tripylon.

York Chance, 125 acr Sur the 14 July 1676 for William York on the south west side of bush river at a bounded red oak and runing vp the river these two ℔ cells of Land In the posestion of Mary Criswell for the Orphants of William York rent ℔ anum —..5..—

C. Poss^r of those two tracts Mary Frizell for ye orp^{ns} of Wm York. This land was form^{rly} call^d Tripolo, cont 50a, but was resur & fo^d to cont. 125a. Poss^r Geo. York, the heir.

Spring Neck, 126 acr Sur the Septemb^r 1697 for Israell Shelton Lyeing at a bounded Chestnut and runing East and by south downe the river and now in the posession as afores[d] Rent ⅌ anum —..5..½·

C. Israel Skelton. Entry incomplete.

Arthurs Choyce, 300 acr Sur the 20th August 1683 for Arthur Taylor on the south side of the west branch of gunpowder river 150 part thereof in the posession of Walter Bosely rent ⅌ anum —..6..—

75 acr more part thereof the posession of Lawrence Richardson rent ⅌ anum —..3..—

75 acr. residue thereof in the posession of Lawrence Richardson for the orphants of James Greear rent ⅌ anum —..3..—

C. Poss[r] Oliver Hareot.

Bosley's Expectation, 200 acr Sur the 10 Octob[r] 1696/7 for Walter Bosley on the south side of the south west branch of gunpowder river beginning at a bounded red oak a bounded tree of 2 tracts Land the one Called Spring neck and the other Arthurs Choyce rent ⅌ anum —..8..—

Black woolfe neck, 150 acr Sur the 3 of June 1667 for Richard Furendall in gunpowder river on the south side of the wester most branch and now In the posession of Edward Felks rent ⅌ anum —..3..—

C. Black Wolve Neck. Poss[r] Ann Felks.

Felkes Forrest, 200 acr Sur the 2 of Decemb[r] 1688 for Edward Felkes Lyeing on the north side of back river and now in the posession of Harebottle for the Orphants of Henry Francis rent ⅌ anum —..8..—

C. Poss[r] Hew Merriday.

Felkes Range, 200 acr Sur the 14 of August 1688 for Edward Felkes Lyeing on the south west branch of gunpowder and now in posession of Edward Felkes rent ⅌ anum —..8..—

C. Poss[r] Ann Felks.

Good Hope, 200 acr Sur the 8 August 1696 for Edward Felks

Lyeing on the south side of the main falls of gunpowder river in the woods begining at a bounded popular by the two bounded white oakes and in the posestion as afores^d, rent ℔ anum —..8..—

C. *Poss^r Ann Felks.*

Salt Peter Neck, 100 acr Sur the 19 Octo^r 1694 for James Denton on the northermost branch of gunp^r. river and on the westermost side of the branch and now in the posestion of William Denton rent ℔ anum —..2..—

Batchelors Meddow, 40 acr Sur the 6 of March 1678 for James Denton on the south side of gunpowder river near Salt peter Creek and now in the posestion of William Denton rent ℔ anum —..1..7

Dentons Hope, 300 acr resurveyed the 27 May 1679 for James Denton 2 ℔cells of Land Called Salt peter Creek and batchelors hope in gunpowder river and now in the posestion of William Denton Rent ℔ anum —..12..—

C. *This Land form^{rly} call^d Batchelo^{rs} hope.*

William & Mary, 50 acr Sur the 20 of August 1695 for William Horne Lyeing at the head of the north East branch of Salt peter Creek begining at a bounded red oak of the Land Called Limbrick Rent ℔ anum —..2..—

C. *Poss^r Horn's orpⁿ.*

Limbrick 100 acr Sur the 5 of Novemb^r 1695 for John Bevins at a bounded oak of Salt peter Creek and on the west side of the branch and was In the posestion of Marcus Tench who has Left this County 12 yeares agoe rent ℔ anum —..4..—

C. *Limmerick. Poss^r Robuck Lynch.*

Midsummer Hill, 201 acr Sur the 18 July 1689 for John Bevins Lyeing on the north side of Salt peter Creek begining at a bounded red oak on a point and now posesed by Francis Dollerhide rent ℔ anum —..8..½

C. *Poss^r Francis Dallahyde.*

Horn point, 64 acr Sur the 6 May 1688 for William Horn in one of the forkes of Salt peter Creek of the said Land of Thomas Richardson at the head of a greate Marsh and now In the posestion of Giles Stephenson rent ℔ anum —..2..7

C. Poss[r] Giles Stevens.

St. Gileses, 200 acr Sur the 11 Novemb[r] 1674 for Giles Stephenson in back river at a marked w[t] oak at the head of a cove on the north side of the river and now in the posestion of Giles Stephenson his son rent ℔ an. —..8..—

C. Giles Stevens Sen[r]. Poss[r] Giles Stevens Jun[r].

James Forecast, 50 acr Sur the 19 of Novemb[r] 1686 for Thomas James at a bounded Spanish oak of the Land of John Rockhold and now in the posestion of Giles Stephenson rent ℔ anum —..2..—

C. Poss[r] Giles Stevens.

Swallow fork, 100 acr. Sur the 3[d] May 1683 for Hendrick Inloes in Seneca Creek at a bounded Spanish oak on a little neck between two branches of the Creek and now in the posestion of John Inlowes rent ℔ anum —..2..—

C. Poss[r] Jno Leakins for Inloes orp[n].

Salebury Plaine, 100 acr Sur the 20 of decemb[r] 1670 for Thomas Pert and Robert Benjor at a bounded the south East End of George Hickesons 50 acr part thereof in the posestion of Inlowes rent ℔ an. —..2..—
50 acr residue thereof in the posestion of Alex[r] Graves rent ℔ anum —..2..—

C. Salisbury plain. Geo. Hickson. Poss[r] 50a Jn[o] Leakins. 50a Alex[r] Graves.

Duck Neck, 100 acr Sur the 2 May 1673 for Hendrick Inlowes in Senico Creek at a marked Spanish oak in a little neck between two branches at the head of the Creek and in the posestion afores[d] rent ℔ anum —..2..—

C. Dutch neck.

The Low Lands, 33 acr Sur the 7 March 1687 for Hendrick Inlowes Lyeing between the mouth of Midle river and Senicoe Creek begining at a bounded white oak by the bay side and posesed as afores^d rent ℔ anum —..1..6

Tryangle Neck, 100 acr Sur the 3 May 1673 for Hendrick Inlowes on the midle river at a marked red oak at the head of a Cove on the north side of up^r river posesed as afores^d rent ℔ anum —..2..—

The Oblong, 150 acr. Sur the 20 June 1687 for Hendrick Inlowes Lyeing on the south side of Midle river on a ridge called river ridge begining at a bounded red oak in the Line of Thomas James Land posesed as aforesaid rent ℔ anum —..6..—

C. Poss^r Willm Holland.

Olivers Reserve, 150 acr Sur the 10 June 1667 for Oliver Sprye in gunpowder river in a branch of the river Called middle branch on the East side of the branch and now posesed by Daniell Scott rent ℔ anum —..3..—

C. Poss^r James Durham for Wm Galloways orpⁿ.

Chestnut Neck, 100 acr Sur the 3 May 1673 for John Chadwell at a marked w^t oak on a point by a marsh on the west side of the westermost branch of Synicoe Creek 50 acr part thereof in the posestion of Daniells Scott rent ℔ anum —..2..—

50 acr Residue thereof in the posestion of John Chadwell rent ℔ anum —..2..—

C. Poss^r Dan^{ll} Scott.

190 acr Sur the 4 July 1676 for John Chadwell between gunpowder river and midle river on a Creek Called Synicoe Creek at a bounded oak by a marsh side 95 acr part thereof in the posestion of Daniel Scot rent ℔ anum —..3..9¾

95 acr residue thereof in the posestion of John Chadwell rent ℔ anum —..3..9¾

C. Stanhercut. Poss^r Dan^{ll} Scott.

Scotts Hopewell, 500 acr Sur the 7 Novemb^r 1696 for Daniell

Scott begining at a bounded red oak stand by a ℔cell of Land formerly taken vp by James Maxwell and now posesed by Daniell Scott rent ℔ anum 1..0..0

 C. Poss^r 256a Dan^{ll} Scott Junr. 244a Jno Howard's orpⁿ.

Fullers Out Lett, 100 acr Sur the 11 Jan^{ry} 1655 for John Fuller Lyeing on the East side of Midle river and now posesed by William Wright, rent ℔ anum —..4..—

Frogmorton, 53 acr Sur the 10 May 1687 for George Oglesby Lyeing on the north side of Midle river and now in the posestion of Henry Cornelius rent ℔ an. —..2..1½

 C. Throgmorton. Poss^r Henry Cornelius. Dead & no heirs.

James Park, 200 acr Sur the 30 May 1678 for Thomas James Lyeing on the South side of Midle river and now in the posestion of George Grover, rent ℔ anum —..8..—

 C. Poss^r Jno Ewins.

Hopewell, 60 acr Sur the 1 of Septemb^r 1687 for Robert Benjor Lyeing on the north side of a Creek Called Sterling Creek and now posesed by Michaell Rutledge rent ℔ anum 5..2..0

Hollands Adventure, 200 acr Sur the 28 Sepr 1676 for George Holland and assigned Francis Watkins on the north side of gunpowder river on a Creek Called Hollands Creek in the posestion of the orphants of the s^d Holland rent ℔ anum 0..8..0

 C. Poss^r s^d Watkins orp^{ns}, in possⁿ of Robt Tasker.

Harmons Hope, 100 acr Sur the 12 August 1667 for Godfrey Harmon on the west side of gunp^r river near the mouth of Salt peter Creek and now in posestion of John Chadwell, rent ℔ anum —..2..—

 C. Hermons Hope. Poss^r Dan^{ll} Scott.

Bettys Delight, 63 acr Sur the 4 Novemb^r 1673 for John Chadwell at the mouth of gunpowder river on an Island Called

Phillips Island at a bounded red oak at the head of a marsh and now in posestion afores^d rent ℔ anum —..1..5

 C. Poss^r Dan^{ll} Scott.

James Pasture, 136 acr Sur in August 1687 for Thomas James on deep Creek begining at a bounded white oak on the north side of back river runing down the river South East 96 perches to a bounded red oak and now in the posestion of Wm Tolfare for the orphants of William Barton Rent ℔ anum —..5..5

 C. Poss^r Lewis Barton.

Long Port, 111 acr Sur the 15 of June 1683 for Major Thomas Long begining at a bounded Spanish oak being a bounded tree of a piece of Land granted to the said Long Called Hopewell 60 acr part thereof in the posestion of Edward Jones for the Orphants of Richard Enock, rent ℔ anum —..2..6
50 acr residue thereof in the posestion of Johana Bumbridge rent ℔ anum —..2..—

 C. All dead. None claims.

Turky Hill, 262 acr Sur the 1 January 1695 for Samuell Sicklemore Lyeing on the East side of the little falls of Gunpowder river begining at a bounded white oak on a ridge and posesed as aforesaid rent ℔ anum —..10..6

 C. Turkey Hill. Poss^r Willm Hitchcock.

Wolfe Harbour, 318 acr Sur the 20th June 1689 for Samuell Sicklemore Lyeing on the north side of gunp^r river begining at a bounded Chesnut on the west side of the mouth of Custers Creek and posesed as aforesaid rent ℔ anum —..12..9

 C. Wolves Harbo^r. Fosters Creek.. Taken away by a survey of Fosters Neck.

Rayma, 100 acr Sur the 28 Aprill 1687 for Samuell Sicklemore Lyeing on the north side of gunp^w river and now in the posestion of John Parker for the Orphants of Thomas Smith Rent ℔ anum —..4..—

 C. Poss^r Tho. Smiths orp^n.

Johns Habitation, 200 acr Sur the 24 Sept[r] 1683 for John Linegar on the south side of a branch of gunp[r] river called back river at a Spanish oak at the end of the South East Line of Arthurs Choice in posestion of Stephen Bently for the Orphants of John Linegar rent ℔ anum —..8..—

C. John Lingager. Poss[r] Step[n] Bentley for S[d] Lingagers orp[ns].

Addition to Priviledge, 59 acr Sur the 15 August 1688 for Robert Benjor Lyeing between Sennica ridge and Salt peter Creek now posesed Alexand[r]. Graves rent ℔ anum 0..2..4

Johns Interest, 200 acre Sur the 14 May 1686 for Michaell Judd Lyeing on the west side of back river now posesed by Abraham Delapp, rent ℔ anum —..8..—

C. Poss[r] James Isum for the orp[n] of Abra: Delap now Jeremiah Downes married y[e] heir.

Robartes Choice, 153 acr Sur the 27 March 1688 for Thomas Robarts Lyeing betweene Patapsco and back river now posesed by the s[d] Robarts rent ℔ anum ———

(In patapsco hundred)

C. Roberts choice sur 27 March 1668. 0. 6. 1½.

Buck Range, 148 acr Sur the 6 february 1687 for John Fuller at the head of back river and now In the posestion of the s[d] Fuller, rent ℔ anum —..4..11

C. Poss[r] Jn[o] Anderson.

Speedwell, 27 acr Sur the 11 of June 1688 for Roger Spinks Lyeing on the south side of gunpowder river now in the posestion of Enock Spinks Rent ℔ anum —..1..1

C. Poss[r] Tho. Littons orp[n].

Richardsons reserve, 214 acr Sur the 5 June 1684 for Thomas Richardson on the East side of the north branch of gunpowder river at a bounded popular standing by the said branch by a Small run and now in the posestion of Orphants of Richard Ellinsworth, rent ℔ anum —..8..7

C. Poss[r] Rich[d] Ellingsworth orp[n].

Richardson's Plaint, 100 acr Sur the 22 Septemb[r] 1688 for Thomas Richardson on the South side of a branch of gunpowder river Called back river at a bounded white oak on a Levill near the s[d] branch and now in the posestion of John Sargent rent ℔ anum —..4..—

    C. Poss[r] John Sergant.

Benjors Horse pasture, 20 acr Sur the 12 Septemb[r] 1683 for Robart Benjor on the south side of the mouth of gunpowder river at a marked white oak standing by a small Island and now in the posestion of Alexand[r] Graves, rent ℔ an. —..1..2½

Hunting Creek, 100 acr Sur the 18 March 1664 for Oliver Sprye vpon the Island back Creek on the north side of the Creek in gunpowder river now posesed by John Chadwell rent ℔ anum —..2..—

    C. Poss[r] Dan[ll] Scott.

Chadwells Range, 80 acr Sur the 24 Novemb[r] 1683 for John Chadwell at the mouth of gunpowder river in an Island Called Phillips Island at a bounded Spanish oak on the north side of the Island and now in the posestion of Alexander Graves rent ℔ anum —..3..2½

    C. 1673.

Benjors Priviledge, 108 acr Sur the 20 Novemb[r] 1659 for Robart Benjor on the south side of Salt peter Creek at a bounded red oak near a bounded white oak of Harmons hope and now In posestion of Alexander Graves, rent ℔ anum —..2..3¾

Swans Point, 100 acr Sur the 1 July 1672 for John Owens on the south side of the west branch of gunp[r]. river at a marked Chestnut in a neck between two brooks Land vncultivated noe heires appeare Escheatable rent sett —..4..—

Wignols Rest, 200 acr Sur the 27 July 1661 for William Wignoll on the western side of gunpowder of the Eastern branch of the s^d river it belongs to the Orphants of John Dorsey, rent ℔ anum —..4..—

    C. Poss^r John Dorsey.

Old Burrough, 350 acr Sur the 13 August 1670 for Peter Sterling at a bounded Chestnut at the head of a Creek on the north side of Sterlings branch now posesed by Luke Raven, rent ℔ anum

    C. Oldborough. Luke Raven.

The Tryangle, 100 acr Sur 14 Novemb^r 1670 for Peter Sterling at a marked chestnutt oak upon a point between the Eastern and midle branch of midle river and now posesed by Luke Raven rent ℔ anum —..4..—

    C. The Triangle. Luke Raven.

Lukes Adventure, 317 acr. Sur the 30 May 1687 for Luke Raven on the north side of Midle river posesed as aforesaid rent ℔ anum —.. 12.. 8½

Seneca Ridge, 100 acr. Sur the 11 June 1685 for Thomas Litefoot on the south side of bush river in the woods no rent payd since it was taken vp.   Litefoot dead who gave the s^d Land to his wife who does not Clame the same as Exec^{rx} for feare of Coll Thomas Taylor who Clames a great debt from the said Estate —.. 4.. —

    C. Not in C.

Best Indeavour, 1000 acr. Sur the 27 Novemb^r 1686 for Thomas Litefoot Lyeing on the East side of bush river Land vncultivated the same as above rent ℔ anum 2.. —.. —

    C. Best Endeavour. Tho. Lightfoot.

London, 100 acr. Sur the 14th Aprill 1674 for John Vaughan on the north side of gunp^r river on the Elk neck creek and belongs to the orphants of the said Vaughan rent ℔ anum —.. 4.. —

    C. Dead no heirs.

500 acr. Sur the 15 May 1683 for Thomas Litefoot on the north branch of gunp^r river beginning at a bounded oak by the said branch rent ℔ anum 1.. —.. —
This Land sould to Mr James Sanders of Anne
arundell County

    C. Not in C.

Expectation, 1000 acr. Sur the 16 Sepr 1683 for Thomas Lite-foot above gunp^r river on the south side of the northern branch begining at a bounded red oak standing by the said branch at a bounded tree of another peace of Land formerly sur for the s^d Litefoot this Land as the rest rent 2.. —.. —

    C. Not in C. Three other tracts of same name, none of which agree with this description.

Oxford 65 acr. Sur the 12 Aprill 1681 for Michaell Judd Lye-ing on the East side gunp^r river in a Creek Called Elk creek Judd ran away and as yet his son will not Clame it, rent ℔ anum 0.. 2.. 7

    C. Sold to Corn Boyle who died wthout heir. Poss^r Theo Kitten.

Watertons Neglect, 6¼ acr. Sur the 1 Augt 1687 for Mical Judd Lyeing on the north side of the fork of gunpow^r river this Land as above rent ℔ anum Charg'd before —.. —.. 00

    C. Poss^r Willm Peckett.

Hollands Gift, 127 acr. Sur the 15 March 1679 for Israel Skelton betwixt the two falls of gunp^r river at a bounded tree of the Land Called Symses Choice and sold to Mical Judd. Judd run away and his son will not as yet Claime rent sup-posed not to be halfe soe much rent —.. 5.. —

    C. Since as I am informed taken away by an old^r Survey.

Patapsco Hundred.

Larkins Addition, 400 acr Sur the 10 Novem^r 1673 for John Larkin on the north side of patapsco river Adjacent to the Land Called Ludlowes Lott rent ℔ anum —.. 16.. —

    C. Not in C.

Hollands Choice, 580 acr Sur the 11 August 1677 for Anthony Holland on the south side of patapsco river in the woods at a bounded oak on the East side of the Holly run rent ⅌ anum 1.. 2.. 2

    C. Poss^r S^d Holland's Orp^n.

Forrest, 1800 acr Sur the 23 March 1678 for Thomas Taylor Esqr on the north side of patapsco river at a bounded tree of the Land of John Pierce rent ⅌ anum £3.. 12.. —

    C. Forest Poss^{rs} 900 a. Wm Chew. 900 a. Coll. Edwd Dorsey. Belongs to said Taylor.

Boddyes Adventure, 700 acr Sur the 14 Septem^r 1676 for Capt John Body on the south side of patapsco river on the north side of Curteses Creek at a Corner of the south west Line of the Land Called Morelys Choice in the posestion of Gardner rent ⅌ an. 1.. 8.. —

    C. Bodys adventure. Poss^r John Gardiner.

Andover, 1640 acr Sur the 12 Septemb^r 1677 for Nicolas Painter on the south side of patapsco river in the woods at a bounded red oak and runing In the Line of Anthony Hollands Land and now in the posestion of Francis Leafe, rent ⅌ an 3.. 5.. 7

    C. Poss^r James Geeniff's orp^n.

Peirces Incouragement, 1000 acr Sur the 11th Oct 1677 for John Peirce on the north side of patapsco river on the western branch at a bounded red oak runing north west rent ⅌ anum £2.. —.. —

    C. Pierce's encouragem^t. Possr's s^d Pierces heirs.

Good Luck, 200 acr Sur the 11 August 1684 for John Thomas on the north side of Patapsco river on the north side of a creek Called Clappers Creek rent ⅌ anum —.. 8.. —

    C. Poss^{rs} 100 a. S^d Thomas 100 a. ye Vestrymen of St Pauls Parish.

Thomases Range, 150 acr Sur the 5 Septem^r 1683 for John Thomas on the north side of Patapsco river rent ℈ anum —.. 6.. —

C. Thomas's range.

Athell Borrow, 600 acr Sur the 2 March 1684 for George Tompson on the north side of Patapsco river by the west side of the midle branch of the river rent ℈ anum 1.. 4.. —

C. Athelborough. Geo. Thomson. Poss^r Giles Blissards orp^n.

Cusacks Forrest, 596 acr Sur the 26 May 1685 for Michaell Cusack on the south side of the west branch of patapsco river as I am Informed it belong to the heires of Capt Richard Hill rent ℈ anum 1.. 3.. 10.

C. Cusack dead and can find no heirs.

Denton, 600 acr Sur the 31 July 1686 for Henry Denton on the west side of the Midle branch of patapsco river belonging to the Orphants of the s^d Denton rent ℈ anum 1.. 4.. —

C. Belongs I'm informed to Willm Bladen Esq.

Hollands Purchase, 300 acr sur the 15 may 1686 for William Holland on the north side of patapsco river on the west side of the midle branch of the said river Rent ℈ anum —.. 12.. —

Timber Neck, 200 acr sur the 28 Octob^r 1670 for John Howard and now in the posestion of the said Howard rent ℈ anum —.. 4.. —

C. Poss^r s^d Howards heirs.

The Levell, 200 acr Sur the 19 July 1688 for Solomon Jones Lyeing on the south side of gunpowder Jones falls rent ℈ anum —.. 8.. —

C. I noe not the man.

Hopewell, 381¼ acr Sur the 15 Jan^{ry} 1686/7 for James Cullen on the north side of patapsco river, rent ℈ an. —.. 15.. 3¼

C. Poss^r Wm Bladen, Esq.

Habnab at a Venture, 350 acr Sur the 30 June 1688 for Thomas Dubin Lyeing on the north side of patapsco river and now belonging to the orphants of the said Durbin rent ℔ anum —.. 14.. —

C. Poss^r 150 a. S^d Durbins orp^n. 200 a. John Eagleston.

Vnited Friendship, 700 acr Sur the 15 Octo^r 1684 for John Larkin Lyeing on the north side of patapsco river rent ℔ anum 1.. 8.. —

C. Poss^{rs} 350 a. Coll. Edwd Dorsey. 350 a. Wm Chew.

Welfare, 104 acr Sur the 24 June 1685 for Michaell Cusack Lyeing on the south side of patapsco river as I am Informed belongs to the Orphants of Capt Richard Hill rent ℔ an —.. 4.. 2

C. Poss^r Capt R^d Hill's heir.

Browns Adventure, 1000 acr Sur the 10 of Octob^r 1644 for Thomas Brown Called browns Adventure Lyeing on the north side of patapsco river and on the north side of Coll Thomas Taylors Land begining at a bounded oak in the said Taylors Line and now in the posestion of Gadsby rent ℔ anum 2.. —.. —

C. Poss^{rs} 870 a. Aaron Rawlins. 130 a. Jno Barker.

Fox Hall, 200 acr Sur the 12 of Octo^r 1694 for Stephen Benson on the north side of patapsco river begining at a bounded red oak rent ℔ anum —.. 8.. —

Jacksons Delight 350 acr Sur the 3 June 1685 for John Prendevill Called Lyeing on the East side of Curteses Creek begining at a bounded Vine near the said Creek rent ℔ anum —.. 14.. —

C. Jackson's Venture—John Prindewell. Poss^r Geo. Westel's orp^n.

Newmans Delight, 450 acr Sur the 16 August 1688 for Roger Newmans Called Newmans delight begining at a bounded oak on the north side of a marshy branch rent ℔ anum —.. 18.. —

C. Poss^r S^d Newmans heir.

Majors Choice, 140 acr Sur the 19th July 1694 for John Thomas Called Majrs Choice Lyeing on the north side of patapsco river begining at a bounded Chestnut of Nicolas Ruxton Called Ruxtons Range rent ℔ anum —.. 5.. 7½

Phillips Rest, 150 acr Sur the 29 August 1695 for Phillip Roper Lyeing on the north side of patapsco river at the head of deerings run begining at a bounded white oak rent ℔ anum —.. 6.. —

C. Not in C.

Uftons Court, 500 acr Sur the 18 March 1667 for George Gale and assigned to David Poole mercht granted to the said Poole by patan the 2d of August 1668 Lyeing on the north side of patapsco river oposite to the Land of Hugh Kensey begining red oak Standing on the Southernmost side of a point Called Whettstone point and now in the posestion of George Hollandsworth for the use of the said Poole rent ℔ anum —.. 10.. —

C. Sur. for Geo. Yates. In Possn of Capn Tho Bale. Possr Nicho Rogers.

Hopewell, 185 acr Sur the 8 June 1676 for Thomas Long on the south side of midle river at a bounded white oak in south Line of the Land formerly Laid out for John Dixon and now in posestion of William Barker for the Orphants of Francis Watkins rent ℔ anum —.. 7.. 5

Bettors Hope, 74 acr Sur the 6 february 1685 for Francis Watkins Lyeing on the south side of midle river and in the posestion of Wm Barker for the orphants as aforesd rent ℔ anum —.. 2.. 11

C. Better Hope. Possr James Crook.

Shrewsbery, 65 acr Sur the 9 february 1697 for Francis Watkins Lyeing on the Stoney run in the woods and posesed as aforesaid rent ℔ anum —.. 2.. 7

C. Possr Willm Farfar.

Shawes Delight, 97 acr Sur the 15 June 1688 for Christopher

Shaw Lyeing on the south side of Midle river and now in posestion of the s^d Shaw, rent ℔ anum —.. 3.. 10

Shawes fancy 100 acr Sur the 10 August 1680 for Christopher Shaw on the west side of Midle river at a bounded Spanish oak of the Land Called hopewell in posestion as afores^d rent ℔ anum —.. 4.. —

Turky Neck, 75 acr Sur the 20 Novemb^r 1673 for Thomas Long on the south side of Midle river at a bounded red oak formerly Laid out for Capt Cornwallis and now in the posestion of John Leakings. rent ℔ anum —.. 3.. —

   C. Turkey Neck. Poss^r James Crook.

Thorrells Neck, 100 acr Sur the 31 July 1661 for Richard Thorrell in back river wth in the mouth of gunpd^r 50 acr part thereof in posestion of James Todd, rent —.. 2.. —

50 residue thereof in pos^n of Joseph Wells for the orphants of John Wells, rent ℔ anum —.. 2.. —

   C. Poss^rs 50 a John Harryman 50 a John Wells orp^n.

Timber Neck, 300 acr Sur the 21 March 1665 for Richd Ball on the north side of patapsco river 65 acr part thereof in posestion of Davis Elder, rent ℔ anum —.. 1.. 6
235 acr residue thereof in posestion of Anthony Demondidier, rent ℔ anum —.. 4.. 6

No name als Stevenson, 120 acr Sur the 3 Oct 1670 for Giles Stevenson on the north side of bush river at a bounded oak in posestion of Jane Peeck, rent ℔ anum —.. 4.. 10

   C. Not in C.

The Wedge, 65 acr Sur the 24 of Novemb^r 1673 for Giles Stephens on the Eastern side of Back river at a bounded Chestnut oak of the Land of Robart Dermon and now in the posestion of George Hopam, rent ℔ anum —.. 2.. 7½

   C. George Hoppam.

Selas Point, 120 acr Sur the 14 of Oct 1670 for Robert Durman on the north side of back river at a bounded Chestnut oake and runing up the river and posesed by Selas Durman, rent ℔ anum —.. 4.. 10

C. Sealas point. Robert Dorman.

Daniells Plaine, 100 acr Sur the 2 of Oct[r] 1695 for Daniell Swindall on the north side of back river near patapsco road begining at a bounded red oak being a bounded tree of the Land of Michaell Gormackson and John Elins and posesd as afore-said, rent ℔ anum —.. 4.. —

C. Daniels Plain. Poss[r] Seala Dorman.

Cherry Garden, 100 acr Sur the 10 of Novemb[r] 1674 for Robart Gardiner in back river in a Marshy Creeke at a marked Chest-nut oake on the East side of the Creek, rent ℔ anum —.. 4.. —

Prospect, 60 acr Sur the 13 of August 1687 for Robert Benjor in one of the branches of back river begining at a bounded white oak be a bounded tree of the Land belonging to M[r] Watkins and now in the posestion of W[m] Farfore, rent ℔ anum —.. 2.. 5

C. Poss[r] Wm. Farfour.

Plaines, 187 acr Sur the 2 of July 1688 for James Todd on the south side of the maine run of back river begining at a bounded white oak being a bounded tree of a parcell of Land formerly taken vp by David Jones and now in posestion of Henry King., rent ℔ anum —.. 7.. 6

C. Plains.

Come by Chance, 282 acr Sur the 24 of Novemb[r] 1694 for John Richardson Lyeing on the west side of Jones falls in patapsco in the woods begining at a bounded Spanish oak and in the posestion as aforesaid rent ℔ anum —.. 11.. 5½

C. Poss[r] John Cole.

Spring Point, 100 acr Sur the 31 March 1662 for Paul Kinsey on the Southern branch of patapsco on the north side and now in the posestion of Thomas Hamon rent ℔ anum —.. 2.. —

The Heath, 200 acr. Sur the 15 Septem[r] 1682 for Charles Gorsuch on the north side of patapsco river at an oak of the Line of Land of Paul Kinsey called Spring point and now posesed by Thomas Harmond rent ℔ anum —.. 8.. —

Harmonds Addition, 29 acr Sur the 11 of Novemb[r] 1688 for Thomas Hamond at a bounded Chestnut oak and in posestion of Thomas Hamond rent ℔ anum —.. 1.. 2

C. Hammonds addicōn. Poss[r] of y[e] above 3 tracts. Tho: Hammond.

Davises Lott, 200 acr Sur the 10 of Octob[r] 1667 for Henry Godrick on the north side of patapsco river at the Eastermost bounds of Robart Loyd and in posestion of the orphant of Alexander Lumly rent ℔ anum —.. 4.. —

C. David's Lott. Poss[r] Alex[r] Lumley's orp[n]. I suppose this to be said Land as is said to be Sur. for W[m] Davis.

Charny, 360 acr Sur the 17 of July 1673 for George Yates on the north side of patapsco river on the west side of the falls of midle branch begining at a bounded red oak by the s[d] falls and posesed by William Prather of Prince Georges County rent ℔ anum —.. 14.. 5

C. Charney.

Yates forbearance 770 acr Sur the 15 June 1683 for George Yates on the north side of patapsco river in the woods begining at a bounded oak at the End of the Line of the Land of Thomas Hoper in posestion of the abovesd Yates rent ℔ anum 1.. 10.. 9

C. Poss[r] John Yates and Son.

Yates forbearance, 140 acr Sur the 17 of July 1673 for George Yates near the main falls of patapsco river begining at a bounded black oak in posestion as aforesaid rent ℔ anum —.. 5.. 7

C. Poss[r] Geo. Yates.

Yates Inheritance, 170 acr Sur. the 22[d] August 1668 for George Yates on the south side of patapsco river at a bounded oak upon a hill side at a bounded tree of Harborenough and posesed by Anthony Johnson rent ℔ anum —.. 3.. 5

C. Poss[r] y[e] heir of John Howard.

MARYLAND RENT ROLLS.

Patapsco hundred

Hectors Hopyard, 300 acr Sur the 25 July 1694 for Hector Marklan begining at a bounded red oak on the East side of the north most branch of Jones falls 200 acr part thereof in posestion of the Hector Marklan rent ℔ anum —.. 8.. —
100 acr residue thereof in the posestion of James Murry rent ℔ anum —.. 4.. —

C. Surveyed for Hector McClain. Poss^rs* 100a sd McClane, 200a James Carroll.*

Hectors Fancy 100 acr Sur the 20 Feb^ry 1695 for Hector Marklan in the woods on the north side of the maine falles of patapsco begining at a bounded white oak of James Murryes Called Athell rent ℔ anum —.. 4.. —

C. Surveyed for Hector McClane.

Morning Choice, 400 acr Sur the 15 March 1695 for John Scutt Lyeing on the north side of patapsco on hunting ridge begining at a bounded white oak in the Line of the Land Called Attrell and In the posestion of the above said Scutt rent ℔ an. —.. 16.. —

C. Morning Choice. Poss^r* Cath. Scutt for y*^e* orp*^ns*. Hew Knowles marr*^d* y*^e* wid*^o*.*

Friends Discovery, 1000 acr Sur the 12 of June 1694 for Jobe Evans Called friends Discovery on a part of a ridge begining at three white oak by a branch of the Herring run and now In the posestion of Francis Mauldin of Calvert County rent ℔ anum 2.. —.. —

C. Poss^r* Fran Malden.*

81

Hamcross, 100 acr Sur the 18 of August 1663 for Warner
Shadwell on the west side of the south branch of Patapsco river
and In the posestion of Jobe Evans for the orphants of one
Drayden In London rent ₩ anum —.. 2.. —

 C. Hamcross. Walner Shadwell. Dryden.

Parishes Range, 2000 acr Sur the 5 of Octo͏ʳ 1678 for Edward
Parish called Parrishes range on the north side of patapsco
river on the fall of middle branch begining at a bounded oak
of Edward Hortons Land 1400 acr part thereof in posestion
Edward Parish rent ₩ an. 2.. 16.. —
300 acr part thereof in posestion of John Wooden of Ann
Arundel County rent ₩ anum —.. 12.. —
300 acr residue thereof George Hogg In Ann Arundell County
rent ₩ anum —.. 12.. —

 *C. Poss͏ʳˢ 1330a Edw͏ᵈ Parish. 370a John Wooding 300a
Geo. Ogg.*

Jobes Addition, 225 acr Sur the 24 of August 1695 for James
Butler caled Jobes Addition Lyeing above the head of Patapsco river in the woods begining at a bounded red oak In
the posestion of James Butler of Prince Georges County, rent
₩ anum —.. 9.. —

 C. Jobs Addicon.

Parkers Pallace, 500 acr sur the 16 of Oct͏ʳ 1695 for Robert
Parker called Parkers pallace Lyeing on the north side of
Patapsco river on Hunting ridge begining at a bounded red
oak of Scuttes morning Choice rent ₩ anum
250 acr part thereof in posestion of Rob͏ᵗ Parker rent ₩ anum
—.. 10.. —
250 acr residue thereof in posestion of Elizabeth Griffith of
Annarundel County, rent ₩ an. —.. 10.. —

 *C. Parkers palace. Poss͏ʳˢ 250a s͏ᵈ Parker 250a Eliz
Griffin.*

Walnutt neck, 100 acr Sur 18 of August 1663 for Hugh Kinsy

on the north side of Patapsco river, 45 acr part thereof In the posestion of Isaac Jackson rent ℔ anum 0.. 10.. —
55 acr residue thereof in posestion of John Willmot rent ℔ anum —.. 1.. 2

Brothers Expectation, 250 acr sur the 30 of Oct. 1695 for George Hollingsworth called Brothers Expectation on the north side of Patapsco river in the woods begining at a bounded white oak at the head of Col Peirces Line of a 1000 acr by the maine falls In the posestion of George Hollingsworth rent ℔ anum —.. 10.. —

    C. Poss^rs 150a Hollingsworth orp^ns 100a Humphrey Lewis.

Brothers Vnity, 100 acr Sur the 30 of Oct. 1695 for George Hollingsworth called Brothers Vnity on the north side of Patapsco river on Hunting ridge begining at a bounded w^t oak by Maidens Choice rent ℔ anum —.. 4.. —

    C. Now in poss^n of Tho Knighton. Poss^r Humphrey Lewis.

Broads Choice, 173 acr Sur the 10 June 1694 for John Broad called broads Choice Lying on the north side of patapsco river begining at a bounded red oak rent ℔ anum —.. 6.. 11

Rogers Road, 100 acr Sur the 10 of february 1695 for Roger Reeves called Rogers road Lyeing at the head of back river between Herring run and Stony run begining at a bounded white oak of James Todd and John Wilmots In posestion of Jane Royston for the orphants of Jno Royston rent ℔ anum —.. 4.. —

    C. Pos^r John Royston's orp^n.

Beares Thicket, 100 acr Sur the 30 of Octr 1695 for James Jackson called beare thickett Lyeing on the north side of patapsco river on hunting ridge begining at a bounded w^t oak of Ashmans hope and In posestion of William Cromwell for the orphants of James Jackson rent ℔ anum —.. 4.. —

    C. Bears thickett. Poss^r s^d Jacksons orp^n.

Selsed, 900 acr Sur the 31 July 1694 for Rowland Thornbury called Selsed Lyeing on the north East branch of Jones falls begining at a bounded white oak on the west side threof In posestion of the orphants of the s^d Thornbury, rent ℔ anum 1.. 16.. —

C. Blessed. Poss^r s^d Thornbury's orp^n Gon into Virginia.

Oultons Garrison, 940 acr sur the 13 May 1696 for John Oulton called Oultons garison on the north side of patapsco river in the woods part of Rangers forest begining at a bounded red oak on the East side of a glade by the garison, rent ℔ anum —.. 13.. 7½

C. Poss^rs 163a Wm Talbott ye residue belongs to ye orp^n of James Murrey.

Copus Harbour, 100 acr Sur the 6 of Septemb^r 1683 for John Copus on the East side of a branch of patapsco river called the northwest branch at a bounded red oak a bounded tree of Gompes Addition and in posestion of Thomas Copus rent ℔ anum —.. 4.. —

Stones Range, 194 acr Sur the 30 of August 1695 for Thomas Stone on the west side of the maine run of back river begining at a Spanish oak of John Broads posesed as aforesd rent ℔ an. —.. 7.. 9½

Long Island Point, 100 acr Sur 31 of Oct. 1671 for William Poultney on the north most side of patapsco river on the north most branch of the river at a bounded Locust at the head of a round bay 50 acr part thereof in posestion of Thomas Stone rent ℔ a. —.. 1.. —
50 acr residue thereof in posestion of John Broad rent ℔ anum —.. 1.. —

C. 50a poss^t by Tho Stone 50a John Broad Poss^r Thos Hodge the whole as I'm informed.

Parkers Haven, 100 acr Sur the 20 of June 1669 for John Kemp on the north west side of Patapsco river on the north west branch on a point on the west side of Collets Creek in posestion of John Thomas for the orphants of the said Kemp rent ℔ anum —.. 4.. —

Kemps Addition, 100 acr Sur the 28 Septemb^r 1683 for John Kemp on the East side of a branch called Harmost branch at a bounded red oak a bounded tree of the Land Called Parkers Haven In posestion of John Thomas for the orphants of the s^d Kemp rent ℔ anum —.. 4.. —

Wilmots folly, 140 acr Sur the 2 of July 1688 for John Wilmot called Wilmotts folly Lyeing In Baltymore County Joyning upon Jones Land posesed by the said Wilmot rent ℔ anum —.. 5.. 9½

The Choice, 100 acr Sur the 13 of Octr 1670 for John Godfrey on the north side of the patapsco river on the north west branch of the s^d river in the posestion of John Wilmot rent ℔ anum —.. 4.. —

Cromwells Range, 200 acr Sur the 19 Octo^r 1695 for Richard Cromwell Called Cromwells Range Lyeing on Hunting ridge begining at a bounded Chestnut tree of Maiden Dayry in the posestion of the sd Cromwell rent ℔ an. —.. 8.. —

Jonas out Lett, 129 acr Sur the 12 of May 1689 for Jonas Bowen Called Jonases out let Lyeing on the north side of patapsco river in the woods begining at a bounded Hickory posesed by the orphants of the s^d Bowen rent ℔ anum —.. 5.. 2.

C. Poss^r Benja. Bowen.

Jonas Addition ,51 acr Sur the 20 of August 1687 for Jonas Bowen Called Jonas Addition Lyeing between patapsco river and back river posesed by the orphants of the s^d Bowen rent ℔ anum —.. 2.. 2½

Hortons fortune, 100 acr Sur the 25 Novemb^r 1670 for Edward Horton at a bounded white oak of the Land of Robert Gorsuch and runing up a branch to a bounded tree of the Land of John Godfrey and posesed by Hugh Jones rent ℔ anum 7.. 4.. —

Gorsuch, 500 acr Sur the 8 July for Robert Gorsuch on the north side of patapsco river posesed by Charles Gorsuch in behalfe of the said Robert Gorsuch rent ℈ anum —.. 10.. —

C. 1659. Poss^r Robt Gorsuch.

Powells point, 70 acr Sur the 3 August 1661 for Howell Powell on the north side of patapsco river Clephas creek posesed by Mary Ruxton for the orphants of Nath^{le} Ruxton. rent ℈ anum & in posestion of his Widdow —.. 1.. 5

100 acr Sur the 12 May 1679 for Nicolas Ruxton on the north side of patapsco river at a bounded white oak in the north Line of Robert Gorsuch posesed by Mary Ruxton for the orphants of Nath^{ll} Ruxton rent ℈ anum —.. 4.. —

C. Poss^r R^d Colegate.

Thomas Adventure, 165 acr Sur the 2^d of Septemb^r 1688 for John Thomas Called Thomases adventure Lyeing on the north side of the patapsco river posesed by the s^d Thomas rent ℈ anum —.. 6.. 7½

C. Thomas's Adventures.

Jurdiston, 299 acr Sur the 8 of february 1688 for John Thomas Called Jurdiston Lyeing in the woods between patapsco and back river 249 acr part thereof in posestion of the said Thomas rent ℈ anum —.. 9.. 11½
50 acr residue thereof in posestion of Joseph Wells rent ℈ anum —.. 2.. —

Wallstowne, 156 acr Sur the 2 June 1682 for Wm Gaine on the north side of patapsco river and on the west side of Welshmans creek adjoyning to the Land Laid out for Howell Powell and in posestion of Nicolas Fitzsymons, rent ℈ anum —.. 6.. —

C. Walltown.

Bennetts Range, 50 acr Sur the 15 decemb^r 1683 for Thomas Everett on the north side of Patapsco river at a bounded red oak at the East End of the Line of Balls Addition posesed by Nicolas Fitzsymon rent ℈ an. —.. 2.. —

Balls Addition 60 acr Sur 30 Septem^r 1670 for Richard Ball at a bounded oak on the East side of Clappers Creek a bounded tree of a tract of Land of Mary Humphryes posesed by Nicolas Fitzsymons rent ꝗ anum —.. 2.. 4

C. Balls addicon.

The Hope 150 acr Sur the 20 March 1665 for Lewis Burgain on the north side of patapsco river on the south side of the Land of Richard Ball Posesed by Jonas Bowen rent ꝗ anum —.. 3.. —

C. Lewis Burgan.

Goosebury Neck, 100 acr Sur the 5 May 1673 for William Ebden in back river at a marked oake in a neck between 2 branches and runing Cross a point for breadth posses^d by Larance Walden rent ꝗ anum —.. 4.. —

C. Gooseberry neck Pos^r Tho Biddison.

Jones Chance 20 acr Sur the 20 May 1673 for Jonas Bowen in beare Creek in patapsco river at a bounded oak of the Land of William Ball upon Clay banks posesed by Jonas Bowen rent ꝗ anum —.. —.. 10

C. Jonas's Chance. Poss^{rs} 100a Jno Thomas for Jno Kemps orp^n 100a John Gardener 100a Benj^a Bowen.

Kinderton, 300 acr Sur the 31 July 1669 for Wm Clapham on the north side of patapsco river and on the westerne side of bear creek 100 part thereof in posestion of John Kemp rent ꝗ anum —.. 2.. —
100 acr p^t thereof in pos. of John Gardner rent ꝗ an. —.. 2.. —
100 acr residue thereof in posestion of Benj Bowen rent ꝗ anum —.. 2.. —

Loyd of L Lott, 200 acr Sur the 26 Octo^r 1667 for Robart Loyd on the north side of patapsco river about a mile from the head posesed by Gabriell Parott rent ꝗ an —.. 4.. —

C. Loyd of Leedloes Lott. Resur & called United Friendship Poss^r Willm Chew. [In a later handwriting poss^d by Geo Parker].

Dearings Increase, 200 acr Sur the 31 of Oct[r] 1667 for John Dearing on the north side of patapsco river posesed by Robert Eager of Annarundell County rent ℔ anum —.. 4.. —

C. *Dearings encrease. Pos[r] Robt Eagle.*

Lunns Lott, 200 acr Sur the 10 of Octo[r] 1672 for Edward Lunn on the north side of patapsco river upon the N. W. branch at a bounded hickery on the west side of the falls of the s[d] branch posesed by Robert Eagar of Anarundel rent ℔ anum —.. 8.. —

C. *Pos[r] George Eager.*

Generalls Point, 150 acr Sur the 3 of August 1661 for George Langford in patapsco river in a Creek Called otter Creek posesed by Martha Bowen for the orphants of Jonas Bowen rent ℔ anum —.. 3.. —

C. *Poss[r] Jonas Bowen.*

Willin, 308 acr Sur the 5 Septem[r] 1679 for Charles Gorsuch on the north side of patapsco river at the head of a branch of beare Creek devids two tracts of Land of Phillip Thomas 160 acr part thereof in posestion of Martha Bowen for the Orphants of Jonas Bowen rent ℔ anum —.. 6.. 5

130 acr part thereof in the posestion of Francis Holland rent ℔ anum —.. 5.. 3

60 acr part thereof posesed by John Copper rent ℔ anum —.. 2.. 5

48 acr residew thereof In the posestion of Charley Gorsuch rent ℔ anum —.. 2.. 9

C. *398a Poss[rs]. 160a Jonas Bowen 130a Jn[o] Fra[s] Holland 60a John Copper 48a Cha Gorsuch.*

Abington, 100 acr Sur the 12 June 1682 for Charles Gorsuch on the north side of patapsco at a bounded white oak standing nigh the head of a bridge posesed by Francis Holland, rent ℔ anum —.. 4.. —

C. *Abbington. Poss[r] John Rouse [added later: post by Fran Holland.*

Jonas Range, 100 acr Sur the 24 May 1684 for Jonas Bowen between back river and patapsco river at a marked red oak on a mountaine posesed by a Martha Bowen for the orphants of Jonas Bowen rent ℔ anum —.. 4.. —

Costrell Hill, 100 acr Sur the 6 March 1667 for Nicolas Corbin Called Costrell Hill Lyeing between Patapsco river and back river posesed by John Barrett for the orphant of Nicolas Corbin rent ℔ anum —.. 4.. —

C. *Corstrell Hill.*

Corbins Rest 200 acr Sur the 6 Decemb^r 1679 for Nicolas Corbin on the north side of patapsco river on the north side of beare Creek branch called bridge branch posesed by John Barrott for the orphant of Nicolas Corbin rent ℔ anum —.. 8.. —

C. *Poss^{rs} ye above 2 Tracts ye s^d Corbins orp^{ns}.*

Welcome, 100 acr Sur the 2 Novemb^r 1684 for Charles Gorsuch on the south side of back river posesed by Richard Crumwell.

C. *And now in poss^n of Tobias Tunbridge.*

Waterford, 200 acr Sur the 13 May 1679 for John Arding at a bounded pine of the Land Called popular neck in bear Creek on the north side of patapsco.

150 acr thereof in posestion of Martha Cage rent ℔ anum —.. 6.. —

50 acr residue thereof posesed by John Wates rent ℔ anum —.. 2.. —

C. *50a Mich^a Temple's heirs.*

The Plaines 300 acr Sur the 18 May 1672 for Phillip Thomas on the north side of patapsco river and on the north side of beare Creek posesed by Samuel Thomas rent ℔ anum —.. 6.. —

Phillips Addition, 200 acr Sur the 18 May 1672 for Phillip Thomas on the north side of patapsco river on a Creek Called beare Creek posesed as above rent ℔ anum —.. 8.. —

C. *Poss^r Tho Roberts for Sam^{el} Thomas.*

Popular Neck, 100 acr Sur the 16 Jan^ry 1672 for Tobias Sternbridge on the north side of patapsco river and on the south side of beare Creeke at a bounded oak by a branch posesed by Tobias Sternbridge rent ℔ anum —.. 2.. —

C. *Poplar Neck.*

Huntington, 135 acr Sur the 29 June 1658 for Tobias Sternbridge on the north side of patapsco river and posesed as aforesaid rent ℔ anum —.. 5.. 6

C. *1688.*

Hares Green 35 acr Sur the 10 Aprill 1682 for Edward Mumford on the north side of patapsco river of a small branch of Humphreyes Creek posesed by Robert Lynch for Samuell Greenwoods orphant rent ℔ anum —.. 1.. 3

C. *Haws Green.*

Sidwell 50 acr Sur the 20 of Decemb^r 1667 for Roger ——— on the south side of back river at a black walnut neare the mouth of a branch posesed by Thomas Smith, rent ℔ anum —.. 1.. —

Todes Range, 400 acr Sur the 24 June 1669 for Thomas Todd on the north side of patapsco river at a bounded oak on a Creek Called Humphryes Creek posesed by Thomas Todd rent ℔ anum —.. 8.. —

C. *Todds range. Poss^rs R^d Fowlers orp^ns as I'm inform'd.*

Joneses Chance, 130 acr Sur the 12 June 1682 for David Jones on the north side of patapsco river on Road Creek on the Eastermost bounds of Powells pumpkin patch posesed by Robert Johnson, rent ℔ anum —.. 4.. —

30 acr residue thereof posesed by James Todd rent ℔ anum —.. 1.. 1

Ardingtons Adventure, 100 acr Sur the 15 of March 1676 for John Arding on the southside of back river at the mouth of the river pos^d by Richd Sampson rent ℔ an. —.. 2.. —

MARYLAND RENT ROLLS.

BALTIMORE COUNTY.

Patapsco hundred

The forrest 100 acr Sur the 16 Septem^r 1672 for Charles Gorsuch on the west side of back river at a bounded oake in the woods runing north west and by north pos^d by Isaac Sampson rent ⅌ an. —.. 4.. —

Vpper Spring Neck, 150 acr sur the 4 of August 1661 for Walter Dixson in patapsco on the Eastern side of bear Creek posesed by William Pearth rent ⅌ an —.. 3.. —

C. *Walter Dickson poss^r Wm Pearle.*

Gunworth, 81 acr Sur the 31 July 1661 for Walter Dixson on the north side of patapsco river at the northern bounded

tree of William Clapham belonging to Francis Petitie noe
heires Land uncultivated rent set ℔ anum —.. 1.. 7¼

*C. 80 acre Sold to Francis Petit who left a daughter.
Supposed to be an alien.*

The Batchellors Hope, 550 acr Sur the 7 of feb^ry 1664 for
Edward Gilfe and Richard Merryday on the north side of
patapsco river noe heires apeare Land uncultivated rent ℔
anum —.. 11. —

C. This land taken away by an old^r Survey as I'm informed.

Dixsons Neck, 450 acr Sur the 7 of June 1667 for John Dixson
on back river w^thin the mouth of gunpowder on the north side
of the said back river sold to Joseph Sumnar and Robert
Garrett who deserted this province 26 yeares agoe Land uncultivated rent set ℔ anum —.. 9.. —

North Conton, 600 acr Sur the 20 of Novemb^r 1652 for Thomas
Sparrow on the north side of patapsco river and now posesed
by John Rous for Sollomon Sparrow rent ℔ anum —.. 12.. —
Sparrows Addition, 45 acr Sur the 24 July 1672 for Soloman
Sparrow on the north side patapsco river on the west side of a
Cove on the west south most Line of Thomas Sparrow posesed
as afores^d rent ℔ anum —.. —.. 11

Alderwood, Acr Sur the 18 of Octo^r 1672 for John Woodvine
on the north side of patapsco river in the woods at a bounded
red oak the s^d Woodvine dead no heires Land vncultivated

£ s d

rent set ℔ annum 0.. 2.. 0 —2.. —

This Land is Lyable to an Escheat

Landisell, 425 acr Sur the 22 Novemb^r 1652 for Richard
Owens on the north side of patapsco river posesed by William
Wilkinson rent ℔ annum —.. 8.. 6

Wilkinsons Spring, 50 acr Sur the 5 March 1681 for William
Wilkinson on the East side of beare Creek in patapsco rivér at
a red oak by a marshy Swamp rent ℔ annum —.. 2.. —

Nashes Rest, 200 acr Sur the 24 of Octo^r 1661 for John Collett in patapsco river in bear Creek posesed by Wm Dennis rent ℔ annum —.. 4.. —

Jones Neglect, 50 acr Sur the 5 March 1675 for Edward Mumford in patapsco river on the East side of a Creek Called beare Creek in posestion of Joseph Perregwa rent ℔ annum —.. 2.. —

    C. Poss^r Step^n Bentley.

Hopewell, 15 acr Sur the 10 March 1681 for Edward Mumford on the north side of patapsco river in blockhouse Creek beginning at a bounded white oak in posestion of Nicol^s Fitzsymon for the orphants of Heathcoat —.. —.. 7

Burmans Forrest, 350 acr Sur the 12 feb^{ry} 1685 for Robert Burman of London M^{r}chant Called Burmans forrest on the south side of back river
100 acr part thereof in the posestion of Joseph Perregwa rent ℔ annum —.. 4.. —
250 acr residue thereof in the posestion of Richard Watkins for Ebenezer Blackiston, rent ℔ annum —.. 10.. —

    C. Poss^r 100 a Joseph Perregoy

Merrymans Lott, 210 Acr Sur the 29 June 1688 for Charles Merryman on the north side of Jones falls
105 acr thereof in the posestion of the said Merryman rent ℔ annum —.. 4.. 2½
105 Acr residue thereof in posestion of Nicolas Hailes rent ℔ annum —.. 4.. 2½

    C. Nich Hale.

Johns Inheritance, 150 acr Sur the 5 of Septemb^r 1667 for John Jones on the north side of patapsco river on the south side of bear Creek and posesed by Charles Merryman for the orphants of John Boaring rent ℔ annum —.. 3.. —

    C. Jones's inheritance Poss^r John Boaring.

East Humphryes, 300 acr resurveyed the 1 Oct. 1679 for Mary

Humphryes on the north side of patapsco river on the west side of Clapper Creek at a black walnutt Stump near a marshy beach at the mouth of the Creek in the posestion of the said Merryman rent ℈ an —.. 6.. —

C. Poss^r Cha. Merryman. I suppose this land to be ye same formerly called West Humphrys.

Swan Harbour, 80 acr Sur the 19 of May 1672 for Charles Gorsuch on the west side of back river begining at a bounded oak and south west and be south posesed by Charles Merryman for the orphant of John Boaring rent ℈ annum —.. 1.. 8

C. Poss^r John Boaring.

In Lowes, 100 acr Sur the 15 of Octr 1670 for Abraham Inloes on the north side of back river at a marked Chestnut oak the westermost bounds of Robert Dermatts Land belonging to the orphants of John Boaring rent ℈ annum —.. 4.. —

C. Inloes. Poss^r John Boaring.

The prospect, 80 acr Sur the 19 May 1672 for Charles Gorsuch on the west side of back river at a bounded white oak belonging to the orphants of William Boaring rent ℈ annum —.. 1.. 8

C. Poss^r James Boaring.

Boarings Range, 50 acr Sur the 10 of decemb^r 1679 for John Boaring on the north side of patapsco river at a bounded white oak by the draught of a branch of bear Creek belonging to the orphants of the said Boaring rent ℈ annum —.. 2.. —

C. Poss^r James Boaring.

Boaring Pasture, 50 acr Sur the 10 of decemb^r 1682 for John Boaring at a bounded red oak in the northwest Line of the Land Called Watterford nigh a branch of bear Creek in patapsco river belongs as aforesd rent ℈ annum —.. 2.. —

C. Poss^r James Boaring.

Martinson, 100 acr Sur the 5th of Aprill 1662 for John Martin on back river wthin the mouth of gunpowder river on the south side of back river posesed by Martin rent ℔ annum —.. 2.. —

    C. Poss^r Robuck Lynch.

Martin, 100 acr Sur the 9th Aprill 1662 for John Martin on the south side of back river posesed as aforesaid rent ℔ annum —.. 2.. —

    C. Poss^r John Harding's orp^{ns}.

Coles Harbour, 550 acr Sur the 28 Aprill 1667 for George Yates assigned David Poole on the north side of patapsco river on the northermost branch posesed by James Todd rent ℔ annum —.. 11.. —

    C. Poss^r 185 a Richd Colegate 365 a Jas. Carroll. Poss^r John Hurst at present.

Black walnut Neck, 300 acr Sur the 10 feb^{ry} 1659 for Capt Thomas Todd on the north side of patapsco river on the East side of a Creek Called Welchmans Creek In posestion of James Todd rent ℔ an —.. 6.. —

    C. Poss^r Mark Swift.

Scudamores Last, 130 acr Sur the 9 of May 1687 for Thomas Scudamore Called Scudamores Last Lyeing on Stony run rent ℔ annum —.. 5.. 2½

    C. Scidemores last, 130 a granted John Hayes 10 Oct. 1704.

Powells Point, 100 acr Sur the 9 July 1667 for Thomas Powell on the north side of Patapsco river posesed by Robert Johnson rent ℔ annum —.. 2.. —

Mountneys Neck, 100 acr Sur the 3 March 1662 for Alexa^r Mountney on the north side of patapsco river In posestion of James Todd rent ℔ annum —.. 2.. —

    C. This land resur & fo^d to be 164 1/2 a. Poss^r John Hurst.

Priveledge, 250 acr Sur the 13 Septem^r 1670 for Richard Ball on the west side of the north west river at a bounded oak the bounded tree of John Dixson in posestion of Nathaniell Linchcomb rent ℔ annum —.. 10.. —

    C. Poss^r Nath. Stinchcomb.

Jones Venture, 80 acr Sur the 16 June 1682 for David Jones on the north side of patapsco river at a bounded tree in the woods 50 acr part thereof posesed by John Harryman rent ℔ annum —.. 2.. —
30 acr residue thereof in posestion of James Todd rent ℔ annum —.. 1.. 2½

    C. Jones's adventure Poss^r James Todd. Todd run away.

Hailes Adventure, 56 acr Sur the 2^d May 1689 for Nicolas Hailes Called Hailes Adventure on the north side of patapsco river begining at a bounded red oak In the woods of Charles Merrymans Line neare ball neck Creek posesed by the said Hailes rent ℔ annum —.. 2.. 3

    C. Hales adventure, Nich Hale. Poss^r Edwd Stephenson

Walton, 120 acr Sur the 3 of Aprill 1662 for John Walton on the south side of back river in the mouth of gunpowd^r river posesed by Nicholas Hailes for the orphant of Jno Arding, rent ℔ annum —.. 2.. 5

Batchelors Delight, 260 acr Sur the 22^d June 1671 for Edward Smith on the south side of bush river at a bounded pine of the Land of John Jones on a branch of beare Creek posesed by Nicolas Hailes for the orphants of John Arding rent ℔ annum —.. 10.. 4

    C. S side Back river.

Ardington, 50 acr Sur the 15 March 1679 for John Arding at a bounded pine of the Land Called popular neck in beare Creek possesed by Nicholas Hailes for the orphants of John Arding rent ℔ annum —.. 2.. —

The Coblers Neglect, 100 acr Sur the 11 of August for John Arding on Wattsons Creek wch comes out of back Creek at a bounded red oak in the south west Line of Waltons Neck In

posestion of Nicholas Hailes for the orphants of John Arding
rent ℔ annum —.. 4.. —

Ardings Marsh, 28 acr Sur the 19 Jan^ry 1686 for John Arding
on the south side of back river posesed as afores^d rent ℔ annum
—.. 1.. 1½

Harleyston, 45 acr Sur the 21 of June 1688 for John Arding
Lyeing on the south side of back river posesed by Nicolas Hailes
for the orphants of John Arding rent ℔ annum —.. 1.. 10

    *C. Harleston. Poss^rs ye above 7 Tracts John Arding's
Orp^ns.*

Addition, 101 acr Sur the 19 of July 1688 for Richard Sampson
Called Addition on the south side of patapsco river rent ℔
annum —.. 4.. —

    C. Poss^r Isaac Sampson.

Maidens Dairy, 248 acr Sur the 20 february 1695 for Thomas
Hoocker Called Maidens Dayry Lyeing on the north side of
patapsco river on hunting ridge begining at a bounded Elm by
a branch of Gwins falls posesed by John Yookly rent ℔ annum
—.. 9.. —

    C. Thomas Hooker. Poss^r Richd Crumwell.

Samuells Hope, 500 acr Sur the 15 June 1694 for Thomas
Hooker Called Samuells hope begining at a bounded white oak
by a Spring Called   Spring posesed by the s^d Hooker
rent ℔ annum 1.. —.. —

Mascalls Rest, 230 acr Sur the   for Richard Mascall
on the west side of patapsco river begining at a bounded white
oak on a point posesed by Thomas Hooker rent ℔ annum
—.. 9.. 1

    *C. Maskals rest. Poss^r Nich. Fitzsimons. [Inserted]
In poss. T. Hooker.*

Hopkins Lott, 81 acr Sur the 24 June 1695 for Robert Hopkins
called Hopkins Lott begining at a bounded water oake of Joseph
Owens Land posesed by the s^d Hopkins rent ℔ annum —.. 3.. 3

Oultons Garisson, 340 Acr Sur the 12 May 1696 for John Oulton Called Oultons Garrison Lyeing on the north side of Patapsco river in the woods part of the Rangers forrest begining at a bounded red oak on the East side of a glade of Jobe Evans by the Garrison posesed by James Murrey rent ⅌ annum —.. 13.. 7½

C. Poss^{rs} 163 a Wm Talbott, ye residue belongs to ye orp^n of James Murrey.

Morgans Delight, 500 acr Sur the 2 June 1694 for James Murrey Lyeing in the woods on part of Little Brittain ridge begining at a bounded hickery of Jobe Evans posesed by James Murry rent ⅌ annum 1.. —.. —

C. Poss^r ye heir of S^d Murrey. Tho Cromwell marr^d ye Wid^o.

Murryes Addition, 89 acr Sur the 25 Octr 1695 for James Murry Lyeing on the north side of patapsco river on hunting ridge begining at a bounded red oak by Thomas Eden rent ⅌ annum —.. 3.. 7

Athell, 617 acr Sur the 12 Novemb^r 1694 for James Murry Lyeing on the north side of patapsco river begining at a bounded red oak neare Davise run 100 part thereof in possestion of Hector Macklane rent ⅌ annum —.. 4.. —
303 Acr part thereof in posestion of Thomas Beale rent ⅌ annum —.. 12.. 1½
214 Acr residue thereof in the posestion of Thomas Odin rent ⅌ annum —.. 8.. 2

C. Poss^r Tho Odell.

Duck Cove, 350 acr Sur the 17 Septemb^r 1670 for Paule Kinsy on the west side of patapsco river begining at a bounded white oak vpon a point by a greate Marsh and running down the river posesed by James Murry rent ⅌ annum —.. 7.. —

C. Poss^r Tho Cromwell for Murreys orp^{ns}

Georges Fancy, 100 acr Sur Jan^{ry} 1685 for George Ashman on the patapsco river on the west side of Curteses Creek in posestion of the Widdow Ashman for the orphant of the s^d Ashman rent ℔ annum —.. 4.. —

Mascalls Hope, 100 acr Sur the 30 June 1669 for Richard Mascall on the north side of Curtises Creek this Land runs into the waters soe Voide —.. 0.. —

 C. Not in C.

Ashmans Hope, 512 acr Sur the 30 Novemb^r 1694 for George Ashman on the north side of patapsco river on hunting ridge begining at a bounded white oak Standing by a greate run in the posestion of the Widdow Ashman for the orphants of George Ashman rent ℔ annum 1.. —.. 6

 C. Poss^r Tho Cromwell.

Davids fancy, 100 acr Sur the 22 June 1671 for David Williams on the north side of patapsco on a branch Called Midle branch at a bounded Locust the bounded tree of David Pooles Land and now In the posestion of Thomas and William Cromwell rent ℔ annum —.. 4.. —

 C. Poss^r Tho Crumwell.

Hunting Quarter, 134 acr Sur the 12th Decemb^r 1679 for William Cromwell on the south side of patapsco on the west side of Curteses Creek now posesed by Thomas Cromwell rent ℔ annum —.. 5.. 4

Beare Neck, 140 acr Sur the 7 July 1671 for William Ball on the south side of patapsco river and on Curteses Creek at a bounded hickery and running vp the fork of the Creek posesed by William Cromwell rent ℔ annum —.. 2.. 10

 C. Bareneck.

South Conton, 245 Acr Sur the 8 of August 1680 for Robert Clarkson on the south side of patapsco river at a bounded white oak by the side of rumly marsh
165 acr thereof in posestion of William Cromwell rent ℔ annum —.. 5.. —

80 Acr residue thereof in posestion of Thomas Cromwell rent ⅌ annum —.. 1.. 10½

Balls Enlargement, 100 acr Sur the 12 July 1673 for William Ball on the south side of patapsco river at a bounded white oak by a branch now in posestion of William Cockey rent ⅌ annum —.. 4.. —

The Plaine, 120 acr Sur the 1 June 1673 for George Hope on the south side of patapsco river at a bounded hickery now in posestion of Blane Todd rent ⅌ a —.. 4.. 10

   C. The Plaine Poss^r Lancelot Todd.

Cockeys Trust, 300 acr Sur the 8 of Aprill 1696 for William Cockey on patapsco river on the north side between the falls of Jones and patapsco begining at a bounded white oak of Rowland Thornburys called blessed now in posestion of Thomas Cockey for the orphants of William Cockey rent ⅌ annum —.. 12.. 0

Rockholds Search, 180 acr Sur the 20 of August 1696 for John Rockhold on the south side of patapsco river begining at a bounded red oak in John Boddyes Line in posestion of the Widdow Rockhold for the orphants of John Rockhold rent ⅌ annum —.. 7.. 3

Vtopia, 320 Acr Sur the 28 decemb^r 1670 for Robert Wilson on the north side of patapsco river at the southermost part of Hugh Kensyes
214 Acr part thereof in posestion of Richard Guest rent ⅌ annum —.. 8.. 8
106 Acr residue thereof in posestion of the Widdow Ashman for the orphants of George Ashman rent ⅌ annum —.. 4.. 2

   C. Poss^{rs} 214 a Rd Crumwell, 106 a Geo Ashmans orp^{ns}

Lowes Neck, 100 acr Sur the 15 May 1683 for Christopher Gest begining at the head of the south East branch of Swan Creek begining at a bounded water oak now posesed by Richard Guest, rent ⅌ annum —.. 4.. —

   C. Low neck.

Long Point, 250 Acr Sur the 16 June 1682 for David Jones at a Spanish oak on the west side of the branch of back river aboute 2 miles from the road from patapsco to gunpowder river posesed by Richard Cromwell rent ℔ annum —.. 10.. —

Cromwells Addition, 16 acr Sur the 12 Jan^ry 1686 for Richard Cromwell Lyeing on the south side of patapsco river in posestion of the s^d Cromwell rent ℔ annum —.. 1.. 2

Leafes Forrest, 200 acr Sur the 18 August 1678 for Francis Leafe in the woods near patapsco river at a Marked red oak on the side of Holly run a bounded tree of the Land Called Holland's Choice and now in posestion of John Martin rent ℔ annum —.. 8.. —

Johnson Intrest, 360 acr Sur the 25 Octo^r 1695 Anthony Johnson on the north side of patapsco in the woods begining at a bounded Spanish oak on the south side of Charles run 200 acr part thereof in posestion of Anthony Johnson rent ℔ annum —.. 8.. —
160 acr residue thereof in posestion of John Gatrill of anarundell rent ℔ annum —.. 6.. 5

C. Johnsons Interest.

Timber Neck, 132 acr Sur the 13 Oct 1694 for William Budd Lyeing at Elk ridge neare patapsco river begining at a bounded popular neare a run Called the Midle run now in the posestion of William Davis rent ℔ annum —.. 5.. 4

Herberts Care, 146 acr Sur the 12 Octo^r 1694 for Elenor Herbert Lyeing at Elkridge begining at a bounded white oak being a bounded tree of Capt. Jn° Dorseys and now in posestion of the s^d Elinor Herbert rent ℔ annum —.. 5.. 10

Adam the first, 500 acr Sur the 8 of Aprill 1687 for Adam Shiply on a ridge Called Elk ridge at a bounded red oak on the north East side of the head of a branch of patapsco river now posesed by Richard Shiply rent ℔ annum 1.. —.. —

Hockley, 100 acr Sur the 23 June 1669 for William Ebden on the north side of patapsco river at the northermost bounded tree

of the Land Called forsters fancy now in posestion of Coll
Edward Dorsey rent $\wp$ annum —.. 2.. —

Brownes fancy, 200 acr Sur the 7 december 1694 for William
Brown near Elkridge begining at a bounded white oak in the
forrest in the posestion of Richard Kertland rent $\wp$ annum
—.. 8.. —

Harborow, 350 acr Sur the 18 August 1663 for Paul Kinsy on
the south side of patapsco river on the south East of the river
now in posestion of the orphants of James Griniff rent $\wp$ an
—.. 7.. —

    C. Poss^{rs} 175 a James Greenif. 175 a Jno Howard's orp^{ns}.

Ropers Increase, 300 acr Sur the 30 Octr 1667 for Thomas
Roper on the north side of patapsco river on the western side
of Ropers Creek now in posestion of Cornelius Howard rent $\wp$
annum —.. 6.. —

Ropers Range, 145 acr Sur the 28 Oct. 1667 for Thomas Roper
on the north side of patapsco river on the west side of the
Midle branch posesed by Turlo Michaell Owen rent $\wp$ annum
—.. —.. 11

    C. Poss^r Tulo Mich^{ll} Owens orp^{ns}.

Lockwood Adventure, 400 acr Sur 11 Octo^r 1677 for Robert
Lockwood on the south side of patapsco river at a bounded red
oak on the East side of Calloways branch now in posestion of
John Howard rent $\wp$ an —.. 16.. —

    C. Poss^r John Howards orp^{ns}.

Halls Pasture, 300 acr Sur the 9 Aprill 1695 for Henry Hall
begining at a bounded red oak on a point by Curteses Creek
posesed by the s^d Hall rent $\wp$ annum —.. 12.. —

    C. Halls palace.

Hopes Lott, 200 acr Sur the 9 August 1695 for George Hope
Lyeing on hunting ridge on the north side of patapsco river
begining at a bounded Elm the Eastermost bounds of William
Slades Land posesed by the said Hope rent $\wp$ annum —.. 8.. —

Hopes Recovery, 31 acr Sur the 12 Novemb^r 1694 for George Hope begining at a bounded oak in the north East Line of Jno Turners Land posesed by the s^d Hope rent ℔ annum —.. 1.. 3½

Denchworth, 250 acr Sur the 10 July 1678 for George Yates on the south side of patapsco river on the branch of Curteses Creek at the Corner tree of Quinton Parker now posesed by George Hope rent ℔ annum —.. 10.. —

C. The above 3 Tracts poss^d by Geo Hope.

Slades Addition, 112 acr Sur the 9 of Aprill 1695 for Wm Slade begining at a bounded water oak by Curtis Creek posesed by the said Slade rent ℔ annum —.. 4.. 6

Slades Camp, 188 acr Sur the 20 february 1695 for Wm Slade Lyeing on the north side of patapsco river in the woods begining at a bounded red oak of James Murrys Land Called athell posesed by the s^d Slade rent ℔ annum —.. 7.. 6

Curtises Neck, 200 acr Sur the 2 Aprill 1662 for Paul Kinsy on the south side of patapsco river on a point of broad Creek posesed by Wm Slade rent ℔ annum —.. 4.. —

The Narrow, 100 acr Sur the 22 March 1678 for George Yates and asigned Francis Leafe on patapsco river & on the north side of Stony Creek and now posesed by William Mackcartee rent ℔ annum —.. 4.. —

C. The Narrows. Poss^r Wm Maccartee.

Wheelocks Lott, 100 acr Sur the 10 Octr 1672 for Edward Wheelock on the south side of patapsco river in bodkin Creek at a bounded white oak posesed by Henry Waters rent ℔ annum —.. 4.. —

Gwins farm, 121 acr Sur the 21 feb^ry 1688 for Richard Gwin on the north side of deep Creek begining at a bounded pine by the Creek side now in the posestion of Henry Waters rent ℔ annum —.. 4.. 11

Smith's Addition, 45 acr Sur the 6 June 1695 for Edward Smith In baltimore County begining at a bounded tree of Homewood Range now in posestion of Richard Banks rent ℔ annum —.. —.. 10

Homewood forrest, 100 acr Sur the 15 July 1678 for Thomas Homewood on the south side of patapsco river on bodkins Creek at a bounded pine at the mouth of a Cove posesed by the s^d Homewood rent ℔ annum —.. 4.. —

Homewood Range, 300 acr Sur the 5 July 1670 for John Homewood on the south side of patapsco river the northermost bounds by the river side of the Land of David Johnson, posesed by Thomas Howard rent ℔ annum —.. 12.. —

    C. Poss^r Tho Homewood.

Beare Neck, 146 acr Sur the 8 Feb 1682 for Robert Procter begining at a bounded pine tree on the south side of the bodkin Creek 100 acr thereof posesed by William Foreman rent ℔ annum —.. 4.. —

46 acr residue thereof belongs to the orphants of Nicolas Lamb rent ℔ annum—this Lyes in Anarundel Co.

Parkers Range, 330 acr Sur the 20 Jan^ry 1673 for Quinton Parker on the south side of patapsco river at a bounded white oak by a small branch now posesed by Joshua Merica rent ℔ annum —.. 9.. 2

    C. Poss^r Joshua Merrica.

Treadhaven Point, 150 acr. Sur the 30 Aprill 1670 for Thomas Richardson on the south side of patapsco river at the mouth of a small Creek and runing up the Creek north and by East posesed by Joshua Merica rent ℔ an —.. 3.. —

Morleys Choice, 300 acr Sur the 18 July 1670 for Joseph Morley on the west side of Curtises Creek posesed by John Gadbey for the orphants of George Norman rent ℔ anum —.. 6.. —

Vnited Friendship, 300 acr Sur the 30 Aprill 1671 for John

Grange on the south side of patapsco river at a bounded pine tree of the Land of John Hawkins by a small branch belongs to the heires of John Rigby rent ℔ anum —.. 6.. —

Pole Almanack Neck, 100 acr Sur the 26 Oct. 1667 for William Davis on the south side of patapsco river belonges to the heires of the said Rigby rent ℔ annum —.. 2.. —

Mascalls Haven, 100 acr Sur the 11 Octr 1670 for Richard Mascall af^d and patten granted in the name of James Wells on the south side of patapsco river at a bounded pine and runing down the river posesed by Jonathan Neale rent ℔ annum —.. 4.. —

   C. Maskalls haven. R^d Maskatt. Poss^r Robt Jubb.

Knighton fancy, 100 acr Sur the 2 Sepr 1671 for Thomas Knighton on the west side of patapsco river at a bounded white oak of the Land of Paul Kinsy noe heires appeares Land vncultivated noe rent payd there 15 yeares rent Set ℔ annum —.. 4.. —

This is Lyable to an Escheat.

   C. No rent paid these 19 years. Sold as Im inform'd to Wm Watson. Dead & no heir.

Wilsons Enlargement, 60 acr Sur the 14 Sepr 1671 for Robert Wilson on the south side of patapsco and on the north side of Curtises Creek at the Southermost Line of the Land of Kinsys no heires Land vncultivated no rent payd the 15 yeares rent Set ℔ annum —.. 1.. 2

As above.

   C. No heirs, rent not paid these 19 years.

Little Towne, 30 acr Sur the 14 Septem^r 1681 for Robert Wilson on the south side of Patapsco river adjoining to the Land Called Harborrow no heires no rent payd these 15 yeares Land vncultivated rent set —.. 3.. 2½

As above.

Radnage, 160 acr Sur the 3 Oct 1667 for George Yates on the south side of patapsco river opposit to the Rocks at a bounded

Locust tree by the river side 60 acr part thereof posesed by Wm Hawkins rent ℔ an —.. 1.. 2

   C. Poss^rs 60a Wm Hawkins 50a Xtopher Cox. 50a Tho Knight Smith.

Hawkins Range, 100 acr Sur the 6 July 1679 for Wm Hawkins on the south side of patapsco river on the side of Rock neck posesed by the s^d Hawkins rent ℔ annum —.. 4.. —

Hawkins Choice, 134 acr Sur the 3 May 1680 for Wm Hawkins in Baltimore County begining at a bounded tree of the Land at the East End of the Land Called Hawkinses Range and now posesed by the s^d Hawkins rent ℔ annum —.. 5.. 4¼

Hawkins Adition, 203 acr Sur the 2 Octo^r 1695 for William Hawkins In Baltimore County begining at a bounded gum of Hawkins Range rent ℔ annum —.. 8.. 1½

Whites Addition, 160 acr Sur the Novemb^r 1678 for Steven White on the south side of patapsco river at a bounded popular by George Yates posesed by William Hawkins for the orphants of Stephen White rent ℔ anum 7.. 2¼

Coxes Range, 200 acr Sur the 15 Novemb^r 1686 for Christopher Cox on the south side patapsco river posesed by him rent ℔ anum —.. 18.. —

   C. Poss^r Luke Read.

Coxes Enlargement, 200 acr Sur the 15 Aprill 1689 for Christopher Cox on the East side of Curtises Creek begining at two bounded oak by the said Creek posesed by the s^d Cox rent ℔ anum —.. 8.. —

   C. Poss^r S^d Read.

Chinkapin Forrest, 61 acr Sur the 23 June 1694 for John Lockett on the north side of deep Creek begining at a bounded pine by the Creek in a Line of the Land branden posesed by the said Lockett rent ℔ anum —.. 2.. 5½

   C. Chinkapink forest. Poss^r ye s^d Locketts orph^n.

Rockholds Range, 200 acr Sur the 22 May 1683 for John

Rockhold on the south side of patapsco river on the head of rock Creek at a bounded oak being a bounded tree of a tract of Land Called Rattle snake neck now posesed by John Lockett rent ℔ anum —.. 8.. —

Pauls Neck, 200 acr Sur the 10 Aprill 1672 for Paul Kensy on the south side of patapsco river now posesed by John Lockett as aforesd rent ℔ anum —.. 8.. —

C. Poss^r John Lockett for R^d Gwin's orp^{ns}.

Newtowne, 200 acr Sur the 25 Aprill 1672 for Edward Halton and Richd Gwin on the north side patapsco river on the falls of the Midle branch of the river now posesed as aforesd rent ℔ anum —.. 8.. —

C. Poss^r Peter Bond.

Brandon, 25 acr Sur the 17 August 1663 for Paul Kinsy on the south side of patapsco on the north west side of deep Creek posesed as aforesaid rent ℔ anum —.. 5.. —

C. Poss^r John Lockett as af^d.

Phillipes fancy, 69 acr Sur the 1st Aprill 1682 for William Cromwell on the south side of patapsco river on the west side of deep Creek at a bounded popular by a water oak of the Land of Jenkin Smith posesed by Thomas Croker rent ℔ anum —.. 2.. 2

C. 61a Rent 2-51/2.

Boons Adventure, 160 acr Sur 10 May 1672 for Humphry Boone on the south side of patapsco river at a bounded pine tree of the Land vpon a point on the north side of Rock Creek in posestion of the said Humphry Boone, rent ℔ an. —.. 6.. 5

Addition to westwood, 100 acr Sur the 30 Novemb^r 1694 for Joseph Strawbridge in the woods on the north side of back river begining at a bounded water oak of the Land Called westwood now posesed by Edward Stevenson rent ℔ anum —.. 4.. —

C. Poss^r Geo Hope.

The Range, 240 acr Sur the 28 decemb[r] 1685 for Henry Constable Lyeing on the south side of patapsco river rent ⅌ an. —.. 9.. 7

C. *Poss[r] The heir of Rigby.*

Batchelors Hope, 100 acr Sur the 9 June 1669 for John— on the south side of patapsco river at a bounded tree of a parcell of Land Called white oak Springe Standing on Jelfs Island bounding on the river to the bounded tree of Paul Kinsy Land no heires appeare Land uncultivated rent set ⅌ anum —.. 2.. —

C. *Sur for Jn[o] Tonnall.*

Owens Adventure, 450 acr Sur the 10 Oct[r] 1694 for Richard Owens on the west side of patapsco river on the north side of Coll Taylors land begining at a bounded oak in Coll Taylors line posesed as above rent ⅌ anum —.. 18.. —

C. *Poss[rs] 225a S[d] Owen. 225a Coll Edw[d] Dorsey.*

Good Endeavor, 40 acr Sur the 1 May 1689 for Charles Gorsuch on west side of patapsco and on the north most side of beare Creek now posesed by John Cooper rent ⅌ anum —.. 1.. 8

C. *Poss[r] Nich Rogers.* [Later entry] *Poss[d] by Jn[o] Copper.*

Robertsons Addition, 38 acr Sur the 12 Septem[r] 1695 for Richard Robertson begining at the said Robertsons South South East Line now posesed by William Mackcartee for the orphants of the said Robertson rent ⅌ anum —.. 1.. 6½

Knightsmiths folly, 94 acr Sur the 10 decem[r] 1695 for Thomas Knightsmith begining at a bounded popular of Stephen White now posesed by the said Knightsmith rent ⅌ anum —.. 3.. 9½

Strife, 185 acr Sur the 30 July 1695 for Tobias Sternbroe between the branch of back river and gunpowd[r] begining at a bounded white oak by the Herring run posesed by the s[d] Sternbroe rent ⅌ anum —.. 7.. 5

C. *Tobias Sternbrow.*

Bonds Forrest, 301 acr Sur the 16 May 1688 for Peter Bond on the head of deep Creek in patapsco river begining at a bounded white oak by a branch and posesed by the s^d bond rent ℔ anum —.. 12.. —

Jenifers delight, 250 acr Sur the 19 Octr 1681 for Jacob Jenifer at a bounded oak on the south side of a Creek Called Swan Creek on the head of back river 150 part thereof in posestion of John Gray rent ℔ anum —.. 6.. —
100 Acr residue thereof in posestion of Thomas Weeks rent ℔ anum —.. 4.. —

Roberts Parke, 200 acr Sur the 17 July 1694 for Thomas Roberts on the north side of patapsco river begining at a bounded red oak by a run descending into Jones falls posesed by the s^d Roberts rent ℔ anum —.. 8.. —

Fellowshipe, 200 acr Sur the 12 June 1696 for John Oulton Lyeing on the north side of patapsco river on a ridge Called little brittane ridge begining at a bounded white oak at the head of the herring run branch the s^d Oulton In England rent ℔ anum —.. 8.. —

C. Poss^r Ed^w Stevenson.

Come by Chance, 257 acr Sur the 24 Feb^r 1694 for John Ferry Lying in Widow neck on the north side of back river begining at the mouth of the north west branch thereof and now belongs to the orphants of John Boaring rent ℔ anum —.. 10.. 3½

Goose Harbour, 41 acr Sur the 5th of Oct. 1679 for Rowland Thornbury on the south side of Gunpowd^r river now In posestion of Joseph Wells for the orphants of the s^d Thornbury rent ℔ anum —.. 1.. 8½

Robert's Choice, 159 acr Sur the 27 March 1688 for Thomas Robert Lyeing between patapsco and back river and posesed by the said Roberts rent ℔ an. —.. 6.. 1

C. 153a.

109

Welshes Addition, 102 acr Sur the 29 June 1688 for Daniell Welsh Lyeing between the falls of patapsco now belongs to the orphants of the s^d Welsh rent ℔ anum —.. 4.. 1

Friendshipp, 100 acr Sur the 20 decemb^r 1670 for Thomas Port and Robert Benjor at a bounded hickory on the north East side of the falls of the north west branch now posesed by Alexand^r Graves rent ℔ anum —.. 4.. —

 C. Poss^r Alex^r Graves. Graves run away as I am informed.

———, acr Sur the 20 May 1669 for George Hickson on the north west branch of patapsco river and vpon the main run of the branch now in posestion of Robert Gibson. I believe Escheatable rent ℔ anum —.. 4.. —

 C. St. Mary Bow. 200a Hickson dead & left no heirs.

Maidens Choice, 450 acr Sur the 17th Aug 1673 for Thomas Cole on the north side of patapsco river at a bounded white oak standing north west belonging to the son of Charles Gorsuch rent ℔ an. —.. 18.. —

 C. Poss^r ye son of Cha Gorsuch, the heir at age.

Stony banke, 50 acr Sur the 16 June 1688 for David Jones on the north side of patapsco river at a bounded oak in the woods Jones dead noe heires appeare Land uncultivated, rent set ℔ anum —.. 2.. —

Jones Range, 350 acr Sur the 15 Jan^{ry} 1661 for David Jones on the north side of patapsco river at a Saplin by a Creek side and runing north north west now posesed by Roger Newman rent ℔ an. —.. 15.. 2

 C. Bel. to ye heirs of Roger Newman in England.

Goose Harbour, 200 acr Sur the 5 decemb^r 1659 ? for Rowland Thornbury on the south side of back river at a bounded white oak by the river side nigh a small marsh now posesed by Joseph Wells for the orphants of the said Thornbury rent ℔ anum —.. 8.. —

300 acr Sur the 5 May 1673 for Giles Stevens in back river at a marked Chestnut by a little Cove on the north side of the river this was sold to Theophilas Hackett since dead no heires appear Land vncultivated Rent sett ℔ anum —.. 12.. —
(This belongs to Mr James ? who purchases the same of the Heyres of Hackett)

C. Paradice. Poss^r James Heath.

Chance, 210 acr Sur the 10 July 1673 for James Ellis on the north side of patapsco river in the woods at a bounded white oak and runing by a Cove Called Rogers Cove Ellis dead rent ℔ anum —.. 8.. 4

C. Ellis's Chance. Poss^r Robt Welsh.

76 acr Sur the 29 Aprill 1678 for William Watson on the north side of Patapsco river in the woods at a bounded white oak and runing East Watson dead no heires rent set. Escheatable.

C. Watson's chance. 176a. Rent 0-7-01/2.

MARYLAND RENT ROLLS.

ANN ARRUNDELL COUNTY.
RENT ROLL 1707

Herring Creek Hundred

Carter

	£	s.	d.
600 Acres Sur: 28th Octob 1651 for Capt Edwd Carter near Herring Creek Bay Rent ℔ Annum	00.	12..	—

Possessors: 300 A: Samll. Chew Junr.
        100 A: William Dorrumple
         50 A: Hen: Archers Orphans
             (who are married to Cha:
              Scot, Willm Gardner & one
              Daughter unmaryed)
         25 A: Thomas Watkins
         25 A: Morgan Jones
        100 A: Walker Emerton

600

C refers to Calvert Paper No. 883 and indicates changes or variations in entries referring to the same tract of land.

C. Possess^rs 300 a Sam Chew jun^r who claims of Robt Paca & He from Wm Hunt & He ye assign of one half of ye patent from Ed^w. Carter, 100 a Wm Dorrumple in Right of his wife ye Wid^o of Robt Sollers, 50 a Hen Arthurs Orp^ns who are married to Cha. Scott Wm Gardiner & one Daughter unmarried. 25 a Tho Watkins, 25 a Morgan Jones, 100 a Walker Emerton.

Carter Bennet

	£	s.	d.
300 A: Sur: 28 Octob 1651 for Richd Bennet Esqr near Herring Creek bay, Rent ⅌ Hun: Possess^d by Coll Wm Holland in Right of his wife the Sister of Francis Holland the Son	—..	6..	—

Bennets Island

| 275 A: Sur: 28: Octob 1651 for Richd Bennet Esqr lying on Herring Creek bay, rent ⅌ Ann Possess^d by Coll Wm Holland in Right of his wife the Sister of Fran: Holland | —.. | 5.. | 6 |

Town Land

| 200 A. Sur: 24th Octob 1651 for Wm Parker on the South Side of Herring Creek Rent ⅌ Ann Possess^d by Christop Vernon in Right of his wife the Relict of Lewis Evans & in behalf of the Orphans of the said Evans | —.. | 4.. | — |

Ayres

| 600 A: Sur: 29: Octob 1651 for Wm Ayres adjoyning to the Land of Capt Edward Carter pattented in the name of Ann daughter & heir of the said Ayres & wife of Sam: Chew, Rent Possess^d by Samuell Chew the son of the said Samuell above mentioned | —.. | 12.. | — |

£1.. 19.. 0

Gordon

300 A: Sur: 18 Novemb 1659 for Alex[r] Gordon on the North Side of Herring Creek & on
the North side of Gotts Creek, rent ℔ Ann
Possess[ors] 200 A: Robert Franklyn
         100 A: Will[m] Horn

     £   s.   d.

—.. 6.. —

    300:

Ram—Got—Swamp

600 A: Sur: 18 Nov: 1659 for Rich[d] Gott on
the North side of Herring Creek, rent ℔ Ann
Possess[rs] 300 A: Rich[d] Gott
         200 A: John Cheshire
          33 A: Sam: Harrison
         100 A: Mordicay Price for Auth[o]
                Hollands Orphans
         100 A: Cap[t] Robert Lockwood

—.. 12.. —

    733   133 A: over & above the Surveys —.. 2.. 8..

Paget

250 A: Sur: 18: Nov[r] 1659 for W[m] Paget on
the West side of a Branch running North out
of Herr: Creek bay called Beaver dam branch
rent
Possess[d] by John Trundle

—.. 5.. —

C.   This Land was escheated for want of ye heirs of Paget
& order'd by his Ldp to be granted to John Trundle ffather of
y[e] possor John Trundle.

Silverston

800 A: Sur: 23[d] Nov. 1659 for Anthony Sallo-
way near the mouth of Bennets Creek rent
Possess[d] by Phillip Cole in Right of his Wife
     daughter & heir of George Skipwith

—.. 16.. —

Kequotan Choyce

		£	s.	d.
300 A: Sur: 5th May 1663 for Stephen Benson				

300 A: Sur: 5th May 1663 for Stephen Benson
in the branches of Herring Creek rent   —.. 6.. —

Poss^{rs} 150 A: George Symons
     100 A: Sam: Guichard in right of his wife
      50 A: Peter Tibedan in right of his
    ——   wife he daughter of Ann Gongoe
    300   as Guichard's is also another
   —— —   daughter of the s^d Gongoe

Jericho

200 A: Sur: 3^d July 1663 for Wm Croseby be-   £   s.   d.
tween the branches of Lyons Creek & the
branches of Herring Creek bay, rent   —.. 4.. —

                                          2.. 11.. 8

Poss^{rs} 100 A: Tho: Tench Esqr for the Or-
              phans of James Rigby whose
              wife was daughter & heir of
              Nathan Smith
     100 A: Christop Vernon in right of his
              wife
    ——   the relict of Lewis Evans & in
    200   behalf of the Orphans of the
              said Evans
C. *Jerico.*

Burrage

500 A: Sur: 20th March 1662 for John Burrage

Burrage Blossom

200 A: Sur: the same day for the s^d Jno Burrage

Burrages End

150 A: Sur: 6 Nov. 1665 for the s^d Jno Burrage

850   The above 3 Tracts ly all together and

	£	s.	d.

joyn the one to the other & ly on the
Ridge to the Westward of Herring
Crek, rent —.. 17.. —

The said three tracts of Land cutting athwart
them all & takeing a part of each of them are
Possess^d by the psons following

> 100 A: John Wilson
> 300 A: Benja: Welch
> 50 A: Tho: Tench Esqr for Nathan Rigby
>   the Orphan of James Rigby
>   as in Jericho aforegoing
> 100 A: Mr Henry Hall being the Glebe
> 272½ A: James Heath
> 27½ A: John Wilson

> 850

*C. 318 a James Smith, 14 a John Wilson, 32 a over y^e
Survey.*

Dan

490 A: Sur: 3 July 1663 for Robert Paca be-
tween the branches of Herring Creek & Lyons
Creek rent —.. 9.. 10
Poss^{rs} 290 A: Tho: Tench Esqr for Nathan
          Rigby as in Jericho
    100 A: John Turner in right of his
          wife the Relict of R^d James
    100 A: Abraham Symons

> 490

C. James Simmons.

Benjamins Choyce

280 A: Sur: 7th July 1663 for Rich Wells on

	£	s.	d.
the Westward of Herring Creek bay in the
Woods, rent —.. 5.. 7¼

Poss^d by Richard Harrison

Dinah Ford's Beaver-Dam

400 A: Sur: 27th Novr 1662 for Tho: Ford
near Herring Creek, rent —.. 8.. —

Poss^{rs} 90 A: Fran: More for Jam: Ford's
Orphans

    62 A: Rob: Brown for Tindalls Or-
phans

  100 A: John Standforth which he holds
only by the Curtisie of Engl^d &
on his death the same Escheats
to his Lo^P

  150 A: Rob: Franklyn

_____

402   Wells   £2.. —.. 5¼

600 A: Sur: 22 Nov. 1659 for Richd Wells
Between Fishing& Creek & Herring Creek bay   —.. 12.. —
Poss^{rs} Samuell Chew & Nehemiah Birckhead

Well's Hills

420 A: Sur: 14 July 1663 for Richd Wells
in the Branches of Fishing Creek, rent   —.. 8.. 5
Poss^{rs} the same as above

West Wells

350 A: Sur: 14th July 1663 for Richd Wells
to the Westward of the Land called Wells be-
tween the Branches of fishing Creek & Herring
Creek bay.

Poss^{rs} 150 A: Sam: Chew & Neh: Birckhead
     200 A: Robert Conaut

_____

350

_____

C.   *Robert Conaught.*

Little Wells

	£	s.	d.
100 A: Sur: 23th July 1663 for Richd Wells between Fishing creek & Herring creek bay near the Land called Wells, rent		—.. 2..	—

Poss^{rs} Sam: Chew & Nehemiah Birckhead

Goury Banks

600 A: Sur: 17: July 1663 for Tho: Ford on the West side the Plant^a of Herring Creek bay about 2½ miles from the bay.   Rent ℔ Ann   —.. 12.. —

Poss^{rs} 300 A: John Rea for Powells Orphans
      150 A: James Wood for Groves Orph^{ns}
      150 A: John Beecher for Groves Orp^{ns}

—————
600
—————

Maidstone

350 A: Sur: 3^d Augt 1663 for Wm Hunt on the West Side the Plant^a of Herring Creek bay about 4 Miles in the woods.   Rent   —.. 7.. —

Poss^{rs} Rich: Bond for Benj^a Chew's Orphan

Hunts Mount

350 A: Granted 29th Sept. 1663 to Wm Hunt lying on the West of Capt. Carters Land & on the West of Herring Creek Bay, rent   —.. 7.. —

————————
£2.. 15.. 5

Poss^{rs} 150 A: Samuell Chew Junr
      83 A: Robert Sollars
    100 A: Thomas Wells
     17 A: Thomas Trott

—————
350
—————

Hunts Chance

	£	s.	d
400 A: Sur: 31: July 1663 for Wm Hunt on the West side the Land of Richd Wells about 2 Miles from Herring Creek bay rent | —.. | 8.. | — |

400 A: Sur: 31: July 1663 for Wm Hunt on
the West side the Land of Richd Wells about
2 Miles from Herring Creek bay rent   —.. 8.. —
Poss^{rs} 200 A: Coll Wm Holland
      200 A: Edward Ward tenant under
          John Godscross who is tenant
          by the curtesie of England &
          upon his death the same Es-
          cheats to his Lords^p

Hollands Hills

190 A: Sur: 7th Augt 1663 for Francis Holland on the westward of Herring Creek bay
near the Land of Carter Bennet, rent   —.. 3.. 10
Poss^r Richd Harrison

Pascalls Chance

200 A: Sur: 6: Decemb^r 1662 for George Pascall on the South side the Land called Gordon,
rent   —.. 6.. —
Poss^{rs} 200 A: Wm Smith for Rob: Gott's
          Orp^{ns}
      100 A: Wm Pearce

    ———
    300
    ———

Birckheads Parcell

600 A: Sur: 10th Feb. 1661 for Christop
Birckhead near the Land Surveyed for John
Burrage, rent   —.. 12.. —
Poss^{rs} 500 A: Nehe: Birckhead
      100 A: Abra: Birckhead

    ———
    600
    ———

C. John Burridge, Abra: Birkhead.

Greenwood

150 A: Sur: 12th July 1663 for Armiger
Greenwood on the north side broadcreek run-
ning out of Herring bay, rent
Poss^{rs} 100 A: Benj^a Capell
      50 A: Mordica Price for Anth: Hol-
            lands Orp^t

      £   s.   d.

—.. 3.. —

   150

Morely

300 A: Sur: 17: July 1663 for Jos: Moreley
about 2 miles from Herring creek bay on the
back of Hollands Hill, rent ℔ Ann   —.. 6.. —
I doe not find this Land was ever Pattented
but it was by Joseph Morely conveyed to W^m
Hunt who dyed without heir & the Land taken
up after, the greatest part by the said Morely
in a Survey of his of 300 A: partly by Rich^d
Wells & partly by Richd Deavour

His Lordship's Mannour on the Ridge

10,000 A: Surv^d: for his Lords^p ... 1662 and
the 1st Aprill 1698 Resurvey'd for his said
Lordship & then found to be 12634 Acres & is
possess^d 11085 A: His Lords^p

325 A: Antho. Smith at the rent	—..	13..	—
250 A: Solomon Sparrow, rent	—..	10..	—
240 A: Wm Rich^dson at the rent	—..	9..	7¼
200 A: Sam: Thomas at the rent	—..	8..	—
100 A: Hen: Hall at the rent	—..	4..	—
100 A: Phillip Dowell at the rent	—..	4..	—
334 A: Seth Bigges at the rent	—..	13..	11½
50 A: John Parrish at the rent	—..	2..	—

12634

Portland Mannour

	£	s.	d.

2000 A: Sur: 6: Decem^r 1667 for Jerome
White Esqr on the South side the west line of
Ann Arrundell Mann^r 500 A: pt. of this Mann^r
was sold to Edwd Talbot & the remainder for
his Lords^p for whom the whole was resurv^d
Aprill 4th 1698 & then found to be 2722 A.

Poss^{rs} 500 A: Widow Talbot, rent   —.. 10.. —

      1090 A: Coll. Hen: Darnell by grant
           from his Lords^p, rent   1.. 2.. —

      1000 A: Hen: Lazenby for Charles
           Calvert Lazenby, rent   1.. —.. —

      132 A: Remains in his Lo^p

2722

Trent

	£	s.	d.

450 A: Sur: 17: July 1663 for Joseph Morely
& John Gray on the back of Hunts Mount on
the west of Herring Creek bay, rent   —.. 9.. —

Poss^{rs} 50 A: Rob: Smith

      62½ A: James Lee for John Wilson's
           Orphan

      62½ A: Tho: Bartlet for Moses Wil-
           son's Orp^n

      50 A: Wm Hollyday

     125 A: James Wood

     100 A: Tho: Trott

450

Smithfield

100 A: Sur: 3^d Aug. 1663 for Nathan Smith
on the West side the Land called Ayres, rent   —.. 2.. —

Poss^r Henry Child

                   6.. 7.. 6¾

Holloway's Neck

100 A: Sur: 24th Octob^r 1651 for Richd Bennet Esqr & pattented in the name of Oliver Holway who dying without Heir the same as Escheat was granted to Tho: Lun, whose daughter & heir Eliz^a intermarryed with Edwd Price for whom with the said Eliz^a the same was reserv^d 1st 9ber 1699 & then found to be 147 A: rent ——.. 5.. 10$\frac{1}{2}$

Poss^r Sam: Maccubin who marryed the s^d Eliz^a the relict of the s^d Price

£   s.   d.

Broughton Ashly

950 A: Sur: 5th Jan^{ry} 1663 for Fran: Holland on the west side of West Wells Hills & Silverston, this Land was resurrv^d for the s^d Francis Holland the 18th Jan^{ry} 1669 for the same q^t rent ——.. 19.. ——

Poss^{rs} 66 A: Coll Wm Holland
     50 A: Jos. Saunders
     60 A: Rob. Connaut
   200 A: John Ward
   100 A: Rob. Gover's heir
     50 A: John Witherd
   150 A: John Chapell
     50 A: Richd Thornbury
     50 A: Richd Tucker
     50 A: John Stephens
     24 A: Sam: Gover
     97 A: John Emerton
      3 A: Dan: Robertson
    ——
   950
  ——

Bednall Green

180 A: Sur: 19th March 1669 for Rob. Wells

	£	s.	d.

at the South East bounds of the Land of Benj^a
Wells to the Westward of Herring Creek bay,
rent   —.. 7.. 4

Poss^r Richd Harrison

Brushy Bay

80 A: Sur: 21 March 1669 for Lyonell Pawly
at a bounded white oak of Jericho, rent   —.. 3.. 2
Poss^r John Preston

Benjamins Addition

49 A: Sur: 30: Sep: 1670 for Benj^a Wells at
a bounded tree of Hollands Hill   Rent   —.. —.. 10
Poss^r Richard Harrison

Souldiers Delight

100 A: Sur: 28th Decem^r 1670 for Lyonell
Pawly at a bounded tree of Goury bank's, rent   —.. 2.. —
Poss^r Coll. Wm Holland

£1.. 18.. 2½

Pascalls Purchase

300 A: Sur: 24th Octob^r 1651 for Edwd Selby
on the west side of Herring Creek

Edward Selby sold this Land to Geo: Pascall
who sold 100 A. pt. thereof to his nephew
James Pascall (the which by mesne convey^a is
now the right of Xtop Vernon) the other 200
A. he sold to Wm Sivick, who left the same to
his only son John Sivick who dying left it by
will to Susanna his Relict, which Susanna sold
thereout to John Wilson 85 A: but proved to
be but 45 A: to Jonathan Jones 61 A: to Xtop
Vernon 30 A: & to James Heath the remaining
part of the said 200 A: the which James the
20th Aprill 1705 caused the whole tract to be
Res^d & was then found to be 374 A. the wch 74
A. Surplus the s^d James Heath obtained a

grant thereof & on the 1st of March 1705 had a
Pattent of Confirm^a as well for the afores^d
Surplus as for his aforesaid remaining pt by
the name of Heath's Landing the which is soe
entred in page 17 the rest of Pascalls Purch:
& that wch only now beares that name is 236
A: at the rent of

Poss^{rs} 130 A: Christop Vernon
     45 A: John Wilson
     61 A: Jonathan Jones

   236

Sanetley

450 A: Sur: 3 Aug. 1663 for Samuell Chew on
the west side the Land called Ayres, rent

Poss^{rs} 400 Eliz^a relict of Jos. Chew for her
        self & the Orpⁿ of the s^d Joseph
     50 Henry Child

   450

Turkey Hill

100 A: Sur: 9th July 1663 for Tho: Prat between the Land of John Burrage & Pascalls
Chance

Poss^r Thomas Pratt

Birckhead's Meadows

50 A: Sur: 7: Jan^{ry} 1663 for Xtop Birckhead
at the North East corner tree of Birckheads
parcell, rent

Poss^r Nehemiah Birckhead

Bersheba

100 A: Sur: 5th July 1663 for John Wilson on
the west side the main branch of Lyons Creek,
rent

£   s.   d.

—.. 4.. 8¾

—.. 9.. —

£   s.   d.

—.. 2.. —

—.. 1.. —

—.. 2.. —

Poss^{rs} 94 A: John Thornbury   £   s.   d.

     6 A: Abra: Birckhead

————

100

————

Chews Rest

300 A: Sur: 19 Aprill 1665 for Sam: Chew
at the Miles end of the Land called Ayres, rent   —.. 6.. —

Poss^r Sam: Chew

Birckheads Lott

434 A: Sur: 3^d March 1663 for Christop.
Birckhead in the woods on the west of the
Plant^a on Herring Creek bay, rent   —.. 8.. —

Poss^{rs} 344 A: Solomon Birckhead

     90 A: Richd Harrison

————

434

————

Smith's delight

300 A: Sur: 2^d March 1664 for Nathan Smith
adjoyning to the Land of Samuell Chew, rent   —.. 6.. —

Poss^{rs} 150: Tho. Tench Esqr for Ja: Rigby's
            Orphan

    150: Samuell Chew

————

300

————

Hopewell

300 A: Sur: 18: July 1663 for Ferdinando
Battee & Andrew Skinner near Herring Creek
beaver dams   —.. 6.. —

Poss^{rs} Widow Battee for her self and the orph^{ns}
    of the s^d Ferdinando

Herring Creek Road

	£	s.	d.

100 A: Sur: 8th Nov. 1665 for John Burrage
near Herring Creek bay, rent   —.. 2.. —
Poss[r] Coll William Holland

Birckheads Chance

50 A: Sur: E[th] Nov. 1665 for Abra: Birckhead in the woods at a bounded Hiccory of
John Wilson in the line of Birckheads parcell,
rent   —.. 1.. —
Poss[r] Abraham Birckhead

Barren point

40 A: Sur: 9th 9ber 1665 for Geo. Pascall on
the East side of Beaver dam branch, rent   —.. —.. 10
Poss[r] William Smith for Rob. Gotts Orp[n]

Daborns hope

40 A: Sur: 21 Nov. 1665 for Tho: Daborn in
Herring Creek Swamp on the So: side of South
Creek, rent   —.. —.. 10
Poss[r] Capt Robert Lockwood

Grammars Chance

350 A: Sur: 5th Xber 1666 for John Gramar
lying on the branch of Lyons Creek, rent   —.. 7.. —
Poss[r] Rich[d] Harrison

Birckheads Chance

750 A: Sur: 3[d] Xber 1667 for George Yate on
Lyons Creek branch, rent   —.. 15.. —
Poss[r] Abraham Birckhead

The Ham

100 A: Sur: 6: Xber 1667 for Rich[d] Bedworth
& Samuell Thornbury in the main bra: of
Lyons Creek   —.. 2.. —
Poss[r] Thomas Tench Esq[r]

126

Morley's Lott

300 A: Sur: 14: Sep: 1667 for Jos: Morely
near the Land called Trent, rent
Poss[r] Rich[d] Harrison

£   s.   d.
—.. 6.. —

Grammars Parrot

400 A: Sur: 22 Sep: 1653 for W[m] Parrot who
Assigned the same to John Grammar who had
the same sur. for himself July 1st 1667, rent
Poss[r] 200 A: Abra: Meares
     100 A: Capt. Beasly
     100 A: Tho: Miles

—.. 8.. —

    400

St. Jeromes

300 A: Sur: 6: Xber 1667 for Jerome White
Esq[r] at the west corner of the Land called
Quick Sale
This Land was granted to Coll. Hen. Darnall
6th Aug[t] 1700 & now in his Possession

—.. 6.. —

Batchellors Choyce

300 A: Sur: 20th Xber 1668 for Ninian Beal
near Lyons Creek, rent
Poss[r]

—.. 6.. —

  C. Poss[r] Jonathan Scarth of London

MARYLAND RENT ROLLS.

Anne Arundel Co.

Daborns Inheritance

250 A: Sur: 27: Aug: 1668 for Tho: Daborn in
Herr. Creek Swamp in the main bra: of broad
creek This Land was Res^d for the sd. Daborn 29th
May 1673 & then added to it 300 A. at new Rent
(the other 250 A. being old Rent) makes the whole
550 A. at

—.. 17.. —

Poss^r John Carr.   £ 3.. 7.. —

Chandlers Grove

100 A: Sur. 31. Mar: 1664 for Tho. Chandler to
the west of Herr. Creek

—.. 2.. —

Poss^r John Whipps.   £ 3.. 9.. —

Prestons Enlargement

65 A: Sur: 1st June 1669 for John Welch at a
bounded tree of the Land called Burrages End,
rent   —.. 1.. 3½
Poss^r Robert Welch.

Bedworth's Addition

52 A: Sur: 27th Feb. 1671 for Richd Bedworth on
the north side of a bra: of Lyons Creek rent   —.. 1.. 0½
Poss^r John Thornbury.

Addition

95 A: Sur: 6. March 1671 for Fran: Holland at a
bounded White Oak of the Land called Wells &
Herring Creek Road   rent —.. 3.. 10
Poss^r Coll. Wm Holland in Right of his wife the
sister of Francis son of the s^d Fra: Holl^d.

Knockers Hall in W. R. H.

*C. Knockers Hall 30a sur 18 ffeb 1671 for ffra
Landry in ye swamp Poss^r Tho Carr.   0-1.*

Portland Landing

200 A: Sur: 17: May 1672 for Jerom White Esqr
on the westward of Portland Mann^r   rent —.. 4.. —
This Land was sold to his Lords^p who granted the
same to Coll. Hen: Darnall 6th Augt 1700 & he is
now poss^r thereof.

The Freindship

50 A: Sur: 20th June 1673 for Wm Andrews &
Tho: Parsons at a bounded tree of Armiger Green-
wood & pattented in the name of the said Parsons
he being the surviv^r   Rent —.. 2.. —
Poss^r Benj. Capell.

Papa Ridge

155 A: Sur: 13th July 1673 for Edwd Parish in
Herring Creek Swamp   rent —.. 6.. 2

Poss^rs 105 Wid° Hurst
     50 Mordica Price
     ───
   155
   ───

Papa's Chance

45 A: Sur: 20 Decemb. 1677 for Rob: Paca in
Herring Creek Bay.   rent —.. 1.. 9½
Poss^r Sam: Chew Junr.

   C. Paca's Chain.

Hollands Range

120 A: Sur: 12 July 1677 for Anth° Holland in
Herr: Creek Swamp at a bounded tree of the Land
of Armiger Greenwood.   Rent —.. 4.. 9½

                             ─────────
Poss^r Benj^a Holland.   £ 1.. 4.. 11

Mavorn Hills

50 A: sur: 12th March 1678 for Wm Tuckbury in
the woods to the westward of the Land called
Jerichoe   —.. 2.. —
Poss^r Charles Hyat of Prin: Geo: Co.

Govers Venture

295 A: Sur: 31 Augt 1678 for Robert Gover at a
bounded tree of Broughton Ashly   Rent —.. 11.. 9½
Poss^r John Ward for Rob. Gover's Orp^n.

Fords Folly

170 A. Sur. 2^d Sept. 1675 for Thomas Ford on the
North of Herring Creek beaver dam   rent —.. 6.. 10¼
Poss^r Francis Moore for Ja: Fords Orp^n.

Hollowayes Everease

54 A: Sur: 15th Sep: 1675 for Oliver Holloway
on Gotts Creek & running west wth Gotts Land
This Land is Esch^t for want of Heirs of Holloway.

The Guift

179 A: Sur: 15th Sep: 1675 for Wm Collier on
Gotts Creek at the end of the west line of Pascall
Chance,   Rt. —.. 7.. 1¾

   C. *The Gift. Possr Robt Franklin.*

Devoyrs Range

220 A: Sur: 24th Augt 1675 for Richd Devoir on
the north of the Land called Hunts Chance, rent —.. 8.. 9½
Possrs Henry Archers Orphans

   C. *Devoirs range.*

Turkey Island

33 A: Sur: 15th Sep: 1675 for Abell Hill at the
Northermost bounds of Paschalls chance,   Rent —.. 1.. 3¾
Possrs 16½ Abell Hills Orpn
      16½ Goldsborrough's Orpn

——————

33

——————

   C. *David Jones for Goldsboroughs orpn.*

Robert's Luck

24 A: Sur: 10th 9ber 1676 for Rob. Franklyn
Junr near the mouth of Herring Creek Swamp
at a bod tree of the Land of Wm Collier,   Rent —.. —.. 11½
Possr Robert Franklyn.

Gullocks Folly

85 A: Sur: 11th Sep: 1678 for Tho. Gullock be-
tween Herring Creek & Puttuxent Rivr near
Birckheads Chance,   Rent —.. 3.. 5
Possrs 42½ Wm Gilborn   ——————
      42½ Joseph Owen   £ 2.. 2.. 3¼

——————

85

Birckhead's Adventure

420 A: Sur. 12th Octobr 1678 for Abra: Birckhead on the North side the main bra: of Lyons
Creek at a bod tree of W & S line of John Gramar
250 A: of this Land is pretended to be taken away
by a survey of Richd Harrisons, wherefore there
is not more paid for but 170 A as pt of this Tract
(but I doubt of this) at the Rent. —.. 5.. 5
Possr Josias Towgood for Rd Purnells Orpn.

Emerton's Addition

20 A: Sur: 17th June 1679 for Humphry Emerton
upon the main bra: of Lyon's Creek.   Rent —.. —.. 9¾
Possr Daniell Robertson.

Emerton's Range

130 A: Sur: 17th June 1679 for Humphry Emerton on the west of Francis Hollands Land Rent —.. 5.. 2½
Possrs 80 A: Sam. Gover
     50 A: John Griffin

130

Gover's Ferrin

419 A: Sur. 12. July 1679 for Robert Gover at a
bod Oak in the west line of Broughton Ashly   —.. 16.. 6
Possrs 209   A. Ephraim Gover
    209½ A. Sam. Gover

419

Conant's Chance

25 A: Sur: 2d Janry 1679 for Rob: Conant by the
side of Herring Creek bay on the North bounds
of Sylvereton.   Rent —.. 1.. —
Possr Coll. Wm Holland.

132

Knighton's Purchase

197 A: Sur: 3^d Jan^{ry} 1679 for Tho: Knighton
about 3 miles to the west of Herr. Cre: bay. Rent —.. 7.. 11
Poss^{rs} 98½ A: Sam: Gover
      98½ A: Rob. Wood

197

Purnells Angle

140 A: Sur: 24th Feb. 1679 for Tho: Purnell at
a Mr Red Birch tree by the side of the main branch
of Lyon's Creek.   Rent —.. 5.. 9

Poss^r Josias Towgood for Purnells Orp^n £ 2.. 2.. 7¼

Spencers Search

17½ A. Sur: 5th M^{rch} 1679 for John Spencer at
a bounded tree of the Land called Ayres on the N W
corner thereof.   Rent —.. —.. 8
Poss^r James Lee for John Wilson's Orp^{ns}.

Gadds Hill

140 A. Sur. 6th March 1679 for John Hall on the
south of Marshes Seat.   Rent —.. 5.. 7
Poss^r John Hall of Baltemore Co.
300 A. Sur: 20th xber 1677 for Robert Paca, the
same being part of the Land called Carter & is the
same now charged to Sam: Chew Junr in page the
first.

Eagles Nest

40 A. Sur. 29th M^{rch} 1679 for Nich: Gross upon
Herring Creek bay   Rent —.. 1.. 7
Poss^r Morgan Jones.

Hillington

50 A. Sur: 26 July 1676 for Abell Hill on the
west side of Dinah Fords Beaver dam.   Rent —.. 2.. —
Poss^r Abell Hill.

Lords County

201 A: Sur: 16: Jan^{ry} 1682 for Nath: Smith, this is layd out as Surplus Land to the Land of John Burrage.   Rent —..   8.. 0½

   C. Possr Thos Tench Esqr for James Rigbys orp^n.

Birckhead's Mill

100 A. Sur: 5th Augt 1682 for Abr: Birckhead on the main bra: of Lyons Creek   Rent R..   4.. —
Poss^r Abraham Birckhead.

Thornburyes Addition

16 A: Sur. 5th Aug. 1682 for Richd Bedworth near Thornburyes Addition   Rent —.. —.. 8
Poss^r Tho: Tench Esqr.

Locust Neck

50 A: Sur: 18th May 1670 for Edwd Parish in Herring Creek Swamp
This Land was sold by Edwd Parish 18 A: to Antho: Holland, the rest to Rob: Lockwood who sold to Theodorus Young & Robt Phillips, Mitley Marry'd Young's widow in whose right he had the Moyety of the s^d rem^a p^t & Phillips left to one Price who gave or sold it to Mord. Price's Brother of whom Mord: Price has the other Moyety of the s^d rem^a pt. These are both Resurv^d & Separately Entred in page the 16.

Truswell

30 A: Sur: 14th May 1683 For Theod: Young & Robert Phillips in Herring Creek Swamp This Land from Young & Phillips is under the same circumstance as pt of Locust Neck is from them & with the same is resurv^d & entred in page the 16:

Range

211 A: Sur: 2ᵈ July 1684 for George Burges near Birckheads Chance at a bounded tree by Pattuxent River vide assigned to George Yate. George Yate's heir lives in Baltemore County but this is supposed to be a mistaken survey of his, for noe pson claims it.

Birckhead's Right

66 A: Sur: 27ᵗʰ May 1684 for Abra: Birckhead adjoyning to his Land of Birckheads chance } —.. 2.. 8
Possʳ Abra: Birckhead.

The Vale of Pleasure

46 A: Sur: 13 Nov. 1684: for Tho: Gullock at a boᵈ tree in the Line of Birckheads Chance   —.. 1.. 10¾
Possʳˢ 23 A: Jos. Owens
     23 A: Wᵐ Gilburn

  46

James's Fancy

55 A: Sur: 15 Nov. 1684 for John James at a bounded tree of Birckheads Chance.   Rent —.. 2.. 2½
Possʳ.

  C. Possʳ James Wilson. Q. if not escheat.

Talbots Search

50 A. Sur: 8ᵗʰ Aprill 1687 for Roger Bishop near the branches of Lyons Creek.   Rent
This was held by John Battee but he affirms that it is Resurᵈ into the Ridge Mannʳ.

Talbots Lane

44 A. Sur: 8ᵗʰ Aprill 1687 for Roger Bishop in the woods near the branches of Lyons Creek   —.. 1.. 9½
Possʳ John Battee.

Harrison's Lot

13 A. Sur. 20 Sep: 1687 for Rich[d] Harrison near
Herring Creek. Rent —.. —.. 6¼
Poss[r] Rich[d] Harrison.

£—.. 9.. —¾

Holland's Addition

47 A: Sur. 16 Octob 1687 for Fran: Holland
lying near Herring Creek. Rent —.. 1.. 10½
Poss[r] Coll W[m] Holland in right of his wife the
sister of Francis Holland the son.

Long Lane

22 A: Sur: 14 Sep: 1698 for Coll Henry Darnall
on the south side Portland Mann[r] Rent —.. —.. 11
Poss[r] John Battee.

Battie's Purchase

53 A: Sur: 14: Sept. 1698 for Coll Henry Darnall
on the south side of Portland Mann[r] Rent —.. 2.. 1½
Poss[r] John Battie.

Wrighton

1.. 8.. 7

*C. Resurv[d] Nov[r] 12, 1684 for Nicholas Terratt
& then fo[d] to be 715a. Poss[rs] 515a W[m] Lydall
for Nich. Terratt's orp[n] 50a Joseph Owens 150
Jeremy Chapman.*

Mitleys Purchase

121 A: Sur: 3[d] Octob[r] 1698 for Xtop Mitley &
Eliz[a] his wife the Relict of Theod: Young the
same being a Resurvey of the moyety of remaing
pt of Locust Neck entred in page 14 & the moyety
of Truswell entred in page 15, the which lying
together upon a Res: was found to be 121 A: Rent —.. 4.. 10
Poss[r] Thomas Harris in right of Mitleys widow.

136

Locust Neck

116 A: Sur: for Mordica
Price & is what was found in the other moyety
of the s^d Rem^a pt of Locust Neck entred in pa:
14 & of Truswell in page 15. Rent —.. 4.. 7¾

18 A: the same being that sold first out of Locust
Neck as in page 14. Rent —.. —.. 8¾

Poss^rs 116 Mor: Price in his own right
     18 ditto Price for Anth: Hollands Orp:

Govers Hills

70 A: Sur: 1 Sep: 1679 for Rob: Gover joyning
to Wells Hills Rent —.. 2.. 9¾

Poss^r John Bowen.

Lott 2.. 6.. 6¼

50 A: Sur: 1st Mar: 1702 for Josias Towgood on
the no: side Lyons Creek at the Southermost Beach
of Gramars Chance. Rent —.. 2.. —

Poss^r Jos. Towgood.

Harrison's Enlargement to Gramars Chance

425 A: Sur: 3 June 1699 for R^d Harrison joyning to the Land of Gramars Chance. Rent —.. 17.. —

Poss^rs 325 A: R^d Harrison
     100 A: Jos. Towgood for Richd Purnell
     ———— an Orphan.
     425
     ————

Heath's Purchase

32 A: Sur: 10th Aprill 1705 for James Heath
lying along the head of Pascall's purchase & between that & Burrages End. Rent —.. 1.. 3½

Poss^rs 19½ A: James Heath
     12½ A: John Wilson
     ————
     32
     ————

C. Poss^rs 5a James Heath. 27a John Wilson.

Fish Pond

58 A: Sur: 4th Xber 1704 for Tho: Tench Esq[r]
at a bo[d] Poplar in the south line of Burr[a] End.

Rent —.. 2.. 4

Poss[r] Tho: Tench Esq[r].

Heath's Landing

138 A: Res: 1st Mar: 1705 for James Heath &
granted by Patt: of Confirm[a] to him, the same
haveing pt of Pascalls Purchase & the Surplus
thereto belonging entred in page 8th   Rent —.. 2.. 9¼

Poss[r] James Heath.

Marshes Seat

150 A: Sur: 24th Octob. 1651 for Tho: March on
the west side of Herring Creek near the west Cre:
This Land pattented in the name of John Hall   —.. 3.. —

Poss[r] Christop Vernon.

mem[d] this should have been the first tract entred
in this Hund[rd].

Oblong

70 A: Sur: 5th M[r]ch 1679 for Nich[o] Ncholson
assi[d] George Holland at a bo[d] Hiccory of Hunts
Hills   R[t] —.. 2.. 10

Poss[r] Sam: Chew Jun[r].
                                              ——————————

                                              1.. 11.. 2¾

Quick Sale

300 A: Sur: 20th Octob. 1663 for John Burage
to the westward of Birckheads pcell   Rent —.. 6.. —

Poss[r] Abra: Birckhead.

Oblong

(entred before)

70 A: Sur: 5th M[r]ch 1679 for Nicholas Nicholson
& Assigned Geo: Holland at a bo[d] tree of Hunts
Hills   —.. 2.. 9¾

MARYLAND RENT ROLLS.

---

*West River Hundred—*1707:

Woolman

100 A: Sur: 26th: Nov. 1651 for Rob: Harwood   £   s.   d.
near the 3 Islands upon a bra: of Road Riv[r]
This Land was after granted to Rich[d] Woolman
& surv[d] for him 4th June 1665 for 150 A   Rent   —.. 3..—
Poss[r] Rob: Brown.

Dart

300 A: Sur: 28th Octob 1652 for Hugh Drew &
Emanuell Drew on the Westside West Riv[r]   —.. 6..—
Poss[rs] 250 A: John Gale
      50 A: Sam: Galloway

300

Sparrows Rest

590 A: Sur: 22 Sept. 1652 for Tho: Sparrow on
the West side Road River
Poss^r Tho: Sparrow

£ s. d.

Rent —..11..10

Northwest River

260 A: Sur. 1 Nov. 1652 for John Brown Xtop
Rowles & John Moseby on the North side West
River   Rent —.. 5.. 3
Poss^{rs} 130 A. Edwd Talbot
       130 A. John Talbott

       ———

       260

       ———

C. Northwest River or Poplar Knowles.

Brownton

660 A: Sur: 28th Octob^r 1652 for John Brown
& John Clark on the West side West River   Rt.   —..13.. 3
Poss^{rs} 500 A. Tho: Tench Esqr for Nathan
             Rigby Orphan of Ja: Rigby
     60 A. Edwd & John Talbott
   100 A. Sam: Galloway

       ———

       660

       ———

Herring

100 A: Sur: 22th Sep: 1652 for Bartho: Herring on the West side of a bra: of Road River
called Herring Creek.
Barth: Herring sold this Land to Tho: Miles
who as 'tis affirmed included it in his Land called
Maryes Mount.

Great Bonnerston

100 A: Sur: 11th Nov. 1659 for James Bonner   £   s.   d.
on the So: side of West River, this Land was
Resd Janry 17, 1670 for Antho: Holland.   Rent   —.. 2..—
Possr Rob: Lockwood

Watkins Purchase

600 A: Sur: 21 Octob. 1652 for Rogr Gross near
Road River—Gross sold this Land to John Wat-
kins for whom it was Resd 10th Octob. 1677 &
then found to be but 554 A: but under the
Rent of   1.. 2.. 2
Possr Capt. Richd. Jones for John Watkins
    Orpns.

Bipartite

100 A: Sur. 12th Nov. 1659 for John Shaw &
Tho. Parsons on the East side of West River,
                              Rent   —.. 2..—
Possr Benja Capell for Matt: Selbys Orpn.

Bonnerston

150 A: Sur. 12th Nov. 1659 for James Bonner on
the North side West River on the West side
Cedar Creek   Rent   —.. 3..—
Possrs   75 A: John Hawkins
        75 A: Sam: Galloway
     ———
    150
     ———

Cumberton

600 A: Sur: 12th Nov. 1659 for John Cumber
upon West River   Rent   —..12..—

Poss^{rs} This Land was Res^d by the s^d Cumber   £   s.   d.
June 14: 1676
Poss^{rs} 300 A. Wid^o Buckerfield
       200 A. John Blackmore
       100 A. Sam: Galloway

       ────

       600
Fordstone
120 A: Sur: 17 Nov. 1659 for Tho: Ford on the
South side of the head of West River   Rent   —.. 2.. 6
Poss^r Samuell Galloway

Hookers Purchase
300 A: Sur: 7th Mar. 1661 for Tho: Hooker
joyning to Taylor's Land a little above the head
of Muddy Creek   Rent   —.. 6..—
Taylors Chance
300 A: Sur: 3^d March 1661 for Tho: Taylor
about 2 miles to the westward of Muddy Creek   —.. 6..—
Poss^r Coll Tho: Taylor

Hale
150 A: Sur: 3^d Mar: 1661 joyning to Taylors
Chance for the s^d Tho: Taylor   Rent   —.. 3..—
Poss^r Coll Tho: Taylor

Barren Neck
  150 A: Sur: 16: June 1663 for Richd Ewen
on the North west side of West River   Rent   —.. 3..—
Poss^r Richd Galloway

Waterton
120 A: Sur: 28th Nov. 1662 for Nicholas Waterman at the head of West River.   Rent   —.. 2.. 5
Poss^r Robert Lockwood

Talbots Ridge

300 A: Sur: 30th Novr 1662 on the Nor. side of
West River at the Upper bound tree of James
Bonner
This Land Res^d by s^d Talbot 1st Octob 1674 &
then found to cont^a but 144 A: the which was
Patt: in the name of Edw: & John Talbot
Poss^{rs}   72 A: Sam: Thomas
          72 A: Wm Richardson
          ___
          144
          ___

£   s.   d.

^h Rent

Rent   —.. 2..10¼

Cumberston Grange

250 A: Sr: 2^d Xber 1662 for John Cumber on
the North side West River   Rent
This Land never Pattented by John Cumber the
Record sayes Caveat entred ags^t it by Walter
Carr, it is alleadged to be all in Elder Surveys.

Galloway

250 A: Sur: 4th Xber 1662 for Richd Galloway
on the North side of West River   Rent   —.. 5..—
Poss^r Sam: Galloway

*C.   This is ye Land of wch ye Gift & favo^r
are compos'd.*

Ewen's Addition

90 A: Sur. 7th Xber 1662 for Richd Ewen on
the North side West River between Barren Neck
& Talbots Ridge   Rent   —.. 1..10
Poss^r Richd Galloway

Talbots Timber Neck

82 A: Sur: 21 Mar: 1662 for Richd Talbot on
the South side of West River on the South Creek
                                         Rent   —.. 1.. 8
Poss^r Capt Rob: Lockwood

Maryes Mount

600 A: Sur: 22th March 1662 for Tho: Miles at the head of Road River   £   s.   d.

Rent   —..12..—

Poss^{rs} 150 A: Coll Tho: Taylor

      100 A: James Lewis

       50 A: John Wooden

      100 A: Richd Wigg

      200 A: Zach: Maccubin in right of his

      ——   wife the daughter of Nicholas

      600   Nicholson.

      ——

C. Mary's Mount.

Parsons Hill or the Peak

150 A: Sur: 11th July 1663 for Tho: Parsons on the West side of West River—Parsons sold this Land to Pet^r Allumby he to Nath: Heathcot who res^d 1st Sep: 1676 for 152 A: Rent   —.. 3.. 1

Poss^r Gerrard Hopkins

Claryes Hope

150 A: Sur: 10 July 1663 for Edwd Parish in the great Swamp near the 3 Islands.   Rent   —.. 3..—

Poss^r Edward Parish the son

C. Clary's hope.

Parishes Park

100 A: Sur: 22: March 1662 for Edwd Parish on the South side of West River at the Head of Cuttlers Creek   Rent   —.. 2..—

Poss^r Benj^a Capell for Matt: Selly's Orp^{ns}.

C. . . . at the head of Cuttle Creek.

Essex

300 A. Sur: 8th July 1663 for Ferdinando Battee on the North side of West River   Rent   —.. 6..—

Poss^r Widow Battee.

Watkins Hope

300 A: Sur: 8th July 1663 for John Watkins on
the North side of West River—but was not Pattented untill 1674 & soe at the rent of
Poss[r] W[m] Richardson

£ s. d.

—..12..—

St. Thomas's Neck

50 A: Sur: 10th July 1663 for Tho: Parsons in
the great Swamp near the 3 Islands,   Rent   —.. 1..—
Poss[r] John Norris

Hogg Harbour

50 A: Sur: 9th July 1663 for Tho: Prat in the
Swamp near the 3 Isl[ds] at the head of the bra:
of Isl[d] Creek.   —. 1..—
Poss[r] Rob[t] Lockwood

Cumbers Ridge

170 A: Sur: 10th July 1663 for John Cumber
Jun[r] at the head of the bra: of Deep Creek near
the 3 Isl[ds] in the Swamp   Rent   —.. 3.. 5
Poss[r] Mordica Price

Addition

18 A: Sur. 8th Xber 1662 for George Skipworth
between barren Neck & Brownton—this was res[d]
by said Skipworth 4th June 1680 for 21 A: R.   —..—.. 9
Poss[r] Rich[d] Galloway

Baldwins Addition

70 A: Sur: 4th Nov. 1663 for John Baldwin at
the head of a bra: of deep Creek & between that
& 3 Isl[ds] in the Swamp.   Rent
35 A: of this Land was res[d] for John Metcalf
into a tract of his called the Range entred in
page 29 & noe more under this name now but
the rem: [a]35 A. in poss. Tho: Crouchly.   R.   —..—.. 7

Bueslands

80 A: Sur. 9th July 1663—for John Cumber in   £ s. d.
Herr: Creek Swamp.   Rent. —.. 1.. 8
Poss^r Capt Rob: Lockwood
   C. Buistands.

Ewen upon Ewenton

400 A: Sur: 1st Nov. 1665 for Cha: Calvert
Esqr & Assigned Richd Ewen on the No: side
West River adjoyning to the Land called Marys
Mo^t: —.. 8..—
Poss^r Richd Galloway

Addition

50 A: Sur: 10th Nov 1665 for James White in
Herring Creek Swamp   Rent —.. 1..—
Poss^r Sam: Galloway

Barwells Choyce

100 A: Sur: 11th Nov 1665 for John Barwell in
Herring Creek Swamp   Rent —.. 2..—
Poss^s John Barwell

Gardiners Folly

100 A: Sur: 29th Augt 1665 for Christop Gardiner in the Swamp between the 3 Islands &
Herr: Creek.—this Land is pretended by Capt.
Lockwood & Ed: Parrish to be in Elder Surveys
but I doubt it, at present none claimes it

Whites Folly

30 A: Sur: 11th 9ber 1665 for James White
lying near the Herring Creek Swamp.   Rent —..—.. 7½
Poss^r Sam: Galloway

Dearing's Gullier alias Hookers Addition

100 A: Sur: 28th Octob. 1667 for John Dearing
in Herring Creek Swamp on the South side of

the South Creek—Tho: Hooker haveing bo^t this
Land res^d the 23^d Augt 1676 & then found to
be 210 A.
Poss^r John Norris.

£   s.   d.

Rent   —.. 8.. 4¾

Normans Damms or Mill-Haven

100 A: Sur: 13: June 1668 for John Norman at
a bo^d White Oak on Muddy Creek.   This Land
was Escheated to his Lo^p for want of heirs
of Norman & granted to John Larkin who res^d
the same 3^d May 1675 & then found to be
201 A: & granted at the Rent of
Poss^r 191 A: Zack: Maccubin in right of his
     wife the daughter of Nicholas
     Nicholson
  10 A: Robert Franklyn
  ——
  201
  ——

—.. 8..   ¼

Browsly Hall

800 A: Sur: 20th July 1669 for Richd Wells on
the Northward of Ann Arrundell or the Ridge
Mann^r
Poss^{rs} 500 A: Sam: Lane
   300 A: James Butler
  ——
  800
  ——

Rent   —..16..—

Selly's Enlargem^t

50 A: Sur: 20th Aprill 1670 for Matt: Selly in
Herring Creek Swamp on the East Side West
River
Poss^r Benj^a Capell for Matt: Selly's Orpⁿ.
  C.   Selby's Enlargem't.
   Sur . . . for Nat Selby.

Rent   —.. 1..—

Parishes Choyce

150 A: Sur: 18 Mar: 1670 for Edwd Parish at a
bo^d Oak of Clary Hope near the 3 Isl^{ds}, Rent —.. 3..—
Poss^r Edward Parish the son

£ s. d.

Parishes Delay

100 A: Sur: 16 Xber 1670 for Edwd Parish in
Herring Creek Swamp at the head of the South
Creek   Rent   —..—..—
Parish sold this Land to John Beck for want of
heires of whom it is Escheated to his Lordsp.

Knocker's Hall

50 A: Sur: 18th Feb. 1671 for Fran: Laundry
in the Swamp   Rent   —.. 1..—
Poss^r Thomas Carr.

Goldsbury's Choyce

128 A: Sur: 13 May 1672 for Rob: Goldsbury in
Herr: Creek Swamp at a bo^d White oak of the
Land of Armiger Greenwood.   Rent   —.. 5.. 2
Poss^r John Holland

The Triangle

36 A: Sur: 2^d May 1672 for Tho. Taylor as
Attorney of Jerome White Esqr at a bo^d Oak of
the Land of the s^d Taylor's   Rent   —..—.. 9
Poss^r Coll^o Tho: Taylor.

Pratts Neck

100 A: Sur: 13 May 1672 for Tho: Pratt in
Herring Creek Swamp at Cattayl slash pond Rent —.. 2..—
Poss^r Samuell Chambers.

Kent

48 A: Sur: 14: Augt 1672 for Ferdinando Battee
at abo^d Oak of Mary's Mount   R.   —.. 1..11
Poss^r Sam: Battee

Dorus's Chance

116 A: Sur: 3 May 1673 for Theodorus Young   £   s.   d.
at a bo[d] Gum by the Catayl slash in the Swamp.

                       Rent   —.. 4.. 8

Poss[rs]   58 A: Tho: Crouchly
       58 A: John Medcalf

   ———
   116
   ———

Pratt's Choyce

166 A: Res: 27: May 1673 for Tho: Pratt at a
Gum at the head of Cattayl pond in the Swamp—
this Res: is upon a Survey of 100 A: Xber 15:
1670 which was let fall this Rent if 166 A. is   —.. 6.. 8

  C. Poss[r] Tho Pratt.

Barwells Enlargem[t]

50 A: Sur 7th June 1673 for John Barwell in
Herr: Cr: Swamp at the Eastern bounds of Bar-
wells Addition   Rent   —.. 2..—
Poss[r] John Barwell

Lockwoods Lott

100 A: Sur: 13: July 1673 for Rob: Lockwood
at a bounded Oak of Waterton in the Swamp, R.   —.. 4..—
Poss[r] Robert Lockwood.

Beaverdam branch

307⅔ A. Sur: 7th May 1674 for Rob: Franklyn lying on the Beaver dam branch   Rent   —..12.. 6
Poss[rs] 100 A: John Weily for Carr's Orp[ns]
       85 A: Rob: Franklyn

   ———
   312
   ———

Francis & Robert

300 A: Sur: 17: Aug: 1678 for Fran: Butler
& Robert Custin in Herr: Creek Swamp, Rent
Poss[r] Edward Parish

£ s. d.

—..12..—

Crouchly's Choyce

200 A: Sur: 13th July 1675 for Thomas
Crouchly in Herr: Creek Swamp   Rent   —.. 2..—
Poss[r] Tho: Crouchly.

Lockwoods Addition

100 A: Sur: 28th July 1675 for Rob: Lockwood
on the North side the No: bra: of deep Creek.

Rent—.. 4..—

Poss[r] Robert Lockwood.

Lockwood's Range

235 A: Sur: 28th July 1675 for Rob: Lockwood
in Herr: Creek Swamp   Rent   —.. 9.. 5
Poss[r] Robert Lockwood

The Favour

125 A: Sur: 10th June 1676 for Sam: Galloway
on the North side West River at a pear tree at the
head of Galloways Creek—And the 20th of June
1682 the same was Res[d] for Rich[d] Galloway at
a marked Oak in the N. NW line of W[m] Rich[d]
sons Land & found but 115 A.   Rent   —.. 4.. 7¼
Poss[r] Benj[a] Laurence

The Guift

125 A: Sur: 10th June 1676 for R[d] Galloway on
the No: side West River in the Woods at a bo[d]
White Oak on a hillside—And the 20th of June
1682 the same was Res[d] for Samuell Galloway at
a bounded tree of Bonnerston & then found to be
but 115 A: Rent   —.. 4.. 7¼
Poss[r] Sam: Galloway.

   C.   The Gift.

150

Hollands Addition

28A: 22th May 1676 for Antho: Holland in
Herr: Creek Swamp
Poss^r Mord: Price for A: Holland's Orp^n

£   s.   d.
Rent —.. 1.. 1½

Cumberton

200 A: Sur: 14: June 1676 for John Cumber in
the woods to the Westward of Cumberston. R. —.. 8..—
Poss^r John Gyles.

  C. Poss^r John Giles.

The Fork

90 A: Sur: 16: June 1676 near the head of West
River by the head of the Swamp. Rent —.. 3.. 7½
Poss^r Widow Waters (sur: for John Waters)

Waters Adventure

90 A: Sur: 16: June 1676 for John Waters at
the Forks at the head of West River. Rent —.. 3.. 7½
Poss^r Wid^o Waters

Proprietaryes Guift

96 A: Sur: 22 July 1677 in the name of W^m
Richardson granted to Nath: Heathcott & joyn-
ing to the land late of Richd Talbot deced —.. 3..10
Poss^r Wid^o Murry, lives in Baltemore Co.

  C. Proprietary's Gift.

The Courant

31 A: Sur: 30th June 1677 for Tho: Hooker in
the Woods on the back of Brownton. Rent —.. 1.. 3
Tho: Hooker poss^r he lives in Balt: Co:

Batty's Due

100 A: Sur: 3: Sep^t 1677 for Ferdin: Battee at
a white Oak in Rich: Talbot's Land. Rent —.. 4..—
Poss^r Sam: Batti^e

Benj^a Fortune

115 A: Sur: 10th Sep^t 1677 for Benj^a Laurence   £   s.   d.
between Ewen upon Ewenton & Ewens Addit.

Rent   —.. 4.. 7¼

Poss^r Richd Galloway

Suffolk

52 A: Sur: 18th July 1677 for Ferdin: Battee
in the Woods on the back of West River,   Rent   —.. 2.. 1

Poss^r Sam. Battee

Hookers Chance

154 A: Sur: 16: July 1678 for Tho: Hooker at
the NW & bW Corner tree of Brownton   R.   —.. 6.. 2

Poss^r Tho: Hooker the Son, he lives in Balt. Co:

Watkin's Inheritance

300 A: Res: 6th Octob 1677 for John Watkins at
a bo^d tree of the Land formerly belonging to R^d
Ewen (this Land was first Surv: for Thomas
Miles 21: Sep: 1652 for 300 A.) is now at the
Rent of   —..12..—

Poss^r Capt. R^d Jones for Watkins Orp^{ns}

Barwells Purchase

115 A: Sur: 26: Mar: 1678 for John Barwell in
Herring Creek Swamp.   Rent.   —.. 4.. 7½

Poss^r John Barwell

MARYLAND RENT ROLLS.

Anne Arundel Co.
Herring Creek Hundred

Pratts Security

150 A: Sur: 7th Aug: 1682 for Tho: Pratt in
Herr: Cre: Swamp at the mouth of Isl^d Creek   —.. 6.. —
Poss^r 50 A: Tho: Pratt the son
    100 A: Saml Chambers

150

Lockwoods Park

50 A: Sur: 6: Aug: 1682 for Rob. Lockwood at
a bo^d w^t Oak of Clary Hope in the Swamp   —.. 2.. —
Poss^r Capt. Rob: Lockwood.

Lockwood's Security

170 A: Sur: 6: Aug. 1682 for Rob: Lockwood
at a bo^d tree of Lockw^{ds} Lott in the Swamp, R: —.. 6.. 10
Poss^r Capt. Rob. Lockwood.

153

Lockwoods Guift

100 A: Sur: 26th: May 1681 for Nich: Waterman in Herring Creek Swamp   R. —.. 4.. —
Poss^r Nich: Waterman, he lives in Cecill Co:

Talbots Angles

157 A: Sur: 6: June 1686 for Edward Talbot on
the west side Beaver dam branch   Rent —.. 3.. 1
80 Acres of this taken away by the elder Sur-
vey of Hopewell soe remains only 77 A: to charge 2.. 6.. 9½
Poss^r Wm Cole—

Tearcoat Thickett

108 A: Sur: 18th June 1686 for Rob: Lockwood in Herr: Cre: Swamp   R. —.. 4.. 4
Poss^r Capt. Robert Lockwood

Little Buckstands

29 A: Sur: 18^{thh} June 1686 for Rob: Lockwood
in Herr: Cree: Swamp   R. —.. 1.. 2
Poss^r Rob: Lockwood

Lockwoods great Park

33 A: Sur: 5: Mar: 1687 for Rob: Lockwood on
the No: side Island Creek in the Swamp,   R. —.. 1.. 4
Poss^r Rob: Lockwood

Lockwoods Luck

52 A: Sur: 5th June 1696 for Rob: Lockwood
between the Swamp & Herr: Creek.   R. —.. 2.. —
Poss^r Rob: Lockwood

Hills Chance

215 A: Sur: 14: Sep: 1698 for Coll. Hen: Darnall lying on the East side of Ann Arr: Mann^r

140 Acres of this is taken away by an eld^r Survey of Hopewell soe remaines 75 Acres only to be charged at the Rent of   —.. 3.. —
Poss^r Wm Cole.

Range

75 A: Res: 6: Xber 1703 for John Metcalf 35 A: whereof haveing been p^t of Baldwen Addition entred in page 23, & beg: at a bo^d Gum of the said Addition in the Swamp.   —.. 3.. —
Poss^r John Metcalph.

Gardiners Chance

40 A: Sur: 5: Octob^r 1671 for Christo: Gardiner on the South Creek in the Swamp.   Rent —.. —.. 9
Poss^{r}r Robert Lockwood
                                                                —.. 15.. 8

Poplar Neck

200 A: Sur: 6: Jan: 1650 for R^d Beard on the South Side of South River   Rent —.. 4.. —
Poss^r Seth Bigges.

Puddington's First

300 A: Sur: 6: Jan^{ry} 1651 for George Puddington on the South Side of South River—This Land I am informed is included in the Lines of Puddington Harbour & Suppose to be therefore let fall by Puddington, at p^{r}sent none claims it nor pays Rent for it.

Burges

300 A: Sur: 21th Jan^{ry} 1651 for William Burges on the South side of South River I doe not find that Coll Burges ever Pattented this

Land, nor did he ever pay any Rent for it nor left it to any pson by name in his will, nor has any one claimed it.

Larkinston

300 A: Sur: 21: Octo: 1652 for Ellis Brown on the South side of South River—This Land Assig^d & Pattented in the name of John Brewer Anno 1663   Rent. —.. 6.. —
Poss^r Capt. Tho: Odell for Brewers Orp^ns
    he lives in Prin: Geo: County

Selby's Marsh

490 A: Sur: 29th: Sep: 1652 for Edward Selby on the west side South River   —.. 9.. —
Poss^rs 250 A: Hezekiah Lincicomb
     100 A: John Gresham
      30 A: ditto
      50 A: Robert Ward
      22 A: James Saunders
I can find noe more Possess^rs of this Land 38 A. is wanting of their Divisions to make the Complem^t but they hold the Land among them.

Wrighton

100 A: Sur: 26: Nov. 1651 for Walter Mansfeild on the West side Road River   Rent —.. 2.. —
Poss^r Thomas Gassaway.

Pytherton

250 A: Sur: 20 June 1652 for Wm Pyther on the west side South River.   Rent —.. 5.. —
Poss^r James Saunders for Parnalls Orp^ns

Townhill choyce

180 A: Sur: 20: June 1652 for Patrick Gossum on the west side of South River and 90 A. Sur:

the same day for Edwd Townhill joyning to the former both now bear the name above & were the possession of Edward Searson & now of his relict the Widow Witchell in all 270 A: Rent —.. 5.. 5

Hasling

200 A: Sur: 20: Octo: 1652 for Jerome Hesling on the south side of South River.   Rent —.. 4.. —
Poss^r Hez: Lincicomb.

Howell

100 A: Sur: 26: Nov: 1651 for Tho: Howell near the 3 Island bay upon a bra: of Road River pattⁿ in the name of Tho: Emerson.   Rent —.. 2.. —
Poss^r Thomas Rutland.

Puddington

160 A: Sur: 17: Xber 1658 for Geo: Puddington on the So: Side South River on the South Side of Burges Branch—this Land resurveyed by Edwd Burges . . . & found to be 222 A. Rent —.. 4.. 5
Poss^r William Nicholson.

West Puddington

340 A: Sur: 18: Xber 1658 for Geo: Puddington on the south side of South River on the North side of Burges Branch.   Rent —.. 6.. 10
Poss^{rs} 227 A: Dr Mord: Moor
      113 A: Rich. Jones for Watkins Orp^{ns}
      ———
      340
      ———

Coxby

100 A: Sur: 6: Xber 1658 for Edwd Cox on the South side South River joyning to Collerby —.. 2.. —
Poss^r Rob: Ward.

Collierby

150 A: Sur: 6 Xber 1658 for John Collier on
the south side of South River joyning to Larkins-
ton Patt: in the name of John Brewer 1678. Rent —.. 3.. —
Poss[r] John Brewer.

Burgh

300 A: Sur: 15th Xber 1658 for W[m] Burges on
the South Side South River joyning to the Lands
of Bessenden & Scorton.   Rent —.. 6.. —
Poss[r] D[r] Mord: Moore.

Bessenden

450 A: Sur: 9th Xber 1658 for Tho: Besson on
the South side South River joyning to Coxby
                           Rent —.. 9.. —
Poss[rs] 100 A: John Perdu
        100 A: David Macklefish
         60 A: Rich[d] Galloway
         30 A: Geo: Miller
       160 A: Tho: Gassaway & John Gassaway

       450

Scorton

80 A: Sur: 18th Xber 1658 for George Wastill
on the South side South River.   Rent —.. 16.. —
Poss[rs] 700 A : D[r] Mor: Moore
       100 A: London Town

       800

Freemans Neck

150 A: Sur: 8th Aug. 1659 for John Freeman
near the head of South River.   Rent —.. 3.. —
Poss[r] Fran: Hardesty.

Lavall

100 A: Sur: 28: Aug. 1659 for Marien Devall
on the westermost bra: of the south Side South
River. This Land Res^d 9th Sepr 1678 into a
Tract of Land called Godwell entred in page 48.

Elk Thickett

150 A: Sur: 30 Aug: 1659 for Arch: Arbuckle
on the west side of South River.   Rent —.. 3.. —
Poss^{rs} 100 A: John Watts
     35 A: Walter Phelps   1.. 17.. —
     15 A: Tho: Jacks

150 Memorand Walter Phelp's 35 A. was Res^d by
— Rob: Davis 20th May 1700 but pattented in the
name of Walter Phelps.

Cheyney Hill

100 A: Sur: 30 A: 1659 for Richd Cheyney on
the South side South River & on the South side
of Flatt Creek.   Rent —.. 2.. —
Poss^r Charles Tilly.

Bessonton

350 A: Sur: 3^d Nov. 1659 for Tho: Besson on
the West side Road River on the North side
Muddy branch   Rent —.. 7.. —
Poss^{rs} 300 A: Sam Chambers
     50 A: Stephen Warman

350

Brewerton

400 A: Sur: 3: 9ber 1659 for John Brewer on
the west side Road River joyning to Bessonton,
       R. —.. 8.. —

Poss[rs] 200 A: Tho: Odell for Brewers Orp[ns]
    100 A: W[m] Brewer
    100 A: John Gresham

    ———

    400

    ———

Younger Besson

50 A. Sur: 3 Nov. 1659 for Tho: Besson the younger on the South side So: River joyning to Bessonton.   Rent —.. 1.. —
Poss[r] Robert Steward.

  C. Stewart.

Townhill

400 A: Sur: 8: Xber 1659 for Edm[d] Townhill on the West side Road River on the No: side of Muddy bra: joyning to Brewerton.   Rent —.. 8.. —
Poss[rs] 200 A: James Lewis
    100 A: W[m] Disney
    100 A: Stephen Warman in right of his
                wife Hester the daughter of
                Nicholas Gassaway.

Lapston

300 A: Sur: 9th Nov. 1659 for Adam Delapp near the mouth of South River joyning to the Land of W[m] Pennington.   Rent —.. 6.. —
Poss[r] Robert Saunders.

  C. Sander's.

Cheyney's Rest

300 A: Sur: 16: Xber 1661 for Rich[d] Cheyney on the So. side South River.   Rent —.. 6.. —
Poss[rs] 180 A: Rich[d] Cheyney's wid[o]

50 A: Benj^a Williams
40 A: Rob: Hopper
30 A: Dan: Clark Orp^ns

─────

300

─────

p. 35   Cheyney's Resolution
700 A: Sur: 16 Xber 1661 for Richd Cheyney
joyning to Cheyney's Rest.   Rent
This Land is by mistake thus Entred for it con-
taines but 400 A: as appears by the Patt: at the
                                    Rent —.. 8.. —

Poss^rs 50 A: Tho: Cheyney
        150 A: John Jacob
        100 A: Wm Jiams
        130 A: Elinor Pindall

        ─────

        430   30 A: over measured   —.. —.. 7½

        ─────

C. Elenor Pindal.

                    Cheyney's Purchase
100 A: Sur: 24th Xber 1661 for Richd Cheyney
on the So: side So: Riv^r on the East Side of
flat Creek   Rent —.. 2.. —
Poss^r Wm Gray, but he is run away.

                    Cheyney's Hazard
100 A: Sur: 24th Xber 1661 for Richd Cheyney
on the South Side South River.   Rent —.. 2.. —
Poss^r John Durdin.

                    Beard's Habitation
700 A: Sur: 4th Jan^ry 1661 for R^d Beard on
the South side West River joyning to West Puddington.   Rent —.. 14.. —
                    And

300 A: added to the South bounds of the said
Beards Habitation by the s^d Beard.   Rent —.. 6.. —

 C. On ye S Side South River.

And

260 A. more added on the north side of the s^d
Beard's Habitation by the sd Beard.   Rent —.. 5.. 3

Poss^rs of the whole 3 tracts 1260 A:

   667 A, Dr Mordica Moore
   333 A, Richd Jones for Jno Watkins
       Orphans
   145 A, Wm Jones
   115 A, James Saunders
   ‾‾‾‾
   1260
   ‾‾‾‾

 C. Dr Mord Moor—James Sanders.

Freemans Fancy

300 A: Sur: 22. Feb: 1661 for John Freeman
1½ mile from the head of South River. Rent —.. 6.. —

              ‾‾‾‾‾‾‾

Poss^r Fran: Hardesty.   2.. 3.. 10½

Covells Folly

500 A: Sur: 16: Feb. 1661 for Ann Covell on
the South side of South River on the West side
of Flatt Creek.   Rent —.. 10.. —

Poss^rs 100 A: Benj^a Williams
   100 A: Walter Phelps
   87½ A: John Selman
   87½ A: Joseph Burton
   25 A: Amos Garrat

 *C. Covels Folly. I cannot discover ye other 100^a Suppose
it to be held by Some of ye above poss^rs by large measure of
their dividends, tho none will own it.*

Netle-Land

200 A: Sur: 23^d Feb. 1661 for George Netlefold on the West side of South River near the
head. This Land Res^d 9th Sept^t: 1678 into a
tract of Land called Godwell entred in page 48.

Fold-Land

200 A: Sur: 26: Feb: 1661 for George Netlefold on the west side South River joyning to Elk
Thicket.   Rent —.. 4.. —
Poss^{rs} 100 A: Benj'^a Williams
   100 A: John Turner

   ___

   200

Puddington's Enlargement

200 A: Sur: 26: Feb: 1661 for Geo: Pudding-
ton on the west side South River joyning to the
Land of George Netlefold.   Rent —.. 4.. —
Poss^r Leonard Weyman.

Puddingtons Addition

100 A: Sur: 26 Feb: 1661 for s^d Puddington
the same being in the same Survey with the last
& lyes on the Southwest with s^d Netlefolds Land.
                                           Rent —.. 2.. —
Poss^r Timothy Shaw in right of his marr^a with
   the Wid^o Frizell.

Plumpton

280 A: Sur: 23: Feb: 1661 on the west side
South River.   Rent —.. 5.. 7¼
Poss^r Geo: Parker of Cal. Co. in right of his
Children by the daughter & heir of Gab: Parrot.

C. Plumton. Sur. . . . for Geo. Walker.

Larkins Hill

450 A: Sur: 3^d Mar. 1661 for John Larkin to
the Westward of Muddy Creek.   Rent —.. 9.. —
Poss^{rs} 350 A: Tho: Larkin
     100 A: Edwd Carter
     :——

     450

————————————

Cheyney Neck

110 A: Sur: 15: Mar: 1661 for R^d Cheyney on
the South side of South River.   Rent —.. 2.. 2½
Poss^r Willm Burroughs.

   C. There is another entry at p. 43 of " C.":
Cheney's Neck, Sur 11 May 1696 for Willm Burroughs on
ye S side of South River Poss^r Willm Burroughs 80 acres
Rent. 3/ 2½

Beaver dam Neck

100 A: Sur: 7: Xber 1662 for Denis Macconough
at the head of Road River.   Rent —.. —.. —
Poss^r John Roberts.
I suppose this to be the same Land that John
Gray after surv^d by this name & is Entred in
page 44. [37]

Love's Neck

50 A: Sur: 12th Jan^ry 1662 for Rob: Love on
the North side Road River between Shaw's
        Creek & Woolman's Creek. Rent —.. 1.. —
Poss^r Thomas Gassaway.

Triangle Neck

100 A: Sur: 3: Aprill 1663 for Robert Loyd on
the South Side of Road River on the No: side
Beaver dam. This Land Res^d & Entred in page
46. Not to be Entred here.

   C. Not in " C."

Uggins Advantage or Powells Inheritance.

50 A: Sur: 16: Ap: 1663 for Richard Uggins
near the head of South River. this Land Res^d by
John & James Powell 9th 7b. 1682 & then found
to cont^a 125 A: at the Rent   —.. 5.. —
Poss^rs 62½ A: Wm Phelps
      62½ A: Tho: Jack

    125

   C. Entered as 50 acres, rent 5/

The Security

66 A: Sur: 28: Aprill 1663 for John Brewer on
the So: side South River   Rent —.. 1.. 4
Poss^rs 33 A: Stephen Warman
      33 A: Dr Mor: Moore

    66

Poplar Ridge

150 A: Sur: 30 Aprill 1663 for Nich^o Gassaway
on the South side South River joyning to the
Land called Bessonton.   Rent —.. 3.. —
Poss^r Willm Bateman.

             1.. 1.. 6½

Haslenut Ridge

200 A: Sur: 3^d Aprill 1663 for John Gray at
the head of Road River. this Land was Res^d the
13th June 1680 for Richd Tydings & then found
to be but 166 A: & granted under the Rent of —.. 3.. 8
Poss^r John Tydings.

   C. Hazlenut ridge.

Wardrop Ridge (in Midle Neck)

100 A: Sur: 12: Octob 1663 for

C. [p. 50] Wardrop Ridge. Sur. 12 Oct. 1663 for Patrick Dunkin on ye N Side South River respecting ye land Call^d Wardrop to ye West. This Land was resur. for sd Dunkin 1 Jan. 1676. Escheated to his Ldpp for want of Leins of ——— and granted y^e ——— to Mr Carroll who is ye p^rsent poss^r

White's Hall

800 A: Sur: 14: Octob: 1663 for Jerome White Esqr on the So: Side the So: Run of South River. Rent —.. 16.. —
Poss^r Joseph Gates of London in Right of his wife & daughter Jane.

Delapton

50 A: 18th Feb: 1662 Sur. for Adam Delapp on the South Side of South River. Rent —.. 1.. —
Poss^r Rob: Saunders.

Puddington Harbour

700 A: Sur: 29: Sep: 1663 for Geo. Puddington on the South side of South River. Rent —.. 14.. —
Poss^{rs} 522 A: Edward Burges
178 A: Wm Nicholson
———
700
—

Abington

875 A: Sur: 26. Jan^{ry} 1663 for Rob: Proctor and John Gater at the head of South River joyning to John Freemans Land. John Gather the son being in poss^o of 148 A: of this Land. had the same 148 A. Res^d the 27th Aug. 1699 & that part then found to be 364 A: soe that the whole of the s^d Land called Abbington is now 1091 A: Rent 1.. 1.. 10

Poss^{rs} 427 A. James Finloe
    100 A. Eliz^a Finloe
    200 A: Wm Ridgly
    364 A: John Gather
    ——————
    1091
    ——————

Midle Plantation

600 A: Sur: May 23: 1664 for Warren Duvall
on the South Side South River between Geo:
Netlefolds Land Ann Covell George Puddington
& George Walkers. Rent —.. 12.. —
Poss^{rs} 547 A: Lewis Duvall
    53 A: Tim: Shaw in right of his wife
    ——————
    600   that was Widow Frizell

Clarkenwell

100 A: Sur: 23^d May 1664 for John Clark on
the So: side South River joyning to Cheny's
Land. Rent —.. 2.. —
Poss^{rs} 50 A: Richd Litton
    50 A: John Durdin Assignee of Eliz^a
        Jones for whom this 50 A. was
        Seperately Res^d 6th Aug. 1681
C. Clerkenwell.

Rich Neck

200 A: Sur: 25th May 1664 for Warren Duvall
& Wm Young on the South side South River on
the west side Jacobs Creek Rent —.. 4.. —
Poss^{rs} 100 A: John Edwards
    100 A: John Bayly for his son to whom
        the same was divided by Robt
        Wade.

Timber Neck

200 A: Sur: 26. May 1664 for Richd Uggins &
John Wheeler on the South Side South Riv^r on
the west side Jacobs Creek.   —.. 4.. —

Poss^{rs} 150 A. Charles Tilley
100 A. Matt: Beard

250 & for the 50 A. above the survey   —.. 1.. —

Poplar Hill

100 A: Sur: 10: July 1665 for Thomas Selby &
Edwd Selby on the No: side of Road River
                    Rent —.. 2.. —

Poss^r Capt. James Saunders.

Indian Range

250 A: Sur: 15: Feb: 1664 for Rob. Franklyn &
Richd Beard near Beards Habitation.   Rent —.. 5.. —
Poss^{rs} 200 A: John Nicolson
50 A: Cha: Cheyney

250

C. John Nicholson, Cha. Cheney.

Burges's Choyce

400 A: Sur: 19th Xber 1665 for Wm Burges on
the South side of South River. this Land was
Res^d 13th Aprill 1704 for Benj^a Burges & then
found to be 747 A. at the Rent of   —.. 14.. 11½
Poss^{rs} 223 A: John Duvall for Hester Iiams
23 A: Jos: Burton
25 A: John Jacobs
61 A: Rich. Iiams
300 A: Richd Snowdon

143 A: Lewis Duvall
67 A: Cha: Cheyney

—

844   91 A: over the survey   1.. 10

Conclusion

50 A: Sur: 25: Sepr 1665 for Richd Forster on
the South side of South River on the South side
of Flatt Creek.   Rent —.. 1.. —
Poss^r Richd Baxter.

    C. Rich^a Forester.

John's Cabin Ridge

30 A: Sur: 20: Nov. 1665 for Richd Beard on
the No. side the Main bra: of Flat Creek this
was since Res^d to 150 A: Rent —.. 3.. —
Poss^{rs} James Saunders.

Shaws Folly

260 A: Sur: p^r mo Xbers 1665 for John Shaw
lying on the West side Road River. This land
was by the s^d Shaw Hes^d 6th Xber 1668 & then
found to be 360 A: Rent —.. 7.. 2
Poss^r John Gresham.

Foster & Lewis

100 A: Sur: 20: Jan^{ry} 1665 for Richd Forster
& John Lewis on the So: side South River on
the West side Jacobs Creek. This Land is
affirmed to me to be within the Survey of Rich
Neck entred in page 39. I doe not find any that
claimes it.

Sharp Point

30 A: Sur: 30 Nov: 1665 for Andrew Roberts
at the head of Road River at the head of Muddy
Creek. I doe not find that ever Roberts payd
Rent for this Land nor doe I find any now claim
it, suppose it a mistaken survey.

Velmeade

400 A: Sur: 10 Jan^{ry} 1667 for John Dearing
on the South side of South River in the Woods.

R. —.. 8.. —

Poss^{rs} 200 A: John Belt
      100 A: Tho: Seaborn
      100 A: Jos. Williams Orp^{ns}

———

400

———

Hiccory Hills

550 A: Sur: 10: Jan^{ry} 1667 for Robert Franklyn on the So: side of South River.   Rent —.. 11.. —
Poss^{rs} 89 A: John Nicholson
     100 A: Jos: Hanslap's Orphan (Char
               Burges of Prin: Geo: County
               for it)
     100 A: Richd Williams
     140 A: Daniell Richardson
     140 A: Jos: Rich^{d}son
      55 A: Tho: Rickets

———

624 & for the 74 A: above the survey   —.. 1.. 5¾

Iron Mine

500 A: Sur: 26: Nov: 1667 for Jerome White
Esqr at the head of South River on the Western
side of the South bra: of the River.   Rent —.. 10.. —
Poss^{r} Richd Snowden.

Arnold Gray

300 A: Sur: 26: June 1668 for Richd Arnold
& John Gray in the woods on the West side of
South River. This Land was Res^{d} 10th Feb.

171

1701 for Sylvester & John Welch & then found
to be 605 A.   Rent —.. 12.. 1½
Poss^{rs} 302½ Sylvester Welch
     302½ John Welch
    —————
    605
    —————

The Landing

70 A: Sur: 1st Augt 1668 for Rob: Proctor on
the North Side of the South Run of South River.
                         R. —.. 1.. 5
Poss^r Fran: Hardesty by Marrying the relict of
John Gather.

Addition

70 A: Sur: 27: Aug: 1668 for Nich^o Gassaway
between South & Road Rivers at a bound poplar
of Bessonton.   Rent. —.. 1.. 5
Poss^r Tho: Gassaway.

Triangle

100 A: Sur: 20th July 1669 for Tho: Taylor
Gent: on the No: of Arrundell Mann^r   Rent —.. 2.. —
Poss^r Solomon Sparrow.

Whites Plaines

2000 A: Sur: 20th July 1669 for Jerom White
bounded on the East by a Line drawn South
from Stockets Run.   Rent £ 2.. —
Poss^r John Taylor of London.

Dodon

664 Sur: 19th July 1669 for Fran: Stocket in
the woods to the Northward of Ann Arrundell
Mann^r on the So: by the Land called Obligation. 1.. 6.. 6
Poss^{rs} 64 A: William Iiams Junr

50 A: Jos. Jones

550 A: Jos. Hanslap's Orphan

---

664 (Cha: Burges of Prin: Geo: Co:)

Bridge Hill

663 A: Sur: 19th July 1669 for Henry Stocket on the Northward of Ann Arrundell Mann[r] in the woods on the South East of Stockets Runn.

Rent 1.. 6.. 6

Poss[rs] 563 A: Aaron Rawlins
100 A: W[m] Iiams

663

C. Will[m] Iiams Jun[r]

Obligation

663 A: Sur: 19th July 1669 for Tho: Stockett to the North of Ann Arr: Mann[r] in the Woods at the No: West corner tree of Taylors Choyce.

Rent 1.. 6.. 6

Poss[rs] 538 A: Tho: Stocket the son
125 A: Mark Richardson

663

Halls Inheritance

180 A: Sur: 24: May 1669 for Xtop Hall on the North side Road River.   Rent —.. 3.. 10
Poss[r] Thomas Gassaway.

Duvalls Addition

165 A: Sur: 3[d] June 1669 for Mareens Duvall on the West side South River.   Rent —.. 3.. 3½
Poss[r] W[m] Roper.

173

Clarks Inheritance

400 A: Sur: 17 June 1669 for Neal Clark on the
West side South River about 3 Miles from the
River adjoyning to Cheyney's Land.   —.. 8.. —
Poss^r George Parker in right of his Children by
the daughter & heir of Gabriell Parrot.

Batchellors Hope

200 A: Sur: 7th June 1669 for James Saunders
on the west side of South River at a bo^d Hiccory
in the No. line of Rob: Franklyn.   Rent —.. 4.. —
Poss^r James Saunders the son.

_____

                                        3.. 11.. 11

C.   Another Batchel^{rs} Hope, 240 a appear in C p. 54:
" Sur. 15 Feb 1665 for Walter Phelps & Nick Gunn on the
N side of South River on y^e E Side of Broad Creek   Poss^r
Charles Carroll.

Addition

190 A: Sur: 9: June 1669 for James Chilcot on
the West side of South River. This Land Res^d
into Godwell & entred in pa: 48.

Franklyn's Enlargemen^t

240 A: Sur: 9th June 1669 for Rob: Franklyn
joyning to the Indian Range.   Rent   4.. 9¾
Poss^{rs} 120 A: Daniell Richardson
       120 A: Jos: Richardson

___

       240 & 25 A: more by Tho: Ricketts above
       ___   the survey   —.. —.. 6

Freinds-choyce

340 A. Sur: 3 June 1669 for Wm Jones and
John Gray on the west side South River.   R. —.. 6.. 9¾
Poss^{rs} 171 A: Daniell & Edwd Maryarte

71 A: Jos: Williams
100 A: John Lamb for Belt's orp[ns]

342

C. Daniel & Edward Margarts.

Champ's Adventure
300 A: Sur: 1st June 1669 for John Champ on
the West side South River adjoyning to Bur-
gesses Choyce.   Rent —.. 6.. —
Poss[r] John Selman.

Rowdown
800 A: Sur: 26: July 1669 for Geo: Yate on
the North side Stockets Run pattented in the
name of Tho: Taylor.   Rent —.. 16.. —
Poss[rs] 750 A: John Taylor
50 A: Wid[o] Rothery

800

Jones's Lot
350 A: Sur: 1st Nov: 1669 for W[m] Jones in the
Woods at a bounded Oak of the Stockets Land. —.. 7.. —
Poss[rs] 175 A: Aaron Rawlins
175 A: Rob: Kirtland

350

C. Poss[r] Aaron Rawlins.

Larkins Choyce
311 A: Sur: 20: Aprill 1670 for John Larkin
on the South Side of South River.   Rent —.. 6.. 2¾
Poss[r] Rich: Poole in right of his wife the
daughter of Mareen Duvall.

Peirpoints Branch

40 A: Sur: 4: Feb: 1669 for Hen: Peirpoint on
the Ridge near Brewer's Land th^t was.   Rent —.. —.. 10
Poss^r Tho: Orum.

   C. Pierpoints Branch.

Margretts Feilds

280 A: Sur: 25 Mar: 1667 for George Saughier
at Pennington's Ponds near the mouth of South
River & near the mouth of the s^d Ponds.   Rent —.. 5.. 7¼
This Land was first Sur: 19: Jan^{ry} 1650 for
Wm Pennington assigned & Patt: to Wm Pell
who sold the same to Geo: Saughier & then Sur.
as above in his own name.   Poss^r Hezekiah
Lincicomb.

   C. At page 40.

Ropers Range

420 A: Sur: 10: Mar: 1669 for Wm Roper on
the South Side South River.   Rent —.. 16.. 9
Poss^{rs} 210 A. Tho: Winter for Fran: John-
              son's orphans
     210 A: Henry Roberts
     ———
     420
     ———

Harris's Range

250 A: Sur: 15th Mar: 1670 for Isaack Harris
at a bounded white oak of Whites Hall.   Rent —.. 5.. —
Poss^r George Parker in behalf of his children
which he had by the daughter & heir of Gab^{ll}
Parrot.

Beaver dam Neck

100 A: Sur: 30: May 1669 for John Gray on
the West side Road River in Muddy Creek.

Rent —.. 2.. —

Poss^r Edwd Cocks tenant to John Roberts.
C. Edward Cox.

Happy Choyce

300 A: Sur: 18: Sep: 1670 for Geo: Yate between South River & Pattuxent Branches.   Rent —.. 12.. —
Poss^r Leonard Weyman.

Morely's Grove

320 A. Sur: 16: 7ber 1670 for Jos: Morely between South River & Pattuxent branches.   Rent —.. 6.. 5
Poss^r Mr Hen: Hall.

Morely's Lott

450 A: Sur: 31 July 1670 for Joseph Morely
between So: Riv^r & Patt: bra: Rent —.. 9.. —
Poss^{rs} Hen: Hall   350 A:
    Wm Roper   100 A:
                    ———

                    450
                    ———

*C. [C 9,] 300 a. Sur. 14 Sepr 1667 for Joseph Morley
near ye Land Call^d Trent. Poss^r Richd Harrison.*

Chilcotts Increase

18 A: Sur: 28: June 1671 for James Chilcot at
a bound Hiccory of West Puddington.   Rent —.. —.. 5
Poss^r Richd Snowden Junr

Wilson's Grove

200 A: Sur: 18: July 1671 for Rob: Wilson between the heads of South & Seavern Rivers.

Rent —.. 8.. —

Poss^r John Duvall.   ———————

Forsters Point

50 A: Sur: 20 July 1671 for John Forster on
the South Side of South River at the head of
flatt Creek. Rent —.. 1.. —
Poss[r] Clement Davis, he is runaway.

C. Foster's Point.

Gathers Range

200 A. Sur: 14th Aprill 1672 for John Gather
at the head of South River. Rent —.. 4.. —
Poss[r] Francis Hardesty by marriage of John
Gathers widow.

Addition

300 A: Sur: 2[d] May 1672 for John Gray on
the South Side South River. Rent —.. 6.. —
Poss[rs] 150 A. Autho: Arnods Orp[ns]
150 A. Tho: Lincicomb

300 A

Taylors Addition

100 A: Sur: 4: July 1672 for Tho: Taylor at a
bounded Oak of Taylors Chance. Rent —.. 2.. —
Poss[r] Coll. Tho: Taylor.

MARYLAND RENT ROLLS.

Duvalls Range

200 A: Sur: 18th June 1672 for Murien Duvall
on the East side the North bra: of Patt. Rivr.

Rent —.. 4.. —

Possr Richd Poole in right of his wife the daughter of Murien Duvall.

*C. Mareen Duvall. Another tract of the same name
appears in C at p. 43. "708 A: surveyed 16 Nov. 1694 for
John Duvall in ye ffork of Patuxt River. Possr. Hezekiah
Lincicumb; and at page 92 "Duvals Range Resur. 25 Nov
1703 for Hezekiah Lynthycom (1527 acres) Begin at ye End
of ye S. 83° Ely Line of Ovenwood Thickett Laid out for Leond
Wayman.*

Davis's Rest

200 A: Sur: 18th June 1672 for Evan Davis on
the South side of South River. Rent —.. 8.. —
Possr Thomas Lincicomb

Bright Seat

400 A: Sur: 20th July 1672 for Edwd Price on
the South Side South River. Rent —.. 16.. —
This Land was Escheated to his Lop for want of
heires of . . . & granted . . . to James Carroll
who now possesses it

Green's Town

50 A: Sur: 29: June 1673 for George Green on
the South side of South River on the South
Side the main bra: of flat Creek. Rent —.. 2.. —
Possr John Grays Widow

Francis's Addition

42 A: Sur: 11th Octob^r 1673 for Tho: Francis near Netlefolds Bra: by the Land of Shaw's.

Rent —.. 1.. 8

Poss^r John Gresham Junr

Wynyates Rest

40 A: Sur: 11th Octob^r 1673 for Thomas Wyn-yate on the Main Branch of Road River. Rent —.. 1.. 8
Poss^r Zach: Maccubin in right of his wife the daughter of Nich: Nicholson

Law's Chance

46 A: Sur: 1st Nov: 1673 for Willm Laws on a bra: of Road River. Rent —.. 1.. 9¾
Poss^r Zach: Cadle.

Sparrows Addition

100 A: Sur: 2^d Feb: 1673 for Tho: Sparrow on Road River Rent —.. 4.. —
Poss^r Tho: Sparrow the son

Hedge Parke

94 A: Sur: 1st Apr^{ll} 1674 for Tho: Hedge in Harwoods Creek in Road River at abo^d tree of Margretts Feilds Rent —.. 3.. 9¼
Poss^r Hez: Lincicomb

Triangle

100 A: first sur^d the 3^d Aprill 1663 for Robert Loyd who sold the same to John Gray & he sold it to Andrew Roberts who the 2^d Aprill 1674 Res^d it, it lyes on the South Side Road River at a bounded Oak of Norman Dams. the Resue is Rent —.. 4.. —
Andrew Roberts Son John sold this Land to Thomas Tench & he to Edwd Carter who now Possesses it

C. (*p 22*)   *The Triangle (36 a) Sur 2 May 1672 for Tho Taylor an attorney of Jerom White Esqr. at a bound Oak of the land of ye said Taylor. Poss^r Coll. Tho Taylor; and C p. 35 " Triangle (100 acres) Sur 20 July 1669 for Tho Taylor on ye N. Side of Ann Arundel Man^r. Poss^r Solomon Sparrow."*

Rowdown Security

477 A: 24th Sep: 1674 for Tho: Taylor Esqr
on the East side the North Bra: of Pattuxent
River.   Rent —.. 19.. 1
Poss^r John Taylor of London

Waterford

800 A: Sur: 19: Sep: 1675 for Wm Jones on
on the North bra: of Patt: River at abo^d tree
of Coll Taylors   Rent   1.. 12.. —
Poss^r John Cheyney

Slatborn

380 A: Sur: 15 Sep: 1675 for Robert Proctor
this Land is within the Lines of Abington &
the Patt: therefore surrendred & vacated

Lincicombs Stop

50 A: Sur: 19th Augt 1676 for Tho: Linci-
comb on the South Side South River at a
Marked tree of Margrets Feild.   Rent —.. 2.. —
Poss^r Hez: Lincicomb

The Plain

120 A: Sur: 28th Xber 1676 for Geo: Yates
on the South Side South River at a Corner
Tree of Plumton.   Rent —.. 4.. 9¾
Poss^r George Parker in right of his Children
which he has by the daughter & heir of Gab:
Parrott.

Rachael's Hope

72 A: Sur: 8th July 1678 for Tho: Mattox on the South bra: of flat Creek in South River.

Rent —.. 2.. 10¾

Poss^r Tho: Mattox (he is run away)
  C. Thos Maddox. Poss^r Tho Madock.

Madocks Adventure

148 A: Sur: 8th July 1678 for Tho: Madocks on the South side of South River at abo^d Oak of Ropers Range.   Rent —.. 5.. 11¼

Poss^r Tho: Ward as Tenant und^r Madock.

Diligent Search

75 Acres Sur: 1st Augt 1678 for Wm Richardson on the bra: of Road River at abo^d Poplar of the Land of Ferdin: Battee.   Rent —.. 3.. —

Poss^r James Lewis

Hesters Habitation

118 A: Sur: 12th March 1678 for Hester Beard on the South Side South River at abo^d Oak on the West side of Burges's Branch.   Rent
This land is affirmed to me to be within the lines of Beard's Habitation.

Lincicomb's Lott

70 A: Sur: 15th Jan^{ry} 1678 for Tho: Lincicomb on the north side of 3 Isl^d Bay at the head of a great Pond   Rent —.. 2.. 10

Poss^r Hez: Lincicomb

Wades Encrease

75 A: Sur: 6th Augt 1678 for Rob: Wade on the South Side River at abo^d White Oak of Johns Cabin branch.   Rent —.. 3.. —

Poss^r Wid^o Davis for Rob: Hoppers Orp^{ns}

Gadwell

Is a Resurvey of 3 Severall tracts of Land
(adjoyning to one another) into one, together
wth the Addition of Surplus & Vacant Land by
George Parker & assigned Wm Parker his son
made the 9th Sep. 1678 the 3 tracts are Lavall
entred in page 33, 100 A: Net land in pa: 36:
200 A: & Addit^n in pa: 42: 190 A. & 315 A:
added as Surplus or Vacant Land in all 805 A.
at the Rent of   1.. 12.. 2½
Poss^r Richard Snowdon

Jacob's Point

21 A: Sur: 10 Nov: 1676 for James Smith at
a bound tree of the Land of James Towning on
the South Side of South River.   Rent —.. —.. 5¼
Poss^r Thomas Symson
  C.   Thomas Simpson.

Roper Gray

480 A: Sur: 4: Augt 1681 for Wm Roper &
John Gray at a bo^d Oak on the Nor: Bra: on
Patt. River.   Rent —.. 19.. 2½
Poss^rs 380 A: Wm Roper
     100 A: Edwd Pen
    ———
    480
    ———

Coap's Hill

40 A: Sur: 4th Augt 1681 for George Coap at
abo^d White Oak of Davis's Rest   Rent —.. —.. 9¾
Poss^r Robert Welch

Green's Beginning

70 A: Sur: 4th Sept. 1682 for John Green on
the So: side So: River in the fork of Netlefold
Creek.   R. —.. 2.. 10
Poss^r John Green

Ayno

400 A: Sur: 3 Sep: 1682 for Henry Hanslap
on the East Side of the North bra: of Pattux^t
River.

Poss^r Tho: Gassaway in right of his wife the
daughter of the s^d Hanslap.

Equality

140 A: Sur: 30th June 1684 for James Saunders at a bo^d Oak by Johns Cabbin bra: Rent —.. 5.. 7¼

Poss^r James Saunders.

Phelp's Choyce

200 A: Sur: 12th; Octob 1682 for Walter
Phelps on the West Side of the North Bra: of
Puttuxent River.   Rent —.. 8.. —

Poss^r Walter Phelps

MARYLAND RENT ROLLS.

South River Hundred—1707:

Pole Cat Hill

391 A: Sur: 21st Feb: 1684 for John Gather
in the fork of Puttuxt River on the South Side
of the North Bra: thereof   Rent   —.. 15.. 7¾
Possr Benja Gather

Brewers Chance

152 A: Sur: 16 Mar: 1684 for John Brewer
on the South Side South River   Rent   —.. 6.. 1
Possr Tho: Odell of Prin: Geo: Co. for Brewers Orphns

Grays Land

17 A: Sur: 15th Janry 1684 for John Gray on
the South Side South River on the North Side
Jacobs Creek   Rent   —.. —.. 8
Possr Charles Tilly

Robin-hoods-Forrest

1976 A: Sur: 5th June 1686 for Richd Snow-
don in the fork of Pattuxent River   Rent   3.. 19.. 0
Possr Richd Snowden
   C. Robinhood Forest.

Gray's Chance

64 A: Sur: 15th Jan^{ry} 1684 for John Gray on
the So: Side So: River on the No: Side of
Jacobs Creek   Rent —.. 2.. 7
Poss^r John Gray's Wid^o who is Marry'd

                                    £ 6.. 13.. 8

Mitchells Chance

205 A: Sur: 29th May 1684 for Wm Mitchell
on the South Side South River   Rent —.. 8.. 2
Poss^r 102½ Edwd Mitchell
     102½ Fran: Peirpoint
   —————
   205

Williams's Angles

15 A: Sur: 16th Feb: 1684 for Benj. Williams
on the South Side of South River Rent —.. —.. 7½
Poss^r Sam: Duvall he lives in Pr: Geo: Co:

Phelps Luck

83 A: Sur: 27th Feb: 1684 for Walter Phelps
on the South Side of South River Rent —.. 3.. 4
Poss^r Walter Phelps

Round About Hill

120 A: Sur: 16 June 1686 for John Gather on
the South Run of South River   Rent —.. 4.. 10
Poss^r Fran: Hardesty by his Marriage with
the wid^o of John Gather

Fortune

54 A: Sur: 6th April 1687 for John Gresham
on the East Side of Road River   Rent —.. 2.. 2
Poss^r John Gresham

Williams's Addition

26 A: Sur: 27 Mar: 1688 for Benj^a Williams
lying on the South Side South River   Rent —.. 1.. 0½
Poss^r John Watts

Linhams Search

38 A: Sur: 11th Mar: 1687 for John Linham
on the South Side So: River   Rent —.. 1.. 6¼
Poss^r James Saunders for Parnalls Orph^{ns}

Selbys Stop

201 A: Sur: 14th Mar: 1687 for Edwd Selby
on the North Side of Road River   Rent —.. 8.. 0½
Poss^r James Saunders

Suttons Addition

20 A: Sur: 28th Mar: 1688 for Tho: Sutton
lying on Burges Creek   Rent —.. —.. 10
Poss^r David Mackintosh

Burges's Right

153 A: Sur: 28th Aprill 1688 for Edward
Burges on the South Side South River   Rent —.. 6.. 1½
Poss^r Edward Burges

Duvalls Range

708 A: Sur: 16: Nov: 1694 for John Duvall
in the fork of Pattuxunt River   Rent 1.. 8.. 4
Poss^r Hezekiah Lincicomb

Tangire

10 A: Sur: 28th Feb. 1694 for Leonard Way-
man on the South Side of the head of So: River
Poss^r Leon^d Weyman   Rent —.. —.. 5
  C. Tangier.

187

MARYLAND RENT ROLLS.

Duvalls delight
1000 A: Sur: 9th Octob 1694 for John Duvall
lying on the North East Side of Patt. Riv^r
Poss^r John Duvall   Rent —.. 2.. —

Cheyney's Neck

80 A: Sur: 11th May 1696 for Wm Burroughs
on the South Side So: River   Rent   —.. 3.. 2½
Poss^r Wm Burroughs

Ridgly's Chance

305 A: Sur: 2^d Octob 1694 for Willm Ridgly
at Rogue's Harbour   Rent   —.. 12.. 2½
Poss^r Wm Ridgly

Turkey Neck

200 A: Sur: 23 Ap: 1697 for Richard Snow-
don in the Fork of Pattuxent Riv^r   Rent   —.. 8.. —
Poss^r Richd Snowdon

What-You-Will

373 A: Sur: 2^d Xber 1699 for John Duvall
lying above the head of South River   Rent   —.. 14.. 11
Poss^r John Duvall

Pinkston's Folly

180 A: Sur: 1st July 1700 for Peter Pinkston
in Rogue's Harbour   Rent   —.. 7.. 2½
Poss^r Peter Pinkston

Elk Thicket Nil
Ovenwood Thicket

200 A: Sur: 26: June 1688 for Leonard Way-
man in the Fork of Puttuxent River   Rent   —.. 8.. —
Poss^r Same Wayman

Elizabeth's Fancy

225 A: Sur: 1st June 1700 for Richd Clark on
the South Side of South River   Rent   —.. 9.. —
Poss^r George Parker in Right of his Children
which he had by the daughter & hier of Gabriel
Parrot

Lugg Ox

780 A: Sur: 10: Octob 1701 for John Duvall
near the head of South River   Rent   1.. 11.. 2
Poss^r Benj^a Wharfield

Souldiers Fortune

100 A: Sur: 8th Xber 1701 for Richd Snowdon
Junr upon the North Bra: of Pat. Riv^r near
Ivy hill   Rent   —.. 4.. —
Poss^r Tim: Ragan

Littletown

280 A: Sur: 22^d June 1703 for John Sumers in
the fork of Puttuxent River   Rent   —.. 11.. 2½
Poss^r John Sumers

Kings Venture

50 A: Sur: 26 May 1704 for Jos: King in the
Fork of Puttuxent River   Rent   —.. 2.. —
Poss^r Jos: King

Walters's Lott

711 A: Sur: 18^{tb} Xber 1705 for Richd Snowdon
Junr in the Fork of Puttuxent on the North
Side of Robinhoods Forrest   Rent   1.. 8.. 5
Poss^r Wid^o Walters for the Orp^n of Walters

Effords Delight

176 A: Sur: 1st July 1703 for Wm Efford on
the No: Side of Robinhoods Forrest at the Head
of Coblers Bra: Rent   —.. 7.. 0
Poss^r Wm Efford

Honest Man's Lot

110½ A: Sur: 12th Xber 1704 for John
Duvall on the No: Bra: at the head of So:
River   Rent   —.. 4.. 5
Poss^r John Duvall

Mitchell's Addition

18½ A: Sur: 9: Mar: 1704 for Wm Mitchell
on the So: Side So. River at Mitchells Chance
Poss^r David Mackintosh   Rent —.. —.. 9

Clark of the Councill

190 A: Sur: 10th 9ber 1701 for Richd Clark
on the North side the No: Bra: of Puttuxent
joyning to Champs Adventure   Rent —.. 7.. 7
Poss^r Henry Hall

Midle Neck Hundred 1707.

Smith's Neck

600 A: Sur: 21: June 1650 for Zephemiah
Smith near South River—This was Res^d the
8th May 1684 for Ann Owen & was found to
contain but 315A: Rent —.. 6.. 3¾
Poss^r Nicholas Sporne of Prin: Geo. Co. tenant
to Owens Orp^{ns}

Howard

650 A: Sur: 3^d July 1650 for Matthew Howard on the South side of Severn River   R. —.. 13.. —
   C. *I do not find This land was ever patented, but ye Survey Supposed to be alter'd by Howard into others.*

Crouchfield

150 A: Sur: 11th Xber 1650 for Wm Crouch on
the North side of Seavern River   Rent —.. 3.. —
Poss^{rs} Rich^d & Alex^r Warfeild for the Orp^{ns}
of John Howard

Todd

100 A: Sur: 8th July 1651 for Thomas Todd on
the South Side of Seavern River   Rent —.. —.. —
This is pt of Annapolis Town & part the liber-
tys begins at the N. E. point of the Town &

extends along the River to the first Creek to the west & then with back lines to the beginning

Locust Neck

100 A: Sur: 22. Nov: 1651 for James Horner on the South side of Seavern   Rent —.. 2.. —

   C. This passed by Tho Brown by ye name of Inheritance as supposed.

Smith

100 A: Sur: 27: Nov: 1651 for Zephaniah Smith joyning to a pcell of Land called Smith's Neck This Land Res^d for Ann Owen the 8 of May 1684 & then found to be but 70 A. Rent   —.. 1.. 5 Poss^r Nich^o Sporne of Prin: Geo: Co: for Owens Orp:

Wyat

90 A: Sur: 22th Novr 1651 for Nich: Wyat on the North side of Severn River (that's a Mistake for the Land is on the South Side S^d River)   —.. 1.. 9¼ Poss^r Sam: Dorsey

Acton

100 A: Sur: 15 Nov. 1651 for Richd Acton near Seavern River   Rent —.. 2.. — Poss^r Sam: Norwood

Porters Hills

200 A: Sur: 20: Nov. 1651 for Peter Porter on the South side of Seavern River   Rent —.. 4.. — Poss^r Tho. Tolly by his Marriage with Kath: Howard widow of Sam: Howard

Baldwins Neck

260 A: Sur: 7th Jan^{ry} 1661 for John Baldwin on the North side of South River   Rent —.. 5.. 3 Poss^r John Baldwin the son

Lydias Rest

400 A: Sur: 24th Octob[r] 1652 for W[m] Har-
Oattly on the No: side of South River. This
Land was Res[d] by John Baldwin the 27th May
1681 & then found to be but 210 A   Rent —.. 4.. 2½
Poss[r] Antho: Ruly

Beard's Dock

250 A: Sur: 15: Aug. 1650 for Rich[d] Beard
on the no: side South River   Rent —.. 5.. —
Poss[r] John Cross

Glevins

200 A: Sur: 25th Nov. 1651 for Tho:
Howell on the South Side of Seavern River
Poss[r] Joseph Hill   Rent —.. 4.. —

Harnes

400 A: Sur: 24th Octob[r] 1651 for W[m] Har-
ness on the No. side of South River   Rent —.. 8.. —
Poss[rs] 300 A. Jos. Hill for Barkers Orp[ns]
      100 A. Jacob Lusby

Warners Neck

320 A: Sur: 20: 9ber 1651 for James Warner
near Seavern River   Rent —.. 6.. 5
Poss[rs] 200 A. . . . Lolly by Marr[a] with Kath:
        widow of Sam: Howard
      120 A: Hen: Pinkney for the Op[n] of
      —— Phill. Howard son of the s[d] Sam.
   320

Gatenby

100 A: Sur. 4 Xber 1658 for Tho: Gates on the
South Side of Seavern River   Rent —.. 2.. —
This Land was Escheated to His Lord[p] for want
of heirs of   & sold by his
Lo[p] to M[r] W[m] Bladen who is the present Poss[r]

Norwood

230 A: Sur: 3: Nov. 1658 for John Norwood
on the So: side of Seavern River   Rent —.. 4.. 8½
Poss[r] Andrew Welplay for Norwood.

Intack

100 A: Sur: 26 Aug. 1659 for John Norwood
on the So: side Seavern on the West side of
Dorsey's Creek   Rent —.. 2.. —
Poss[r] And[w] Welplay for Norwood

Norwoods Fancy

420 A: Sur: 27th Aug[t] 1659 for John Norwood
on the So: side Seavern R: on the West side the
Round bay   Rent —.. 8.. 5
Poss[r] 210 W[m] Yeildhall
    210 Edw[d] Hall
    ———
    420

Clink

100 A: Sur: 27: Aug: 1659 for W[m] Galloway
on the So: Side Seavern River   Rent —.. 2.. —
Poss[r] Tho: Brown

Comb

150 A: Sur: 28: Aug: 1659 for Tobias Butler
This Land lyes at the head of South River & is
pretended to be in Elder Surveys but I beleeve
the same is Escheatable to his Lo[p] for want
of Heirs of Butler, it lyes near Freemans Neck
which belongs to Gather & possess[d] by Fran:
Hardesty, this Land at psent is claimed by noe
person.

Nelson

100 A: Sur: 28th Aug[t] 1659 for Neal Clark on
the East Side South River   Rent —.. 2.. —
Poss[r] Tho: Reynolds

Saughier

250 A: Sur: 23^d: Sept: 1650 for George
Saughier near Durands Creek. I doe not find
that ever Saughier Alien^a this Land nor does
any one claim it & it lying in the same place
with Georgeston Ente^d in 58 I question if it be
not the same Land tho not the quantity.

Broome

220 A: Sur: 30th Aug: 1659 for Richd Beard
on the North Side of So: River on the West side
of bro^d Creek. this was again Sur: 31 Octob
1670 & Ass^d Coll. Hen. Ridgly   —.. 4.. 5
Poss^r Coll Hen: Ridgly of Prin: Geo: Co: for
Hen: Ridglys Orp^{ns}

Brampton

100 A: Sur: 30: Aug: 1659 for R^d: Beard on
the North side South River on the East side bro^d
Creek   Rent   —.. 2.. —
Poss^r John Maccubbin

Brownly

150 A: Sur: 4th Sept: 1659 for Tho: Brown
near the head of Seavern River on the West side
                                        Rent   —.. 3.. —

Poss^r Tho: Browne

Cosill alias Brushy Neck

200 A: Sur: 2d Nov. 1659 for John Collier on
the South side of Todds Creek on the South
side Seavern River. This Land was Res^d by
Tho: Francis the 7th Octob. 1683 for 390 A: by
the name of Brushy Neck & after for Sam:
Young the 28th Octob. 1699 for 200 A: & soe
confirmed   Rent   —.. 4.. —
Poss^r Sam: Young.

Georgeston

190 A: Sur: 3ᵈ Sept. 1659 for George Saughier
near Durands Creek   Rent   —.. 3.. 10½
Possʳ Rob: Lusby.

Withers Durand

250 A: Sur: 16: Xber 1661 for Sam: Withers
on the South Side Seavern River near Howells
Creek   —.. 3.. —
Possʳ 200 A: Wᵐ Bladen
     50 A: Edwᵈ Moore
   ——
   250

Richardson's Folly

200 A: Sur: 19: Janʳʸ 1661 for Laurence
Richardson on the So: Side of Seavern River
near Round bay.   Rent   —.. 4.. —
Possʳˢ 100 A: Tho: Bland
     100 A: John Rockhold
   ——
   200

Covells Cove

430 A: Sur: 16: Feb: 1661 for Ann Covell on
the North side South River joyning to Nelson
                       Rent   —.. 8.. 7¼
Possʳˢ 300 A: Ann Lamberts Exʳˢ
     80 A: Sam Whitter
     50 A: John Ingram for Robinson's
   ——
   430   Orphans.

Hogg Neck

250 A: Sur: 18ᵗʰ Feb. 1661 for Edwᵈ Hope on
the North side South River   Rent   —.. 5.. —
Possʳ Charles Ridgly

Wardrap

200 A: Sur: for James Warn^r 20th Feb: 1661
on the No: side South River on the east side of
Broad Creek   Rent   —.. 4.. —
Poss^r Moses Maccubins

Wardridge

600 A: Sur: 20th Feb. 1661 for James Warner
& Henry Ridgly on the No: side So: Riv^r Rent   —.. 12.. —
Poss^r 200 A: Coll. Hen: Ridgly
      200 A: d^o for his son Hen^s: Orp^{ns}
      200 A: Charles Ridgly

  600

West Quarter

100 A: Sur: 17: Mar: 1661 for Jacob Brem-
ington on the So: side of Seavern Riv^r on the
North side Howell Creek   Rent   —.. 2.. —
Poss^r Joseph Hill

Adventure

50 A: Sur: 15th Sp: 1663 for Wm Frizell on
the North side So: River at the bounds of
Nich^o Wyat   Rent   —.. 1.. —
Poss^r Coll Hen: Ridglys Orphans

Landing Place

50 A: Sur: 15 Aprill 1663 for Neal Clark on
the North side of So: River joyning to Nelson   —.. 1.. —
Poss^r Tho: Reynolds

Turkey Quarter

150 A: Sur: 15: Aprill 1663 for Neal Clark
on the No: side of the head of So: River between the Land of James Warner & Nich^o Wyat
                     Rent   —.. 3.. —

Poss^r Neal Clark

Hambleton

350 A: Sur: 27: Octob. 1662 for Edward Skidmore on the North side South River at a
marked Pine in the mouth of Maccubins Cove
Poss^r Samuell Young

$$\text{Rent} \quad \text{—.. } 7.. \text{—}$$

Wyats Ridge

450 A: Sur: 16: Decemb. 1662 for Nicholas
Wyat between the Bra: of South River & the
main Bra: of Broad Creek   Rent   —.. 9.. —
Poss^r 225 A: Samuell Dorsey
    225 Coll. Hen: Ridgely for his
    ——   son Henry's Orphan's
  450

Todds Range

120 A: Sur: 18: Xber 1662 for Tho: Todd on
the South Side Severn River   Rent   —.. 2.. 5
Poss^{rs} 100 A: Samuel Norwood
    20 A: Town of Annapolis Comon

  ——

  120

Howards Heirship

420 A: Sur: 26: Jan^{ry} 1662 for Cornelius
Howard on the South Side Seavern Riv^r at
the head of Hockly Creek   Rent   —.. 8.. 5
Poss^{rs} 300 A: Caleb Dorsey
    64 A: Joseph Howard
    60 A: Cornelius Howard

  ——

  124

        4 A: over the Survey   —.. —.. 1

Howards Hope

100 A: Sur: 26: Jan^{ry} 1662 for Samuell
Howard on the South Side of Severne Riv^r —.. 2.. —
Poss^r Joseph Howard

Howard's Interest

180 A: Sur: 28th Jan[ry] 1662 for John Howard
on the South Side of Severne River   Rent   —.. 3.. —
Poss[r] John Dorsey son of Joshua Dor:

Charles's Hills

200 A: Sur: 27th Jan[ry] 1662 for Charles
Stephens on the South side Severn Riv[r] on the
North side Mountain Neck   Rent   —.. 4.. —
Poss[r] Cornelius Howard

Withers Outlett

100 A. Sur: 4: Mar: 1662 for Samuell Withers
on the South Side Severne River on the West
side ferry Creek   Rent   —.. 2.. —
Poss[r] Joseph Hill

Smith's Rest

150 A: Sur: 5: Mar: 1662 for Walter Smith
on the North Side South River. 50 A: p[t] of
this is in possession of Jacob Lusby and the remaining 100 A: in possess[n] of John Davidge
who the   Res[d]
the same & found to contain 121 A: by the
name of Dabidges Meadows the whole now is
171 A. at   Rent   —.. 3.. 5¼

Edwards Neck

100 A: Sur: 5th Mar: 1662 for John Edwards
on the north side South River at a point at
the mouth of Fishing Creek   —.. 2.. —
Poss[r] Anthony Ruly

Wardrop Ridge

100 A: Sur: 12 Octob 1663 for Patrick Dunkin
on the north side South River respecting the
Land called Wardrop to the West. This Land
was Res[d] for s[d] Dunkin 1st June 1676 at the
rent of   —.. 4.. —

Escheated to his Lo^p for want of Heirs of . . . & granted the . . . to Mr Cha: Carroll who is the psent poss^r

Woodyard

150 A: 15th Octob 1663 Sur: for John Howard & Char: Stephens near the round bay on the So: side Severne River 400 A: of this —.. 2.. — Land is in possessⁿ of Sam: Norwood the rem^a 50 A. is res^d into a tract of Land called Good Mothers endeavour entred in page 79 & the s^d 100 A: now only und^r this name

Salmons Hill

100 A: Sur: 26: Octob 1663 for Ralph Salmon at the head of Plumb Creek on the south side of South River　Rent　—.. 2.. —
Poss^{rs} 50 A: Ruth Howard
　　　50 A: Guy Meek

　100

James's Hill

100 A: Sur: 21: June 1663 for John James on the south side Severne River joyning to the Land of Samuell Withers　Rent　—.. 2.. —
Poss^r William Bladen

Chance

100 A: Sur: 12th Octob. 1663 for Wm Frezill on the North side South River on the East side green ginger Creek　Rent　—.. 2.. —
Poss^r Thomas Rutland

Hope

100 A: Sur: 15th Octob 1663 for Henry Sewell on the South Side Severne River about a mile from the head of Plumb Creek　R.　—.. 2.. —
Poss^r Richd Warfeild

Wyat's Hill

60 A: Sur: 16: Octob 1663 for Nich⁰ Wyatt
on the South side Severne River   Rent   —.. 1.. 2½
Possʳ Edwᵈ Dorsey

The Landing

100 A: Sur: 20ᵗʰ Octo: 1663 for Tho: Underwood on the North side Severne at the head
of Ferry Creek   Rent   —.. 2.. —
Possʳ Thomas Cockey from James Anford & he
      from Thomas Underwood but I doubt the
      sale from Anford, he left noe heir

Wayfeild

100 A: Sur: 21 Octob 1663 for Nich⁰ Wyat
on the South side Severn River in the woods   —.. 2.. —
Possʳ Richᵈ Warfeild

Bear Ridge

175 A: Sur: 12: Octob 1663 for Nich⁰ Wyat
on the South side Severne River   Rent   —.. 3.. 6
Possʳ Josua Dorsey

MARYLAND RENT ROLLS.

MIDDLE NECK HUNDRED 1707.

Baldwins Addition

120 A: Sur: 2^d Nov. 1663 for John Baldwin
on the North Side South River in the Woods at
the head of the Plant^a he liveth upon   —.. 2.. 5
Poss^r John Baldwin

C. p. 52. Entry identical; but on C. p. 20 appears Bald-
wins addition 70 a. sur. 4 Nov. 1663 for John Baldwin at the
head of a bra. of Deep Creek & between that & 3 Islands in
the Swamp. 35 a. of this land was resur. for John Metcalf
into a Tract of his call^d The Range & no more und^r this name
now than the remain 35 a. in possⁿ Tho Crouchly.

Hockley in the Hole

400 A: Sur: 27: Jan^{ry} 1663 for Edward Dorsey
Joshua Dorsey & John Dorsey on the So: side
of Severne River in the Woods   Rent —.. —.. —
this Land was Res^d for John Dorsey the 17th
March 1683 & found to cont^a 842 A: the 400 A:
first Surv^d being Old Rent the remainder New,
the whole now at   1.. 5.. 8
Poss^r Caleb Dorsey.

Chance

200 A: Sur: 27: Jan^{ry} 1663 for Cornelius Howard on the South side of Severne River 100 A: pt of this tract Sur: into a tract called Howards Inheritance & there entred, the s^d Ho^{ds} Inherit^a is in page 80—& but 100 A of this tract now remaining.   Rent —.. 1.. —

Poss^r Tho: Tolly by his Marriage with Cath: Howard the wid^o of Sam: Howard.

Ropers Yard

200 A: Sur: 7: Jan^{ry} 1650 for John Edwards Patt: in the name of Tho: Roper Anno 1664 on the No: side South River.   Rent —.. 4.. —

C. Patent Surrender^d & had New Warrant.

Come by Chance   Nil

C. p. 67. Come by chance 200 a. granted 28 May 1692 to Michael Birmingham & Escheat to his Ldpp for want of heirs of Michael Cusack granted und^r Such Rent as to ye s^d Cusack. Poss^r Joseph Hill, the same is 214 a.

Advantage

40 A: Sur: 29: Feb: 1663 for Richd Moss on the South Side Severne in the Woods.   Rent —.. —.. 10

Poss^r Wm Pennington

Mountain Neck

190 A: Sur: 8: Aprill 1664 for Tho: Hamond on the South Side Severne River.   Rent —.. 3.. 10

This Land has always paid for 250 A: & soe much Coll Hamond sayes it is, tho' he knows not how it comes to be soe the Record being as above the 60 A: rem^a Rent is   —.. 1.. 2½

Poss^r Coll. John Hamond.

Brushy Neck

150 A: Sur: 28: May 1664 for John Baldwin
on the North side of South River.   Rent —.. 13.. —
Poss[r] John Baldwin the son.

Grimeston

100 A: Sur: 4th June 1664 for W[m] Grimes on
the South Side Severne River at the head of the
South bra: of Plumb Creek.   Rent —.. 2.. —
Poss[r] William Grimes

Reads Lott

40 A: Sur: 2[d] May 1665 for W[m] Read at a
bounded Oak of Robert Clarkson's at the head of
Beasly Creek   Rent —.. —.. 10
Poss[r] Jos: Hill for Barkers Orp[ns].

C. . . . at ye head of Brasley Creek.

Timber Neck

40 A: Granted 15th Sep: 1665 to John Maccubin on broad Creek   Rent —.. —.. 10
Poss[r] John Maccubin

Horn Neck

300 A: Sur: 7[th] March 1664 for Rob: Clarkson
at a bounded water Oak by the River side
Poss[r] Joseph Hill   Rent —.. 6.. —

The Chance

15 A: Sur. 16: Nov. 1664 for Thomas Roper at
a bounded Hiccory in the Woods joyning to the
Land of W[m] Frizell   Rent —.. —.. 3½
At p[r]sent none claims this Land.

C. Patent Surrender[d] & new warr[t].

Bruton Grimes

50 A: Sur: 3[d] June 1664 for John Bruton &
W[m] Grimes in the Woods on the South side Severne River   Rent —.. 3.. —

Upon reading the Cert. of this Land to Coll Hamond he informed me that Wm Grimes possesses this Land but Grimes denyes it nor can I find any one th^t claimes it.

C. 150 a. . . . nor that it ever was patented.

Bruton

50 A: Sur: 4th June 1665 for John Bruton in the woods on the South Side Severn Riv^r. Upon reading the Cert: of this Land to Coll Hamond he informed me that the same was in possess^n of Wid^o Ruth Howard, but she denyes it, nor does any one else claim it.

Bells Haven

100 A: Sur: 25th August 1665 for Tho: Bell at Bessons Creek. This Land was Res^d the 3^d June 1684 for Richd Burnett & Eliz^a his wife & then found to be but 55 A: at the Rent   —.. 1.. 1¼
Poss^r Richd Burnett's daughter with Samuell Dryer.

Read's Lott

100 A: Sur: 16: Nov: 1665 for Willm Read near Severne River   Rent —.. 2.. —
Poss^r Jos: Hill for Barkers Orp^{ns}

Pierpoints Lott

150 A: Sur: 3^d Nov. 1665 for Hen: Peirpoint in the woods about 2 miles from Severn Riv^r this Res^d by the s^d Peirpoint June 4: 1673 & then found to be 207 A: under the Rent of   —.. 5.. 3
Poss^r Amos Peirpoint.

C. Hen Pierpont . . . Amos Pierpont.

Fullers Point

120 A: Sur: 12: Aprill 1664 for Phillip Thomas at a marked White Oak by the bayside.   Rent —.. 2.. 5
Poss^r Robert Johnson.

Batchellors Hope

240 A: Sur: 15: Feb: 1665 for Walter Phelps
& Nich: Green on the Nor: Side of So: River on
the East side broad Creek.   Rent —.. 4.. 10
Poss^r Charles Carroll.

Howard & Porter's Range

500 A: Sur: 18th Feb. 1665 for Cornelius How-
ard & Peter Porter on the South Side Severne
River by a bra: near the Land of John Howard —.. 10.. —
Poss^{rs} 250 A: Ruth Howard wid^o.

  176½ A: Theophilus Kiton
  100   A: Adam Shiply
  ———
  526½ 26½ over the Survey.   —.. —.. 5½

Howards Thickett

50 A: Sur: 19th Feb: 1665 for John Howard on
the South Side of Severne River at a bound
White Oak of Cha: Stephen's Land. This is
Res^r into a tract of Land called Good Mothers
Endeavour page 79 & soe noe more here to be
charged.

Neglect

30 A: Sur: 15: March 1665 for Patrick Dunkin
on the North Side South River by broad Creek.
                Rent —.. —.. 7
Poss^r James Steward

Peasly's Neck

250 A: Sur: 1st Xber 1666 for Fran: Peasly on
the South side Severn River near Bessons Creek.
Joseph Hill possesses this whose Fa. Richd Hill
the 24: Sep: 1674 res^d it & found to be but 159
A: & that is all he payes Rent for 3.. 2¼   —.. 3.. 2¼

Orphans Inheritance

200 A: Res: 21: May 1666 for Eliz: Sisson on
the South side Severn River at a bounded Red
Oak on a Point by the side of Road Bay. Rent —.. 4.. —
This Resurvey is by means of 2 Assignem^{ts}
vizt 100 A: from Wm Crouch & 100 A. from
John Howard & after Res^d into one as above Is
possessed by Edward Hall & Wm Yeildhall.

Upper Tauton

280 A: Sur: 15th Xber 1662 for Laurence Rich-
ardson on the South Side Severne River at a
M^rked Red Oak.   —.. 5.. 8
Poss^{rs} 160 A: John Dorsey (son of Joshua)
     120 A: John Young for Rockholds heirs.

___
280

Wyat's Harbour

100 A: Sur: 20: May 1667 for Nich^o Wyat at
a bounded Cedar on Wyat's Point.   Rent —.. 2.. —
Poss^r Sam: Dorsey.

Harris's Mount

100 Sur: 20 Nov: 1667 for Willm Harrison the
North side South River.   Rent —.. 2.. —
Poss^r Sam^{ll} Young.

Encrease

50 A: Sur: 31st Xber 1667 for John Minter on
the South Side Severne Riv^r.   Rent —.. 1.. —
Poss^r Richd Warfeild.

First Choice

60 A: Sur: 21: Xber 1667 for Matt: Howard
on the South Side Severn River near the Land
of Ra: Salmon's.   Rent —.. 3.. 2½
Poss^r Wid^o Ruth Howard.

Remainder of Warner's Neck

120 A: being the remainder of 320 A: Sur: 10th
of June 1667 for James Warner on the South
Side of Seavern River at the mouth of Warners
Neck, the other 200 A. is now Survd into Howards Inheritance entred in page 80: the 120 A.
at the rent of   —.. 2.. 5
Possr Henry Pinkney by his Marriage wth the
widow of Phill: Howard

Howard's & Porter's Fancy

333 A: Sur: 30 Xber 1667 for Cornelius How-
ard at a bod Poplar of Howard's & Porter's
Range.   Rent —.. 6.. 8
Possrs 150 A: John Marriot
       183 A: Peter Porter
       ———
       333

Jane's Inheritance

50 A: Sur. 30 Xber 1667 for Jane Sisson upon
Sunken ground Creek on the South Side Severne
Rivr.   Rent —.. 1.. —
Possr Thomas Ward.

Dorsey

60 A: Sur: 22: Augt 1668 for Edward Dorsey
on the South side A. A.: River   Rent —.. 1.. 2
Possr Wm Bladen.

Piney Point

50 A. Sur: 17: Sep: 1668 for Thomas Phelps on
the South side Clarkson's Creek.   Rent —.. 1.. —
Possr Joseph Hill

Ropers Neck

300 A: Sur: 28: Sep: 1668 for Thomas Roper
on the North side South River at the point on
the West side Ropers Creek.   Rent —.. 6.. —
Possr Cornelius Howard

Encrease

100 A: Sur: 14: June 1669 for Cornelius How-
ard on the South side Severne Riv^r near Plumb
Creek   Rent. —.. 2.. —
Poss^r Thomas Brown

*C. Brown bo^t this Land of Hen Sewall who bo^t of Corn.
Howard.*

Browns Encrease

250 A: Sur: 14: June 1669 for Willm Hopkins
on the South side Severne River at the North
bounds of Brownston.   Rent —.. 5.. —
Poss^r Thomas Brown

Guy's Rest

100 A: Sur: 14th June 1669 for Guy Meek on
the South Side Severne River.   Rent —.. 2.. —
Poss^r Guy Meek

C. Poss^r John Meek.

Gardner's Warfeild

60 A: Sur: 10 Augt 1669 for Richd Warfield
& Edward Gardner at Nich^o Wyat's Norther
most bound tree   Rent —.. 1.. 2½
Poss^r Richd Warfeild

Broome   Nil

220 A: Sur. 31. Octob^r 1670 for Richd Beard &

*C. 1 Broom 220 a. Sur. 30 Augt 1659 for R^d Beard on y^e
N. Side of South river on ye W. Side of Broad Creek. This
was again Sur. 31 Oct. 1670 & assign'd Coll. Henry Ridgeley.
Poss^r Coll. Henry Ridgeley for Henry Ridgeley's orp^{ns}.*

Todds Harbour

120 A. Sur. 16: Xber 1670 for Thomas Todd
on the west side Severne River at a bounded
Red Oak & running down Todds Creek.   Rent —.. 4.. 10
Town of Annapolis

Venall's Inheritance

100 A: Sur: 7: July 1671 on the East side of
the North Run of South River at a bounded Pine
of Tobias Butlers, 50 A: pt of this Land was sold
by Venall to John Barker to be sold the same to
W[m] Ridgly who now possesses it the other 50 A:
was Escheated to His Lords[p] for want of heirs
of Venall & the 14th Aug[t] 1680 was Res[d] &
granted to Rich[d] Rawlins by the name of Rawlins purchase & is now in Possess[n] of Rich[d] son of
the s[d] Richard, the whole R.   —.. 4.. —

Guy's Will

100 A. Sur: 28: June 1671 for Guy Meek between the heads of South & Severn Rivers at a
bounded White Oak of Guy's Rest.   Rent —.. 4.. —

Hereford

260 A: Sur: 18: July 1671 for Robert Wilson
between the heads of South & Severne Riv[rs] at a
bo[d] tree of John Gather's   Rent —.. 10.. 5
Poss[rs] 234 A: John Marriot
      26 A: Theo: Kitton

    —
    260

Peirpoints Rock's

80 A: Sur: 15 Xber. 1665 for Henry Peirpoint
on the North side South River on the North
west side broad Creek.   Rent —.. 1.. 7¼
Poss[r] Amos Peirpoint
  C. *Henry Pierpont . . . Amos Pierpoint.*

Howard's Hill

200 A: Sur: 9: May 1672 for Cornelius Howard on the South Side Severne River on the
North side of Underwoods Creek   Rent —.. 4.. —
Poss[r] Cornelius Howard the son.

Freinds Choice

100 A: Sur: 6: May 1672 for Wm Grimes and
Nicholas Shepheard on the South side Severne
River at a bounded Oak on a point.　　　Rent —.. 2.. —
Poss^r Sam: Dryer
　C. Sheppard.

Grimes Addition

100 A: Sur. 6: May 1672 for William Grimes
on the South Side of Severne River at the fork
of Plumb Creek　　　　　　　Rent —.. 2.. —
Poss^r George Valentine

———————

MARYLAND RENT ROLLS.

Anne Arundel Co.

Midle Neck Hundred, 1707
Long Venture

250 A: Sur: 2ᵈ. July 1672 for John Stinson between the head of South & Severne Rivʳˢ at a bound Oak of Hen: Peirpoint   Rent —.. 10.. —
Possʳ Richard Rawlins.

Proctors Forrest

100 A: Sur: 2ᵈ. July 1672 for Robert Proctor on the North side South River by the Land of Robert Clarkson   Rent —.. 4.. —
Possʳ Edward Romney.

Henry's Addition

30 A: Sur: 20: May 1673 for Hen: Sewall in round bay at a boᵈ Red Oak by Wᵐ Galloways Land
Possʳ Hen: Sewalls Orphans.   Rent —.. 1.. 2

Warfeilds Forrest

182 A: Sur: 7: June 1673 for Richᵈ Warfield in the woods.   Rent —.. 7.. 3½
Possʳ John Warfield.

The March

110 A: Sur: 7 June 1673 for Edward Gardiner at a boᵈ Oak of Howard & Porters Range   Rent —.. 4.. 5
Possʳ Ruth Howard Widᵒ.
   C. The Marsh.

Hair Hill

100 A: Sur: 3ʳᵈ July 1673 for Peter Porter in the

Woods about 3 miles from the head of Severn at
a bo^d White Oak   Rent —.. 4.. —
Poss^r Peter Porter.

Green Spring

200 A: Sur: 16: June 1673 for Rob: Proctor in
the line of Jerom White Esqr called Whitehall &
running therewith N. W.   Rent —.. 4.. —
Poss^r Wid^o Ruth Howard.

Shepheard's Range

100 A: Sur: 3: Xber 1673 for Nicholas Shepheard
on the South Side of Severne River   Rent —.. 4.. —
Poss^r Samuell Dryer.

Howard's Hills

150 A: Sur: 14: Mar: 1665 for John Howard &
Assigned Philip Howard on Severn Ridge at a bo^d
Poplar of Howard & Porter's fancy   Rent —.. 3.. —
Poss^r Wid^o Ruth Howard.

Warfeilds Right

50 A: Sur: 10: Mar: 1674 for Richd Warfeild on
the South Side Ann Arrundle River near Round
Bay   Rent —.. 1.. —
Poss^r Richd Everard.

Todds Pasture

29 A: Sur: 16 Nov. 1674 for Thomas Todd in
Todds Neck   Rent —.. —.. 7¼
   In the Town of Annapolis as is affirmed.

Advance

42 A: Sur: 13: July 1674 for Daniel Edge between South & Severn Rivers on Norwood's Creek
Poss^r William Gibbons.   Rent —.. 1.. 8¼

Brent Wood

100 A: Sur: 27: Aug: 1674 for Rob: Gudgeon be-

tween the bra: of Severn & South Rivers   Rent —.. 4.. —
Poss[r] John Dorsey.

Lancasters Plaines

180 A: Sur: 28: Aug 1674 for John Hudson on the
South Side of Severn River by Indian Bra: R. —.. 7.. 2½
Poss[r] Henry Pinkney for Phill: Howard's Orphans.

Howards Mount

80 A: Sur: 20: Feb. 1665 for John Howard on the
South Side of Severn River near Round Bay.
Poss[r] Phillip Norwood   Rent —.. 1.. 7¼

Widow's Addition

130 A: Sur: 10: Jan[ry] 1678 for Elizabeth Read on
the South Side of Severn River   Rent —.. 5.. 2½
Poss[r] Joseph Hill for Barker's Orphans.

Ross

136 A: Sur: 16: Jan[ry] 1678 for Guy Meek on the
South Side of Severne River at a bound tree of
Matt: Howard   Rent —.. 5.. 5
Poss[r] John Meek.

   C. 1668.

Ridgly's beginning

40 A: Sur: 15: Jan[ry] 1678 for W[m] Ridgly on the
North Side South River in Hogg Neck   Rent —.. 1.. 7¼
Poss[r] s[d] W[m] Ridgly.

Charles's Hills

271 A: Sur: 17: Mar: 1678 for Charles Stephens
on the west side Severn River   Rent —.. 10.. 10
Poss[r] Tho: Brown Jun[r] who marr[d] the wid[o] of
Cha: Stephen.

Proctor's Chance

30 A: Sur: 1[st] July 1679 for Rob: Proctor at a
m[r]ked Hiccory of the Intack on the west side

Severn River   Rent —.. 1.. 2½
Poss^r And^w Welplay for Norwoods.

Pettycoats Rest
100 A: Sur: 8: July 1679 for Wm Pettycoat at a
bound tree of the Advance   Rent —.. 4.. —
Poss^r Tho: Freeborn.

Henry's Encrease
43 A: Sur: 8: July 1679 for Hen: Sewall on the
South Side Severn River   Rent —.. 1.. 8¾
Poss^r Tho: Brown.

Rocky Point
50 A: Sur: 13: Octob. 1679 for Ann Lambert on
the North Side South River on the South Side
Forked Bra: Rent —.. 2.. —
Poss^r Ann Lamberts Exers.

Betenson's Adventure
82 A: Sur: 17: Mar: 1679 for Edward Betenson
on the North Side South River   Rent —.. 3.. 3½
Poss^r John Betenson.

New Worcester ats Tolly's Point
103 A: Sur: 1st Octo: 1679 for Thomas Tolly by
the bay side & by Lusby's Creek. This was Res^d
by the s^d Tolly 9th Nov. 1683 for 140 A: Rent —.. 5.. 7¼
Poss^r Joseph Hill.

Brooksby's Point
350 A: Sur: 5: 8ber 1680 for John Brooksby on
the South Side of Severn River by Indian Branch
Poss^{rs} 290 A: John Marriot   Rent —.. 14.. —
      60 A: Tho: Abbrix

——————
350
——————

215

Warfeilds Plains

300 A: Sur: 30th Mar. 1681 for Richd Warfeild
on the South Side of Severne River   Rent —.. 12.. —
Poss^r John Warfeild.

Sheply's Choyce

200 A: Sur: 30th Mar. 1681 for Adam Sheply on
the South Side Severn River by the Riverside
Poss^{rs} 100 A: Peter Porter   Rent —.. 8.. —
     100 A: James Barnes of Balto. Co:

———

200

Brandy

300 A: Sur: 29th Sepr 1681 for Richd Warfeild at
the head of Severn River   Rent —.. 12.. —
Poss^r Alexand^r Warfeild

Medcalf's Chance

80 A: Sur: 30th Sept. 1681 for John Metcalf be-
tween the Bra: of South River at a bo^d Hiccory of
Howard & Porter's Range   Rent —.. 3.. 2½
Poss^r Amos Garret.

Weston

130 A: Sur: 1st Octob. 1681 for Guy Meek on the
South Side of Severne River on the bra: of Plumb
Creek   Rent —.. 5.. 2½
Poss^r John Meek

Meek's Rest

210 A: Resurv^d 1st Octob. 1681 for Guy Meek on
the South Side Severn River the Record says this
Res: was made by Assignm^t of 140 A: from Hen:
Hanslap but mentions not how the rest to make the
complement of 210 A: became, only concludes th^t
quantity   —.. 8.. 2½
Poss^r John Meek

Howards Adventure

500 A: Sur: 9th Octob. 1681 for Matthew Howard
at the head of Severne River   Rent 1.. ———
Poss^r Charles Hamond.

Chilton

40 A: Sur: 19: Octob. 1681 for Abra: Child at the
Land of Thomas Brown on the South Side of Sev-
erne River   Rent —.. 1.. 8
Poss^r Amos Garret.

The Freindship

30 A: Sur: 3: May 1682 for Wm Frizell on the
North Side South River on the East Side broad
Creek   Rent —.. 1.. 2½
Poss^r John Frizell.

   C. The Friendship.

Favour

123 A: Res^d 27 June 1682 for Benj^a Bond on the
No. Side of South River at a bo^d Red Oak on a
point at the mouth of Oatly Creek   Rent —.. 4.. 11¼
This Res. was from 290 A. at first Poss^r Henry
Carter by his marriage with the wid^o of ———
Jefferyes.

Addition

50 A: Sur: 11: Aug: 1682, for Richd Warfeild
above the head of Severn River at the Land called
Hair Hall   Rent —.. 2.. —
Poss^r Richd Warfeild.

Geff's Encrease

180 A: Sur: 12: Augt 1682 for Thomas Geff on
the North Side South River at the bound tree of
Wardrop Ridge   Rent —.. 7.. 2½
Poss^r Charles Carroll.

Cardwell

300 A: Sur: 4th Sep: 1682 for John Marriot at

3 miles above the head of Severn Riv^r   R. —.. 12.. —
Poss^r John Marriot.

Narrow Neck

41 A: Sur: 6th Sep: 1682 for Wm Yeidhall on the
South Side of Severn River by the Round bay at
the head of the Sunken ground   —.. 1.. 7¾
Poss^r Tho: Ward.

Angle

70 A: Sur: 12: Sep: 1682 for John Cross on the
North side South River att the bound tree of Bell
Haven   Rent —.. —.. —
This Land was sold by John Cross to Gervase Win-
terbottom for want of Heirs of whom it Escheats
to His Lords^p.

Mill Meadow

240 A: Sur: 13: Sep: 1682 for Richd Hill at the
head of Seavern River at Hen: Sewall's Land   R.—.. 9.. 7¼
Poss^r Joseph Hill.

The Levell

264 A: Sur: 11: Sep: 1682 for John Cross on the
North Side South River joyning to Zepha: Smith's
Land   Rent —.. 10.. 6¾
Poss^r 164 Jos: Hill
        100 A: Rob. Johnson
        ————
        264
        ————

The Mayden

40 A: Sur: 29: Sep: 1682 for Mary Howard on
the South Side Severne River at a Poplar of
Howards & Porters Range   Rent —.. 1.. 7¼
Poss^r Wid^o Ruth Howard.

Shepheard's Grove

120 A: Sur: 12: May 1683 for Nicholas Shepheard

about 3 miles above the head of Severn Riv^r Rent —.. 4.. 9¾
Poss^r Nich^o Shepheard.

C. *Sheppard's Grove.*

Norwoods Angles

103 A: Sur: 22: June 1683 for And^w Norwood on
the Bra: of Todds Creek   Rent —.. 4.. 1½
Poss^r Thomas Freeborn.

Edges Addition

50 A: Sur: 22: June 1683 for Daniell Edge between South & Severn Rivers   Rent —.. 2.. —
Poss^r Wm Gibbons.

Howards Addition

70 A: Sur: 21: June 1683 for Phillip Howard
between South & Severn Rivers   Rent —.. 2.. 9¾
Poss^r Wid^o Ruth Howard.

Addition

48 A: Sur: 8th July 1684 for Tho. Lytfoot as-
signed to George Tate between South River &
Severn at bo^d tree of Chance   Rent —.. 1.. 11¼
Poss^r Joseph Hill (This was some of Cusacks
Land).

C. *Lightfoot.*

Boyds Chance

60 A: Sur: 26 June 1684 for John Boyd in the
wood between South & Severn Riv^{rs} Rent —.. 2.. 5
Poss^r Gerr^d Topping for Moonshots Orp^{ns}.

Orphan's Addition

85 A: Sur: 1: July 1684 for Robert & Laurence
Gudgeon in the woods between South & Severn
Rivers   Rent —.. 3.. 5
Poss^r Caleb Dorsey.

Childs Reserve

62 A: Sur: 6: Mar: 1683 for Abra: Child on the
South Side Severn River in the Round bay   Rent —.. 2.. 6
Poss^r Abra: Child.

Metcalfs Mount

70 A: Sur: 21: June 1683 for John Metcalf in
the woods between the North Run bra: of So.
River   Rent —.. 2.. 9¾
Poss^r Amos Garret.

   C. Medcalf's Mount.

The Range

384 A: Sur: 4: July 1684 for Tho: Lytfoot about
a mile from the head of Severn River   Rent —.. 15.. 4½
Poss^r Jabus Peirpoint.

   C. Lightfoot, Pierpoint.

Angle

7 A: Sur: 2: July 1684 for Richard Hill on the
South side of Severn on Dorsey Creek   Rent —.. —.. 3½
In the Town of Annapolis.

Burntwood Comon

50 A: Sur: 1st July 1684 for Robert & Laurence
Gudgeon on Rockholds Creek   Rent —.. 2.. —
Poss^r John Young for Rockholds Orp^{ns}.

The Addition

60 A: Sur: 2^d July 1684 for Capt. Richard Hill
on the South Side of Severne River on the South
Side of Todds Creek   Rent —.. 2.. 5
Poss^r Joseph Hill.

   C. The Addiccon.

Clark's Luck

60 A: Sur: 14: Octob. 1684 for Neal Clark on the

North Side of South River at Hog Neck   Rent —.. 2.. 5
Poss^r Tho: Reynolds for Griffiths Orp^ns.

Garret's Town

59 A: Sur: 6: July 1684 for Tho. Windell & Ass^d
to Mich: Cussack on the North Side So: Riv^r on
the East side Broad Creek   Rent —.. 2.. 4½
Poss^r Joseph Hill.

Rich Neck

284 A: Sur: 20: Mar: 1684 for John Hamond on
the East Side the No: bra: of Patt: River at Hun-
the East Side the No: bra: of Patt: River at Huntington at a bo^d Hiccory standing by the bra: &
bound on the River West   Rent —.. 11.. 4½
Poss^r Coll. John Hamond.

Dunkens Luck

52 A: Sur: 23 Feb. 1684 for Pat: Dunken on the
No: Side So: Riv^r on the west side Hamilton
Creeke.   Rent —.. 2.. 1
Poss^r Samuel Young.

MARYLAND RENT ROLLS.

Middle Neck Hundred, 1707

Norwoods Recovery

104 A: Sur: 6: June 1686 for Andrew Norwood
on the North side of South River   Rent —.. 2.. 2
Poss^r And^w Welplay for Norwood.

Ridgley's Forrest

264 A: Sur: 3 June 1686 for Hen: Ridgley on the
East side of the No: bra: of Patt. Riv^r at Huntington   Rent —.. 10.. 6¾

Milland

100 A: Sur: 16: Octob. 1683 for Rob: Proctor on
the North side South River on the main bra: of
broad Creek   Rent —.. 4.. —
Poss^r Thomas Freeborn.

Shepheards Chance

240 A: Sur: 12: June 1686 for Nich^o Shepheard
on the South Side of Severn River   Rent —.. 9.. 7¼
Poss^r Nich^o Shepheard.
Poss^r Nich Sheppard.

    C. Sheppards Chance.
      2

Addition

22 A: Sur: 16: Sep: 1685 for John Hamond on
the So: side of Severn River   Rent —.. —.. 10¾
Poss^r Col John Hammond.

C. Addicōn

Clark's Enlargem^t

265 A: Sur: 20: June 1686 for Neal Clark on the
North side of South River   Rent —.. 10.. 7¼

Brown's Chance

98 A: Sur: 29 Mar: 1687 for Thomas Brown on
the South Side of Severn River   Rent &.. 3.. 11¼
Poss^r Stephen Gill for Daniell Macconas.

Mayden Croft

128 A: Sur: 17: June 1688 for Laurence Draper
on the bayside between So: & Severn Rivers M^r
Bladen affirms to me this Land to be in Elder Surveys of his

Jeffs Search

39 A: Sur: 5th June 1688 for Wm Jeff on the No:
side So: River   Rent —.. 1.. 6¾
Poss^r Tho: Rutland.

Ridgly's beginning

28 A: Sur: for Hen: Ridgly Octob 4th 1694 lying
at Huntington on Patt. River No: bran.   R. —.. 11.. 3½
Poss^r Coll Ridgly for his son Henry's Orphan's.

Howard's Luck

190 A: Sur: 26 Octob 1694 for John Howard at
Huntington on Patt: Riv^r North branch   R. —.. 7.. 7¼
Poss^r Rich^d & Alex^r Warfeild for the Orp^{ns} of
John Howard.

Ridgly's Lott

273 A: Sur: 8th Xber 1694 for Hen: Ridgly lying
between Huntington & Elk Ridge   Rent —.. 10.. 11½
Poss[r] Coll Ridgly for Henry Ridgly's Orp[ns].

Hiccory Ridge

262 A: Sur: 1: Nov. 1694 for Charles Stevenson
the bra: of Severn River   Rent —.. 10.. 6
Poss[r] W[m] Stephens.

Griffith's Lott

197 A: Sur: 4: Nov. 1694 for W[m] Griffin between
South & Severn Rivers   Rent —.. 7.. 10¾
Poss[r] Tho: Reynolds for Griffiths Orp[ns].

Majors Fancy

186 A: Sur: 12: Mar: 1694 for Maj. Edward
Dorsey between South & Severn Rivers   Rent —.. 7.. 5½
Poss[r] Samuell Dorsey.

Freeborn's Enlargement

80 A: Sur: 17: Octob[r] 1694 for Tho: Freeborn on
the North Side South River   Rent —.. 3.. 2½
Poss[r] Thomas Freeborne.

Baldwin's Chance

415 A: Sur: 16: Octob. 1694 for John Baldwin on
the North Side So: River at Baldwins point   R. —.. 16.. 7¾
Poss[r] John Baldwin.

Harris's Beginning

122 A: Sur: 5th Xber 1694 for John Harris lying
at Huntington on Patt. River No: bra: Rent —.. 4.. 10¾
Poss[r] Wid[o] Sarah Crouchly at Rich[d] Wiggs.

Grimes Enlargem[t]

187 A: Sur: 29th Nov: 1694 for W[m] Grimes on
the South Side Severn River   Rent —.. 7.. 6
Poss[r] W[m] Grimes.

What-you-please

72 A: Sur: 14: Feb. 1688 for Charles Stephens
between South & Severn Rivers   Rent —.. 2.. 10
Poss^r Wm Stephens.

   C. *Wm Stevens.*

Peirpoints Range

200 A: Sur: 13: Feb. 1688 for Johns Peirpoint in
the woods   Rent —.. 8.. —
Poss^r same Peirpoint.

Timber Neck

303 A: Sur: 14: Feb: 1688 for Cha: Stevens in the
Woods   Rent —.. 12.. 1½
Poss^r 101 A: Eliz^a Steven
     101 A: Sarah Stephens
     101 A: Willm Yeildhall in right of his
     ——— wife Mary daughter of Cha: Stephens
     303

Stony Hills

36 A: Sur: 12th Xber 1695 for Richd Everet in
A. A. Co.   Rent —.. 1.. 5½
Poss^r Laurence Gary.

Browns Forrest

387 A: Sur: 24 Feb. 1695 for Tho: Brown on the
West side the No: Bra: of Patt. Riv^r   Rent —.. 15.. 6
Poss^r Saml Brown.

Dryers Inheritance

254 A: Sur: 25: Feb. 1695 for Sam. Dryer on the
West Side the No: Bra: of Patt. River   Rent —.. 10.. 2
Poss^r Same Dryer.

Ridgly's Forrest

264 A: Sur: 3: June 1686 for Coll. Hen: Ridgly
on the East side the No: Bra: of Patt. River Rent —.. 10.. 6¾
Poss^r Charles Ridgly.

Turkey Island

333 A: Sur: 27: Sep: 1694 for Neal Clark lying
at Rogues harbour bra: head of Patt: River   Rent —.. 13.. 4
Poss^r Neal Clark.

Warfeilds Range

1080 A: Sur: 10: Xber 1694 for Rich^d & John
Warfeild lying on Middle River   Rent 2.. 3.. 2½
Poss^{rs} 540 A: John Warfeild
   240 A: Benj. Warfeild
   150 A: Caleb Dorsey
   150 A: Geo. Yate

  1080

Owen's Range

162 A: Sur. 15 Feb. 1688 for Richd Owen in A.
A. Co.   Rt. —.. 6.. 6
Poss^r Ambrose Nelson

Chelsy

117 A: Sur: 21: Nov. 1695 for Lan: Draper in
A. A. Co.   Rt.
Mr Bladen affirms to me this Land is in Elder sur-
veys of his about Withers Durand.

Hamonds Forrest

362 A: Sur: 31: Octob. 1694 for John Hamond at
the head of Severn River   Rent —.. 14.. 6
Poss^r the same Hamond.

Huntington Quarter

259 A: Sur: 28: Nov. 1694 for Hen: Ridgly Senr
& Hen: Rid: Junr lying at Huntington   Rent —.. 10.. 4½
Poss^r Coll. Henry Ridgly.

Desert

158 A: Sur: 12: May 1696 for Thomas Blackwell
on Patt: Riv^r   Rent —.. 6.. 4
Poss^r John Dorsey.

Come by Chance

200 A: or thereabout granted the 28th May 1692 to
Michaell Birmingham & Escheat to his Lords^p for
want of heires of Michael Cusack granted und^r
such Rent as they were to the s^d Cusack,   Rent —.. 8.. —
Poss^r Jos: Hill.

Ruly's Search

74: A: Sur: 26: July 1696 for Autho: Ruly lying
on the No: Side of South Riv^r   Rent —.. 2.. 11½
Poss^r Saml Ruly.

Good Mothers Endeavour

285 A. Res^d 23. Aprill 1698 for Elinor Howard
50 A: p^t thereof being Howards Thicket entred in
page 66 & 50 A: p^t of the Woodyard entred in pa:
61 the rem^a is Surplus   Rent —.. 5.. 7½
Poss^r Wm Maccubin in Right of Elin^r Howard.

Howard's Search

121 A: Sur: 10: Nov: 1696 for John Howard at
the h^r bounds of Howards Mount   Rent —.. 4.. 10¼
Poss^r Rich^d & Alexa. Warfeild Ex^{rs} John Howard.

Howards Discovery

50 A: Sur: 19: Xber 1696 for John Howard in
A. A. Co.   —.. 2.. —
Poss^{rs} Rich^d & Alex: Warfeild Ex^{rs} John Howard.

What is left

105 A: Sur: 20 Xber 1701 for Amos Peirpoint on
Lowsers Branch   Rent —.. 4.. 2½
Poss^r Saml Peirpoint.

Addition

80 A: Sur: 1: Nov: 1701 for Sam: Young at bo^d
white Oak in Rob: Clarksons line   Rent —.. 3.. 2½
Poss^r Saml Young.

Addition

50 A: Sur: 5: Aug. 1702 for Wm Jones on the
South Side Severn River   Rent —.. 2.. —
Poss^r Wm Jones.

Smiths Addition

45 A: Sur: 6th June 1695 for Edwd Smith on the
North side of Severn   Rent —.. 1.. 9¾
Poss^r Tho: Banks, his Heir in England.

Ben's Discovery

380 A: Sur: 23: Xber 1704 for Benj^a Warfeild on
the West side of Fowlers bra: at the end of the
N & W line of Grimeston   Rent —.. 15.. 2½
Poss^r same Ben: Warfeild.

   C. Benj^a Discovery.

Young's Range

300 A: Sur: 15 Mar: 1704 for John Young at the
head of Severn River above Severn Bridge at a bo^d
Popular in the Main Run   Rent —.. 12.. —
Poss^r Saml Young.

Howards Inheritance

449 A: Sur: 23: Mar: 1669 for Sam: Howard 100
A. p^t thereof having been p^t of a tract of Land
called Chance entred in pa: 63 & 200 A: more p^t
thereof having been p^t of Warner's Neck entred in
page 67 the remainer is Surplus   Rent —.. 9.. —
Poss^r Tho: Tolly by his marriage with Kath: the
    widow of the s^d Samuell Howard.

Burle Bank or Burles Hill

450 A: Sur: 15 June 1650 for Rob: Burle bo^d on the No. with Chesepeak bay. This Land is affirmed by Stephen Burle to be the same Land now called Burles Hill Sur: 15 June 1658 & they found to cont^a but 200 A: for wch q^t it was Res^d 21 July 1666   Rent —.. 4.. —

Poss^r Stephen Burle.

Holmans Hope

100 A: Sur: 15: June 1650 for Abra: Holman bo^d on the East with Chesepeak Bay. This Land was layd out in the Neck of Land that makes the bay & mouth of Magothy Riv^r but none now claimes nor can the certain place of any line of it be found.

Pen Lloyd als Swan Neck

570 A: Sur: 2^d Xber 1650 for Edwd Lloyd on the No: side of Severn River. Mr Lloyd Sur^d this Land again the 15th Sep: 1659 & then was found to be 600 A: & called Swan Neck the which upon a further Res: 22 May 1667 of 370 A: was found to be 471 A: so that the whole tract was found to be 671 A: —.. 13.. 5¼

Poss^r 471 A: Coll. Hamond from Capt. Conaway
      100 A: d° from Tho: Reynolds
      100 A: Fran: Mead

    ———

    671

C. Pen Loyd als Swan neck Sur: 2 Xber 1650 for Edwd Loyd on ye N. Side of Severn River. Mr Loyd Sur: this land again 15 Sep. 1659 & then was fo^d to contain 600 a & call^d Swan Neck 300 a part whereof he sold to Tho: Turner who sold to James Connaway who resur: ye same May 22, 1667 & fo^d to be 471 a. The oth^r 300 a ye sd Loyd sold

100 a pt thereof to R^d Horner 100 a more to Xtoph^r
Rolles & 100 a to James Smith who resur: his 100 a
ye 30 Mar 1674 & fo^d to be 250 a, ye 471 a of Con-
naways & ye 100 a of Horners are now ye Right of
Coll Hammond ye 100 a of Rolles now in possion
of Fr^a Mead & ye 250 a of Smiths now Philemon
Smith, the whole Cont^a 921 a

Scotland

600 A: Sur: 26: Nov. 1652 for Richd Ewen near
Fishing Creek on the Bay side a little above the
north point of Severn River — .. 12.. —
Poss^r 200 A: Thomas Homwood
      200 A: Lewis Jones
      100 A: Joshua Merikin from Ja: Heath
       50 A: ditto Merriken
       50 A: Joshua Merikin son of Hugh Merriken

      600

Young's Land

250 A: Sur: 28th Sep: 1652 for Richd Young on
the No: side of Severn River near Burks Creek.
And alsoe 250 A: Sur: 30th Sept 1652 for the s^d
Young joyning to the former on the No: thereof R. — .. 10.. —
Poss^{rs} 100 A: Wm Pennington
       75 A: A: Josua Merriken
       75 A: Tho: Hanson
     150 A: Rich^d & Ralph Moses Orphans
       75 A: each
     100 A: Edward Gibbs lives on but know
         not his title.

Covell

200 A: Sur: 27 Octob 1651 for John Covell joyning to the Land of Wm Durand   Rent — .. 4.. —
Poss^r Tho: Tench Esqr for James Rigbys Orphan

Hawkins

600 A: Sur: 27: Sep: 1652 for Ralph Hawkins
near Maggothy River. Wm Hawkins of Patapsco
River is Son & Heir of the said Ralph Hawkins,
he does not claim this Land nor has his father ever
alienated it th^t appears, but the Land is now in
other Surveys possessed.

Little Hawkins

150 A: Sur: 30 Sep: 1652 for Ralph Hawkins on
the South Side of Maggothy River   Rent —.. 3.. —
Poss^rs 125 A: Wm Hawkins of Balto. Co.
    25 A: layd in the Town at Maggoty.

150

Homewoods Lott

210 A: Sur: 1^3: Feb^ry 1650 for James Homewood
on the East Side of Goury's Creek   Rent —.. 4.. 2½

Homewood

210 A: Sur: 13: Feb^ry 1650 for James Homewood
at the mouth of Maggoty River & Patt: in the name
of Thomas Homewood. This Land was Res^d by
the s^d Tho: Homewood the 2^d Aug. 1666 & then
found to be but 140 A.   Rent —.. 2.. —
Poss^r John Ingram for James Homew^ds Orphan.

MARYLAND RENT ROLLS.

Broad & Town Neck Hundred, 1707
Town Neck

250 A: Sur: 18: Nov. 1658 for Nath: Utie on the
East side of Severn River   Rent —.. 5.. —
Poss^r Coll. Charles Greenbury

    C. See also p. 98 of original Mss.

    C. Town Neck Resur. 2 Xber 1714 for Robt
Goldsborough. Beg. at a bounded Pine on a small
creek side Being ye Orig^{ll}. Bound^r Pat. 10 Ap.
1717. 275 a.

Hopkins Plantation

215 A. Sur; 5th Sept. 1659, for Wm Hopkins on
the No: side Severn River joyning to Henry Cat-
lines.   Rent —.. 4.. 3¾
Poss^{rs} 107 A: John Brice for Worthingtons Orp^{ns}
    145 A: Wm Crouch for John Howard's
        Orp^{ns}

---

    252   37 A: over.   Rent —.. —.. 9

Howardston

100 A: Sur. 16: Sep. 1659 for Phillip Howard on
the north side of Severn River   Rent —.. 2.. —
Poss[r] John Brice for Jn[o] Worthingtons Orp[ns]

Asketon

350 A: Sur: 8: Sep: 1659 for John Askew on the
East side Severn River joyning to W[m] Crouches
Land   —.. 4.. 7¼
Poss[r] Rich[d] Hampton

Pendenny als Expectation

200 A: Sur: 14 Sep: 1659 for Edward Lloyd
Esq[r] on the No: side of Severn River—M[r] Lloyd
sold this Land to Tho: Meares who Res[d] it the 17
Mar. 1664 & added 100 A. more to it calling the
whole Expectation   —.. 6.. —
Poss[r] John Brice for Worthington's Orphans

Rigby

125 A: Sur: 20 Sep[r] 1659 for James Rigby being
two pcells on the North side Severn Riv[r] on the
South side Broad Creek   Rent —.. 2.. 6
Poss[r] Thomas Tench Esq[r] for James Rigby's
    Orphans

Fuller als Whitehall

150 A: Sur: 21: Sep: 1659 for W[m] Fuller on
the No: side Severn River on the No: side of
Homew[ds] Creeke   Rent —.. 3.. —
Poss[r] Coll. Cha: Greenbury

Maidenston

250 A: Sur: 22: Sep. 1659, for Eliz[a] Strong on
the No: Side Severn River on the East side broad
Creeke   —.. 5.. —
Poss[r] Widow Rider

Clarkston

100 A: Sur: 5th Octob^r 1659 for Matt: Clark near
Dorrells Creek   Rent —.. 2.. —
John Ingram for Ja: Homewoods Orp^{ns}

Brownston

100 A: Sur: 20: Octob^r 1659 for Tho: Brown on
the North side Severn River joyning to Hen: Cat-
lins   —.. 2.. —
Poss^r Charles Rivers for his wifes Children left
  them by W^m. Hopkins

Crouches Triangle

60 A: Sur: 18: Mar: 1661 for Wm Crouch on the
No: side of Severn River near the back line of No:
Crouchfeild litle Neck   Rent —.. 1.. 2½
Poss^r Phillip Jones

  C.   Crowch's Triangle.

Woolchurch Rent

10 A: Sur: 12 Xber 1662 for Hen: Woolchurch
on the No: side Severn River being Sev^{rll} pcells
of Town Land   Rent —.. 2.. 2½
Poss^r Wm Bladen

  C.   Woolchurch.

Leonard Neck

290 A: Sur: 17: Feb^{ry} 1662 for Hen: Woolchurch
on the South side Maggoty River on the West side
Magotty Creek   Rent —.. 5.. 9¾
Poss^{rs} 146 A: Tho: Hanson
      124 A: Edwd Gibbs
       20 A: Joshua Merriken, it did belong to
              to the Orp^{ns} of Wm Coventry for
              want of Heirs of whom I suppose it
              be Escheat to his Lo^P.

Litle Piney Neck

80 A: Sur: 20th Octob^r 1662 for Wm Hopkins on
the South side of Maggoty River between the
Wester most brd: of Forked Creek & Piney Neck
Creek   —.. 1.. 7¼
Poss^r Charles Rivers for his wifes Children left
   them by Wm Hopkins

Pytherston

60 A. Sur: 22 Sepr 1659 for Wm Pythers on the
E^t side broad Creek   Rent —.. 1.. 2½
Poss^r Thomas Homewood

Hopkins Chance

100 A: Sur: 20. Octob. 1662 for Wm Hopkins on
the South side of Maggoty River   Rent —.. 2.. —
Poss^{rs} 50 A: Henry Hilliard
        50 A: Daniell Hilliard
        ———
        100

Hopkins Fancy

100 A: Sur: 25 Octob. 1662 for Wm Hopkins on
the No: side of Severn River in Eaglenest bay
Poss^r John Gadsby
                                             Rent —.. 2.. —

Barren Neck

150 A: Sur: 13: Xber 1662 for Richd Devois on
the West side Ferry Creek at the head of Strongs
Cove   Rent —.. 3.. —
Poss^r Wm Taylard
   C. Devour.

Howard's Inheritance

130 A: Sur. 23 Jan^{ry} 1663 for Matt. Howard on
the North side of Severn River   Rent —.. 2.. 7¼
Poss^r John Brice for Worthington's Heires

Midle Neck

50 A. Sur. 9 Feb. 1662 for Tho: Underwood on the
North side Severn Riv[r] by a bra: of Ferry Creek
Poss[r] Tho: Cockey for Rich[d] Moses Orp[ns]   R. —.. 1.. —

Durands Place

100 A. Sur: 14 Feb. 1662 for Alice Durand on the
North side of Severn River on the West Side Du-
rands Creek   Rent —.. 2.. —
Poss[r] W[m] Bladen

The Plain

100 A. Sur. 16 Feb. 1662 for Rob. Tyler & Abr.
Dawson on the no. Side Severn River   Rent —.. —.. —
   C. Rob[t] Taylor. . . . Vacated on Record.

Slayd's Hope

50 A. 20th Feb. 1662 Sur. for W[m] Slayd on the
No. side of Severn River   Rent —.. 1.. —
Poss[r] Edw[d] Peak

Truroe

50 A: Sur: 20: Feb. 1662 for Tho. Turner on the
north side of Severn River   Rent —.. 1.. —
Poss[r] Coll Hamond

Lusby

50 A: Sur: 6: Mar. 1662 for Rob: Lusby on the
No. Side Severn River on the W. side Ferry Creek.
                                          R. —.. —.. —
This Land was Alienated by Jacob Lusby to
Thomas Bucknall to whose Orphans it belongs if
any left else it is Escheat

Broad Creek

200 A. Sur. 5 Octo. 1659 for W[m] Fuller on the
No. Side Broad Creek.   Rent —.. 4.. —
Poss[rs] 75 Hen: Merriday

75 Mary Eagle
50 Rob. Jubb for Jona; Neal's Orp^{ns}

─────

200

Skidmore

200 A: Sur: 21. Ap^l 1663 for Edwd Skidmore at a
M^{r}ked W^t Oak on the So: Side Fishing Creek

Rent —.. 4.. —

Poss^r John Ching for Sam: Skidmore's Orp^{ns}

Burle's Town

100 A: Sur. 16, March 1662 for Rob. Burle on
the Et side Ferry Creek   Rent —.. 2.. —
Poss^r Rob:· Boone

Brushy Neck

100 A: Sur: 19: Octob 1663 for Rob. Tyler on
the No: side of Severn Riv^r at a M^{rk} Red Poplar
in the line of Tho: Turner   Rent —.. 2.. —
Poss^r 50 A: Coll Hamond
     40 A: Wm Clark
     10 A: Alex^r Gardiner

─────

100

Deep Creek Point

100 A: Sur. 19: Octob 1663 for Abra: Dawson
on the N^o side of Deep Creek   Rent —.. 2.. —
Poss^r Tho: Dawson

Heires Purchase

90 A: Sur: 3: Feb. 1663 for Sarah Marsh for the
use of Tho: Marsh her son at the Ferry place Rent —.. 1.. 9¾
Poss^r Sebastian Olly's Widow

Netlam

50 A: Sur: 1st June 1663 for John Askew on the
No: side of Severne River   Rent —.. 1.. —
Poss^r Edmund Talbot

Wolf Neck

100 A: Sur: 2ᵈ June 1662 for Wᵐ Slaid on the
No: side Severn River on the West side Ferry
Creek   R. —.. 2.. —
Possʳ Mary Eagle

  C. Wᵐ Slayd.

Strawberry Plain

100 A: Sur: 8ᵗʰ June 1663 for Wᵐ Hopkins on
the No: side Severn River between Swan Neck
& litle Piney Neck   Rent —.. 2.. —
Possʳ Coll. John Hamond

Greenbury

50 A: Sur: 14. July 1663 for John Green on the
North side Severn River near Netlam   Rent —.. 1.. —
Possʳ Tho: Reynolds

Woodham

50 A: Sur: 18: Aug. 1663 for Abra: Holman on
the North side Severn River on the Nor. side Broad
Creek   Rent —.. 1.. —
Possʳ Joshua Merrikin

Brushy Neck bottom

100 A: Sur: 9. Octob. 1663 for Wᵐ Hopkins on
the South side of Magoty River   Rent —.. 2.. —
Possʳ 50 A. Wᵐ Penninton

    50 A. John Hunt of Baltemᵒ Co.
    ———
  100

  C. Bushy Neck Bottom.

Deep Creek Neck

50 A. Sur: 20: Octob 1663 for Rob: Tyler on the
West side of Deep Creek North of Severn Rivʳ

                            Rent —.. 1.. —

Possʳ John Worrall

Forked Creek Point

100 A: Sur: 20. Octob 1663 for Rob: Tyler on
the South side of Magoty Riv^r.   Rent —.. 2.. —
Poss^r Alex^r Gardiner

Homewood's Purchase

260 A: Sur: 2^d Feb: 1663 for John Homewood
on the No. Side of Severn Riv^r near Homew^ds
Creek.   R. —.. 5.. 2
Poss^r Tho: Homewood

Wadlington

150 A: Sur: 3. Feb: 1663 for John Homewood
on the Nor: Side of Severn Riv^r by Homew^ds
Cre   Rent —.. 3.. —
Poss^r Tho: Homewood

Brushy Neck

150 A: Sur: 20: May 1664 for Edwd Bates on the
South Side of Maggoty River   Rent —.. 3.. —
Poss^r John Sumerland

Ralph's Neck

100 A: Sur: 18 Feb. 1663 for Ralph Hawkins on
the South Side of Maggoty River   Rent —.. 2.. —
Poss^r Wm Hawkins lives at Potapsco

Hawkins Habitation

100 A: Sur: 19; Feb. 1663 for Ralph Hawkins on
the North Side of Severn Riv^r in bro^d Neck   Rent —.. 2.. —
Poss^r Wm Bladen

Swan Cove

50 A: Sur: 19: Feb. 1663 for Emanuell Drew on
the East side of Ferry Creek   Rent —.. 1.. —
Poss^r Henry Merriday

C. Eman Dreie.

Homewood's Parcell

60 A: Sur. 20. Feb. 1663 for John Homewood on
the North Side of Severn River in Broad Neck

Rent —.. 1.. 2½

Poss^r Tho: Homewood

Deep Creek Point

50 A: Sur: 2^d Feb. 1663 for Thomas Turner on
the South of Maggoty River joyning to Swan Neck —.. 1.. —
Poss^r Coll. John Hamond

Long Neck

50 A: Sur: 24 Feb: 1663 for Elis^a Dorrell on the
North of Maggoty River   Rent —.. 1.. —
Poss^r Wid^o Boston

Gray's Sands

50 A: Sur: 23: Feb: 1663 for Tho: Turner on
the North side of Maggoty River   Rent —.. 3.. —
Poss^r 90 A. Wm Clark
    60 A. Zach: Gray
    ———
    150

Crouches Triangle

40 A: Sur: 12: May 1664 for Wm Crouch on the
No. Side of Severn Riv^r Rent —.. 1.. 9¾
Poss^r Rebeckah Hancock

  C. Crowch's Triangle cf. ante.

Litle Netlam

50 A: Sur: 20: May 1664 for John Askew on the
No. side of Severn River   Rent —.. 1.. —
Poss^r Edmund Talbot

Merrikin

50 A: Sur: 1: June 1664 for Christian Merrikin

on the No. side Severn Riv^r on the No: side
Scotchers Creek   Rent —.. 1.. —
Poss^r Joshua Merrikin

Tanyard

120 A: Sur: 2^d June 1664 for Thomas Thurston
on the North Side Severn Riv^r in Bro^d Neck   R. —.. 2.. 5
Poss^r Wid^o Ann Lewis

Cole's Point

50 A: Sur: 7th Octob^r 1665 for Thomas Cole on
the Eastern side of Fullers Creek on Severn River —.. 1.. —
Poss^r James Heath

Solomons Desire

10 A: Sur: 13: Nov: 1665 for Wm Hill on the
No. Side Severn Riv^r   Rent —.. —.. 2½
Poss^r Phillip Jones

Orwick

190 A: Sur: 30: Nov: 1665 for James Orwick on
the Mountaines begins at a Hiccory by the bay
side of Tho. Homewoods Land   Rent —.. 3.. 9¾
Poss^r John Ingram for Ja: Homewood's Orphan

Mosses Purchase

100 A: Sur: 29: Nov. 1665 for Rich Moss on the
Mountaines by Maggoty River   Rent —.. 2.. —
Poss^r John Ingram for Ja. Homewoods Orpⁿ

Hopewell

30 A: Sur: 14: Feb. 1665 for Wm Hopkins on the
Nor: side of Severn River   Rent —.. —.. 7¼
Charles Rivers poss^r for his wifes Children left
them by Wm Hopkins

Midleland

40 A: Sur: 14. Feb. 1665 for Hen: Cattlyn on

the North side of Severn River at the River side

Rent —.. —.. 9¾

Poss^r Cha: Rivers as in Hopewell

C.   Hen. Catline.

Brown & Clark

50 A. Sur. 14: Feb. 1665 for John Brown & John
Clark on the North Side Severn Riv^r R. —.. 1.. —
Poss^r Charles Rivers as in Hopewell

Tyler's Lott

100 A. Sur: 15: Feb. 1665 for Rob. Tyler on the
North side Severn River by Matt: Howards Land
Poss^r Charles Rivers for his wife Children as in
Hopewell

Rent —.. 2.. —

Great Pyney Neck

100 A: Sur. 15th Feb. 1665 for Wm Hopkins on
the North Side of Maggoty River   Rent —.. 2.. —
Poss^r Charles Rivers for his wifes Children

Howard's Folly

100 A: Sur: 20th Feb. 1665 for John Howard on
the South Side of Maggoty River   Rent —.. 2.. —
Poss^r John Clark

Smith's Range

100 A: Sur: 22. Mar: 1665 for Herman Solling on
the North Side of Severn River   Rent —.. 2.. —
Poss^r Charles Rivers for his wifes Child^n as in
Hopewell

Range

50 A: Sur: 20. May 1666 for Eliz^a Hill on the
Nor. Side Severn River at the bo^d tree of Green-
bury   .R. —.. 1.. —
Poss^r Morrice Baker

Crouches Milldam

70 A: Sur: 17: May 1666 for Wm Crouch at the
Nor: Side Severn River near Cro^s Triangle   R. —.. 1.. 5
Poss^r Thomas Albrix

———————————

MARYLAND RENT ROLLS.

ANNE ARUNDEL COUNTY.

Broad & Town Neck Hund[d], 1707
Crouch's Calf Pasture

30 A. Sur: 17: May 1666 for William Crouch on
the No: side of Severn River   Rent —.. —.. 7¼
Poss[r] Phillip Jones for Tho: Jones.

Chance

25 A: Sur: 6. Aug[t] 1666 for Geo. Yate on the E[t]
side of Severn River   Rent —.. —.. 6
Poss[r] W[m] Bladen.

Homewoods Range

150 A: Res. 3[d] Aug. 1666 for John Homewood
on the North Side of Maggoty River on the
North side of Homewoods Creek   Rent —.. 3.. —
This Land was first layd out for 390 A. after
for 140 A. & at last for 150 A. as above
Poss[r] John Ingram for James Homew[ds] Orp[n].

The Complement

100 A: Sur. 3[d] Aug. 1666 for Thomas Homewood near the Mountains on Maggoty Riv[r] Rent —.. 2.. —
Poss[r] John Ingram for Ja: Homewoods Orp[n].

Homewood's Chance

300 A: Sur. 3[d] Aug[t] 1666 for John Homewood
at mr[k] Red Oak at the mouth of Youngs Cove
near the head of Ferry Creek   Rent —.. 6.. —
Poss[r] Rob. Eagle.

Pettybone's Rest

280 A. Sur. 31. July 1666 for R^d Pettybone
near Burles Pond near Maggoty River   —.. 5.. 7¼
Poss^r Wid^o Lewis.

Blays Neck

200 A: Sur. 1st Aug. 1666 for Edwd Blay at
the head of Homewoods Creek in Severn Riv^r
Poss^r Robert Eagle.   R —.. 4.. —

Rich Neck

90 A: Sur: 30 July 1666 for John Rockhold
being a Neck of Land & bounding on the So: wth
Fuller   —.. 1.. 9¾
Poss^r Tho. Homewood.

Linnenston

300 A: Sur: 24: May 1667 on the Mountaines
for Paul Darrell at a bo^d Hiccory by a Valley
side of Maggoty River   Rent —.. 6.. —
Poss^{rs} 150 A. John Peasly
     150 A. John Ingram for Robinsons Orp^{ns}.

300

Baker's Encrease

80 A: Sur. 28. Ap^l 1667 for Morrice Baker on
the North side of Severn River near Greenbury
Poss^{rs} 50 A: Wm Gosnell   R. —.. 1.. 7¼
     30 A: Tho. Reynolds

80

Addition

400 A. Sur. 3^d July 1668 for James Connaway
& Tho: Turner on the North Side Severn Riv^r R. —.. 8.. —
Poss^r Coll John Hamond.

Graves End

30 A. Sur. 1st June 1669 for Geo. Norman at a

bo^d Oak on the No. Side of Severn Riv^r by the
bayside   R. —.. —.. 7¼
Poss^r Edmund Talbot.

Normans Fancy

25 A: Sur: 14 June 1669 on the North side of
Severn River for Geo: Norman   Rent —.. —.. 6
Poss^r John Gadsby.

Brutons Hope

40 A: Sur. 24. March 1667 for John Bruton at
a bo^d tree of the Land formly Layd out for Rd.
Salmon   Rent —.. —.. 9¾
Poss^r Edward Hall.

Hogg Neck

70 A: Sur . . . for Wm Davis on the North side
Severn River being a Neck of Land   —.. 1.. —
Poss^r Tho. Homewood.

Wheelocks Chance

50 A: Sur. 19. July 1670 for Edward Wheelock
at a bo^d tree of John Ray's   R. —.. 1.. —
Poss^r John Hanson.
   C.   Poss^r Tho. Hanson.

Pawsons Plain

400 A: Sur: 24 8ber 1670 for John Pawson between the bra: of Magotty & Potapsco Riv^r on
the head of Beaver Dam Creek   Rent —.. 16.. —
Poss^r 200 A: John Peasly
     200 A: d^o as Exc^r of Patt: Murphy.
     ———
     400

Cornfeild Plain

100 A. Sur: 23 Octob 1670 for Thomas Turner
on the East side of Cornfeild Creek   Rent —.. 4.. —
Poss^r John Ingram for Ja: Homewoods Orphan.

Homewoods Addition

150 A: Sur: 23rd Octob 1670 for Tho. Homewood   R^t —.. 6.. —
Poss^r John Ingram for Ja: Homewood's Orphⁿ.

Forked Neck

50 A: Sur. 23rd Octob 1670 for Tho. Turner &
James Conaway on the So: side Magotty Riv^r
Possr Coll. John Hamond.   Rent —.. 1.. —

Hopkins Encrease

100 A. Sur. 18: Octob^r 1670 for Wm Hopkins
on the South Side Maggoty River at bo^d tree of
the Land of Edwd Wheelock   Rent —.. 4.. —
Poss^r Chas. Rivers for his wifes Children.

*C. Patent in Tho. Tolly's hand as marrying
wth ye Wid^o Howard.*

Deep Point

60 A. Sur. 14, June 1669 for Wm Hopkins on
the South side Magotty River on the So: Side
of Deep Creep Creek
This is affirmed to me to be taken away by Tho.
Dawson's Deep Creek point entred in 85.

Baker's Folly

100 A. Sur: 26. Octob^r 1670 for Richd Bayly on
the North side of Maggoty River at Sandy Point
Poss^r Willm Clark.   R. —.. 4.. —

Sturton's Rest

110 A: Sur: 26. Octob 1670 for Geo: Sturton
on the No: side of Maggoty River on Cedar
point   —.. 4.. 2
Poss^r Hen. Maynard.

Huckleberry Ally

100 A. Sur. 3^d Nov. 1670 for John Homewood

in Rich Neck at a Chestnut of Wadlington Rent —.. 4.. —
Poss^r Thomas Homewood.

C.. Hickleberry ally.

Slades Addition
50 A: Sur. 3^d July 1671 for William Slade at
the head of Slades Branch   Rent —.. 1.. —
Poss^r Mary Eagle.

Alcots Triangle
70 A. Sur. 3 July 1671 for Sam. Alcot on the
East side of Severn in Levy Neck branch   R. —.. 1.. 5
Poss^r Tho: Homewood.

Flushing
100 A. Sur. 6: July 1671 for Thomas Turner
between Severn & Magotty Rivers   Rent —.. 2.. —
Poss^r Coll John Hamond.

Ferfatt
30 A: Sur. 6th July 1671 for R^d Bayly between
Severn & Magotty Rivers   Rent —.. —.. 7¼
Poss^r James Carr.

Bate's Chance
80 A: Sur. 7th July 1671 for Edward Bates on
the No. side of Severn River at a bo^d pine tree
of John Askew   Rent —.. 1.. 7¼
Poss^r Richard Hampton.

Litle Brushy Neck
75 A: Sur: 12. Feb: 1671 for Wm Hopkins on
the side of Magoty River at a bound pine by
Hopkins Creek
This Land was Res^d by the s^d Hopkins 30 July
1682 & then found 150 A: Rent —.. 6.. —
Poss^r Richd Sarrell.

Stincicombs Addition
36 A: Sur. 30. Octob 1671. for Nath Stincicomb
in the broad Neck & run N. E.   Rent —.. —.. 8¾
Poss^r Wid^o Lewis.

Ratle Snake point

50 A: Sur: 16: Feb. 1667 for Wm Illingsworth
at Ratle Snake point   Rent —.. 1.. —
Poss^r Wm Bladen Esqr by his purchase of the
same as Escheat for want of Heirs of . . .

Addition

150 A: Sur: 21: Mar. 1665 for Xtop^r Rolles on
the E. side of Eagle nest Bay on the No: of
Severn   Rent —.. 3.. —
Poss^r 50 A: John Harwood for John Cusin.
   C.   Pos^{rs} John Gadsby 50^a, Rd Hampton 100^a.

Choice

50 A: Sur. 22. Mar. 1665 for Jno Dearing about
a quarter of a mile from Eagle Nest Bay   Rent
   C.   This Survey as I'm inform'd lett fall.

Dearings Encrease

100 A: Sur: 22. Mar: 1665 for Jno Dearing on
the north side of Eaglenest bay   Rent
   C.. This Survey as I'm inform'd lett fall.

Brown's Quarter

20 A. Sur. 21: Nov. 1667 for James Brown at
the East of Durand's Creek   Rent —.. —.: —
I cannot find any owner or claimer of this Land
but is pretended to be in Elder Surveys.

Smith's Range

112 A: Sur. 1st Octob 1678 for Wm Hopkins on
the North Side of Severn Riv^r on a bra. of
Magotty River   Rent —.. 4.. 6
Poss^r Charles Rivers for his Wifes Children as
in Hopewell.

Friendship

160 A: Sur: 3^d Octob 1678 for Joseph Freind
and Wm Cook on the So: side of Maggoty River
Poss^r Jos: Connaway.   Rent —.. 6.. 5

Grays Range

100 A: Sur. 7: Jan^{ry} 1675 for John Gray on
the No. of Maggoty by Grays Sands   Rent —.. 4.. —
Poss^r Zachary Gray.

Strongs Leavings

125 A: Sur: 12th July 1675 for Edwd Whee-
lock on the E^t sid^e Severn Riv^r on Ferry
Creek   R. —.. 5.. —
The last poss^r of this Land was Geo. Eager for
Wheelocks Orphans.

Browns Peace

52 Acres Sur: 26. June 1676 for Tho. Brown
on the West side Severne River   Rent —.. 2.. 1
Poss^r Tho: Brown.

Homewood's Town

635 A. Sur: 20. Aprill 1678 for Tho. Homewood
near Danills Inheritance   Rent 1.. 5.. 5
Poss^r John Ingram for Ja^s Homew^{ds} Orp^n.

Tylers Lott

100 A. Sur. 5. July 1679 for Rob. Tyler on the
North Side of Maggoty Riv^r Rent —.. 4.. —
Poss^r John Wood.

Hallets Lott

50 A: Sur. July 6: 1679 for Jacob Hallet on the
No: Side Magotty River   Rent —.. 2.. —
Poss^r Wm Clark.

Randall's Fancy

5½ A: Sur: 8: July 1679 for Christop Randall
on the No. side Severn Riv^r at a bo^d Stump of
Hopkins Fancy   Rent —.. —.. 3
Poss^r John Gadsby.

Brown's Folly

270 A: Sur: 9th July 1679 for Tho: Brown at a
bo[d] Oak of Hopkins   Rent —.. 10.. 9¾
Poss[r] Same Brown.

Cuckold's Point

100 A. Sur. 10. Octob 1679 for Will[m] Cockee
on the No. Side Maggoty River   Rent —.. 4.. —
Poss[r] Same W[m] Cockee's Orp[n].

Randalls purchase

102 A: Sur. 23. Apr: 1680 for Christop Randall
on the No. Side Severn River by Norman's
Fancy   —.. 4.. 1
Poss[r] John Gadsby.

Martin's Nest

150 A: Sur: 23. Aprill 1680 for Martin Faukner
on the North Side of Severn River   Rent —.. 6.. —
Poss[r] William Bladen.

Sewells Encrease

500 A: Sur. 25. May 1680 for Henry Sewell on
the North Side Severn River   Rent 1.. —.. —
Poss[r] 250 A: Amos Garret
       150 A: Phillip Sewell.
       100 A: Josua Sewell

———
500

Philk's Rest

316 Sur: 24. Aprill 1680 for Edw[d] Philks, on
the No: Side Severn River   Rent —.. 12.. 7¾
Poss[r] 158 A: Will[m] Smith
       158 A: John Todd

———
316

Eagleston's Range

206 A: Sur: 25 May 1680 for Bernard Eagleston

on the No. Side of Severn River at the mouth of
Cypress Swamp Creek   Rent —.. 8.. 3
Poss[r] Abra. Child.

Grays Encrease

300 A: Sur. 16. June 1680 for John Gray on the
No. Side Severn River by Martins Nest   R. —.. 12.. —
Poss[rs] 190 A. John Gadsby
          50 A. Joseph Smith
          60 A. John Brice
          ———
          300

Hopkins Addition

100 A. Sur. 17. June 1680 for W[m] Hopkins between Maggoty & Severn Riv[rs]   Rent —.. 4.. —
Poss[r] Cha: Rivers for his Wifes Children.

The Contest

100 A: Sur. 17. June 1680 for Will[m] Hopkins
near Maggoty River   Rent —.. 4.. —
Poss[r] Charles Rivers for his Wifes Children.

Randalls Range

100 A: Sur: 17: June 1680 for Christop Randall
on the So. Side Maggoty River   Rent —.. 4.. —
Poss[r] John Gadsby.

Bear Neck

225 A. Sur. 19: June 1680 for Fran: Mead
at the mouth of Cattayl Bra: on the South Side
of Maggoty River   Rent —.. 9.. —
Poss[rs] 161 A: Fran: Mead
          64 A: Tho. Robinson
          ———
          225

Greenberry's Forrest

450 A: Sur. 15. June 1680 for Nich Greenberry
by Cattayl Creek north side Severn   Rent —.. 18.. —
Poss[r] John Brice for Worthington's Orphans.

Lewis's Addition

325 A: Sur: 20. Sep. 1678 for Henry Lewis by
Cypress Swamp Creek   Rent —.. 13.. —
Poss^r John Brice for Worthington's Orp^{ns}.

Phelp's Encrease

300 A: Sur. 20. June 1680 for Walter Phelps by
Cypress Swamp on the West side of it   Rent —.. 12.. —
Poss^r Tho: Riccaut.

Sutton's Choyce

307 A. Sur. 20 July 1680 for Tho: Sutton on
the So: Side Maggoty River   Rent —.. 12.. 3½
Poss^r Tho: Robinson.

Aldridge's Beginning

300 A: Sur. 20 Aug. 1680 for Nich: Aldridge
on the So: Side Maggoty Riv^r Rent —.. 12.. —
Poss^r Nich^o Aldridge.

Hanslaps Range

300 A: Sur: 20. Aug. 1680 for Henry Hanslap
on the North Side So:River joyns to Phelps Encrease   R. —.. 12.. —
Poss^r Wid^o Eliz^a Chew tho' she denys to pay
Rent for it.

Blands Quarter

200 A. Sur: 14: Aug. 1680 for Tho: Bland on
the No. Side Severn River   Rent —.. 8.. —
Poss^r Jos. Smith.

Freindship

100 A: Sur: 24: May 1681 for Thom: Brown &
Wm Hopkins about 2 miles from the head of
Severn in the Woods   Rent —.. 4.. —
Poss^r Widow Stevens.

Hopkins Forbearance

142 A: Sur: 9th Aug. 1681. for Wm Hopkins on

the South Side of Maggoty River at great Pyney
Neck   Rent —.. 5.. 8¼
Poss^r Charles Rivers for his Wifes Children.

Somerland's Lott

60 A: Sur: 3^d Augt 1681 for John Somerland on
the South Side Maggoty River near the head of
Bates Branch   Rent —.. 2.. 5
Poss^r John Somerland.

The Heart

60 A: Sur: 3^d Augt 1681 for Wm Bewsey on
the So: Side of Maggoty Riv^r on the point of a
fork of Back Creek   Rent —.. 2.. 5
Poss^r Wm Cockee in right of his Wife Mary
Crouch.

C. William Cocky.

Roper Gray

480 A: Sur: 4th Aug. 1681 for [Nil]

C. Not in C.

Hall's Parcell

100 A: Sur: 6: Aug: 1681 for Josiah Hall on
the North Side of Maggoty Riv^r on the E^t side of
Bayly's Creek   Rent —.. 4.. —
Poss^rs 50 A: Benj^a Gardiner in Right of his
           wife Ann Hall
     50 A. . . . Hall the other sister
     ———
     100

Cockey's Addition

130 A: Sur. 6: Augt 1681 for Wm Cockey on
the North Side of Maggoty River   Rent —.. 5.. 2½
Poss^r John Wood.

Lunns Addition

55 A: Sur. 7. Aug. 1681 for Edward Lun betw^n
Severn & Maggoty Rivers   Rent —.. 2.. 2½
Poss^r Wm Cockey of Balt. County.

Woodcocks Nest

30 A: Sur. 7: Aug. 1681 for Thomas Wood on a
bra. of Maggoty River   Rent —.. 1.. 2½
Poss[r] John Somerland.

Rowles Chance

11 A: Sur. 9. Aug. 1681 for Christop Rowles on
the South Side of Magotty River on litle piny
Neck point   Rent —.. —.. 5½
Poss[r] Christop Rowles Orp[n].

Diamond

200 A: Sur. 28: Sep: 1681 for Tho: Brown four
miles above the head of Severn River   Rent —.. 8.. —
Poss[r] Amos Peirpoint.

Greenifston

700 A: Sur: 29. Sept. 1681 for James Greeniff &
assigned Nich Painter four miles above the head
of Severn River   1.. 8.. —
Nich. Painter made a will in this Province
wherein he disposed of his Lands but it's sayd
he made another will after in England and there
again Divised them, none claimes this Land at
present.

Wheeler's Lott

200 A: Sur. 23 Jan[ry] 1681 for John Wheeler on
Cattayl Creek   Rent —.. 8.. —
Poss[r] Matt: Beard.

Content

150 A: Sur: 4: Aug. 1681 for Geo: Saughier
joyning to Aldridges Beginning   Rent —.. 6.. —
Poss[r] R[d] Cromwell.

Proctor's Park

518 A: Sur: 4: May 1682 for Rob. Proctor on
the North side of Maggoty River   Rent 1.. —.. 8¾
Poss[r] Hen: Maynard.

Foothold

135 A: Sur: 7: Sep: 1682 for Tho: Pennington
on the So. Side of Maggoty at Luffmans Lands   —.. 5..
Poss^r 67½ A: Alex^r Gardiner
    67½ A: William Pennington

———

135

Addition

22½ A. Sur. 29. Sep: 1682 for Samuell Underwood on the No: Side Severn Riv^r Rent —.. —.. 11
Poss^r John Hurst of Balt. Co.

Howards Addition

22½ A: Sur: 28: Sep: 1682 for Matt: Howard
on the Nor: Side Severn River by Underwoods
Land   Rent —.. —.. 11
Poss^r Wm Crouch for Jno Howards Orp^n.

Burles Park (Nil)

200 A. Sur: 21: May 1689 for
  C. Not in C.

Cockey's Addition

25 A: Sur. 23 May 1683 for Wm Cockee joyning
to his other Land   Rent —.. 1.. —
Poss^r Tho. Cockee.
  C. Thomas Cockey.

Orwicks Fancy

150 A. Sur. 15th May 1683 for James Orwick
on the North side of Severn River on the East
side of Eaglenest Bay   Rent —.. 6.. —
Poss^r Mary Eagle.

Milford

717 A. Sur. 17. July 1683 for Robert Proctor
on the North side of Maggoty River   Rent —.. 8.. —
Poss^{rs} 200 A: John Wood
The rest of this Land Rob. Proctor never sold &
is Escheat for want of Heires of him.

Dorsey's Addition

50 A. Sur: 19. Octob 1683 for Joshua Dorsey in
the Woods at a bo[d] Hiccory on John Howards
Land   Rent —.. 2.. —
Poss[r] John Dorsey.

Mutuall Consent

50 A: Sur. 20 June 1683 for W[m] Cockey between Severn & Magotty Rivers   Rent —.. 2.. —
Poss[r] John Hurst of Baltemore Co:

Howards Pasture

200 A. Sur: 18 July 1684 for Tho: Lytfoot assign[d] Geor: Yates & from him to Geo. Burges on
the North of Magotty River   Rent —.. 9.. 5½
Poss[r] John Gresham Jun[r].

*C.. Howards Pasture, 200 a. Sur. 18 July
1683 for Math Howard on y[e] W Side y[e] heead
of Maggoty river Poss[r] John Brice for Worthingtons orpn[s].*

*The next entry in C is The Health 236 a with
text identical with that here given for Howards
Pasture. Evidently copyists error in mixing up
two different entries.*

Peasly's Lott

109 A. Sur. 20 July 1684 for John Peasly on
the North side of West River.   Rent —.. 4.. 4½
Poss[r] Wid[o] Boston.

Gibbs's Folly

200 A: Sur. 5. July 1684 for W[m] Gibbs on the
South Side of Maggoty River at abo[d] tree of
Suttons Choyce   Rent —.. 8.. —
Poss[r] Tho: Robinson.

Chance

32 A: Sur: 3: Sep. 1684 for Robert Taylor on
the South Side of Maggoty River   Rent —.. 1.. 3½
Poss[r] Alex[r] Gardiner.

Murphys Choice

125 A: Sur. 19. July 1684 for Pat: Murphy on
the N. E. side of Grayes Creek in Mag. Riv[r] Rent —.. 5.. —
Poss[r] Zachary Gray.

Luck

155 A: Sur. 27: Aug. 1684 for Mary Gardiner
on the So: Side of Magotty River   Rent —.. 6.. 2½
Poss[r] Edw[d] Gibbs for Mary Gardiner.

Nicholson's Addition

32 A. Sur: 29 Aug: 1684 for John Nicholson
on the So: Side of Cornfeild Creek on the No. of
Mag. Riv[r]   —.. 1.. 3½
Poss[r] Wid[o] Boston.

Homewoods Outlett

60 A. Sur. 24: Mar. 1684 for James Homewood
on the No. side of Maggoty River   Rent —.. 2.. 5
Poss[r] John Ingram for Homew[ds] Orp[n]

Litleworth

132 A: Sur: 25th July 1684 for Cap[t] Richard
Hill on the North side of Severn River   R. —.. 5.. 3
Poss[r] Jos. Hill.

Bettys Point

90 A: Sur: 7: Aprill 1684 for Rich[d] Bayly on
the West side Maggoty Creek   Rent —.. 3.. 7¼
Poss[r] Joshua Merrikin.

Pyney Plain

70 A: Sur: 8-Apr. 1684 for Rich[d] Bayly on the
North side of Maggoty River   Rent —.. 2.. 9¾
Poss[r] Wid[o] Ann Lewis.

    C. Piny Plain.

Bennets Chance

124 A: Sur: 25 May 1684 for John Bennet on

the North side of Homewoods Creek near Blay's
Branch   Rent —.. 4.. 11½
Poss^r Tho: Homewood.

Floyds Chance

60 A: Sur. 17 June 1686 for John Floyd on the
South side of Maggoty Riv^r Rent —.. 2.. 5
Poss^r John Floyd.

Gray's Adventure

184 A: Sur. 24 July 1685 for John Gray and
Ass^d Ralph Bazill on the No. Side of Maggoty
Creek   Rent —.. 7.. 4½
   C.—Poss^r Jno Cooly's orp^{ns}.

Mosses Purchase

32 A. Sur: 24 Apr. 1685 for Richd Moss on the
So. Side of Maggoty River   Rent —.. 1.. 3½
Poss^r Tho: Cockey for R^d Mosses Orp^{ns}.

Luffman's Due

131 A: Sur: 5th Sept. 1685 for Wm Luffman on
the South Side of Maggoty River   Rent —.. 5.. 3
Poss^{rs} 65½ John Hurst of Baltemore Co.
      65½ Wm Pennington.

   ——

131

Bayly's Content

24 A: Sur. 24: Aprill 1685 for Richd Bayly on
the South Side of Maggoty Riv^r Rent —.. —.. 11½
Poss^r Joshua Merrikin.

Gray's Lott

239 A: Sur: 24: July 1685 for John Gray on
the No: Side of Magotty River   Rent —.. 9.. 6¾
Poss^r Thomas Bank's heires in England.

Tryall

164 A: Sur: 15 Aprill 1685 for Edward Jones
on the South Side of Maggoty River   Rent —.. 6. 6¾
Poss^r Henry Brown.

Ray's Chance

115 A: Sur: 27 Mar: 1687 for John Ray on the
So. Side of Maggoty River   Rent —.. 4.. 7¼
Poss^r Joshua Jones by Marriage with Ray's
daughter.

Dorrills Luck

76 A. Sur: 27th Mar. 1687 for Paul Dorrell on
an Island the mouth of Maggoty River   Rent —.. 3.. 0½
Poss^r John Ingram for Robinsons Orp^{ns}.

The Pound

68 A. Sur. 6. June 1687 for Tho: Richardson
& Assigned to Richd Beard on the So: Side of
Maggoty on the West of Beards Creek   Rent —.. 2.. 8¾
Poss^r Matt: Beard.

Huckleberry Forrest

1611 A: Sur. 6: June 1687 for Tho: Richard-
son & assigned Richd Beard on the So. Side of
Maggoty   Rent 3.. 4.. 5½
Poss^{rs} 545 A: Matt: Beard.

         138 A: Tho. Robinson

         330 A: Tho. Johnson

         114 A: Edwd Hall

         375 A: John Harwood by his marrying
                    the relict of Cosins

         130 A. Fran: Mead

         100 A. Escheat to his Lott for want of
     ——   heirs of Ann Bernard.

   1611

Midleborough

11 A. Sur: 26: Mar. 1688 for Nich. Greenbury
on the No. side of Severn River   Rent —.. —.. 5½
Poss^r Charles Greenberry.

Ironstone Hill

115 A: Sur: 10 May 1687 for Edward Gibbs
on the South Side of Maggoty River   Rent —.. 4.. 7½
Possr Edwd Gibbs.

Bennets Park

81 A: Sur: 7: Octob 1687 for John Bennet on
the South Side of Homewoods Creek   Rent —.. 3.. 3
Possr Tho: Homewood.

Clarks Purchase

70 A: Sur: 20 June 1686 for Wm Clark on the
No. Side of Maggoty River   Rent —.. 2.. 9¾
Possr Wm Clark.

Gadsby's Adventure

33 A. Sur. 28 Xber 1694 for John Gadsby on
the No: side Severn River   Rent —.. 1.. 4
Possr Same Gadsby.

Neal's Purchase

198 A: Sur: 23: June 1694 for Jonathan Neal
on the Nor: Side of Maggoty River   Rent —.. 7.. 11¼
Possr Rob: Judd for Jona: Neal's Orphns.

Nicholsons Addition

36 A: Sur: 16: Jan. 1694 for John Nicholson on
the No. side of Severn   Rent —.. 1.. 5½
Possr Wido Boston.

Homewood's Enlargemt

100 A: Sur: 6: Aug. 1695 for James Homewood
lying on the North of Maggoty Rivr   Rent —.. 4.. —
Possr John Ingram for Ja: Homewoods Orpns.

Kendall's Purchase

100 A. Sur. 6: Aug. 1695 for John Kendall on
Magotty River   Rent —.. 4.. —
Possr Jacob Peacock by Marr: Kendalls Widow.

Penningtons Search

100 A: Sur. 6. Sep: 1695 for Wm Pennington
North of Severn River   Rent —.. 4.. —
Poss^r . . . Pennington.

  C. Poss^r William Pennington.

Marsh's Forrest

60 A. Sur. 30. Octob^r 1696 for John Marsh
lying near the Bra. of Severn River   Rent —.. 2.. 5
Poss^r same Marsh.

Homewood's Search

78 A: Sur. 20. Jan^{ry} 1698 for Tho. Homewood
on the So: side of Magotty River   Rent —.. 3.. 1½
Poss^r John Ingram for Ja^s Homew^{ds} Orp^n.

Mosses Discovery

80 A: Sur: 19: July 1702 for Ralph Moss on
the North side Blay's Branch near Maggoty R:
                       Rent —.. 3.. 2½
Poss^r Hen. Brown for Rd: Mosses Orp^{ns}.

Davistone

240 A: Sur: 17 Xber 1702 for Thomas Davis at
the head of Severn near Rogues Harb^r Rent —.. 9.. 7¼
Poss^r Same Davis.

Laylards Enlargem^t

54 A: Sur: 10 Jan^{ry} . . . for Wm Laylard on
the So: Side of Maggoty River   Rent —.. 2.. 3
Poss^r Same Laylard.

Dawson's Guift

80 A. Sur: Jan^{ry} 1701 for Mary Fuller near
Maggoty   Rent —.. 3.. 2½
Poss^r Tho: Dawson.

Contents of the Hundreds in the Whole County

Herring Creek Hund: £ 36.. 10.. —¾
West River Hund: 19.. 5.. 1¾

South River Hund.	61..	2..	9½
Midle-Neck Hund:	49..	6..	5
Broad & Town Neck H.	44..	6..	5½

£210.. 10.. 10½

Lands in Ann Arrundell County Escheatable to His Lords^p

pa

100	pt. Dinah Ford's Beaver dam upon the death of John Standforth who holds by the Curtisy of England	3
200	pt Hunts Chance upon the death of John Gadscross who holds by the same Curtisy	5
54	Holloways Encrease	12
100	Parrishes delay	25
150	Comb	57
70	Angle	74
50	Lusby	84
517	pt. Milford	96

267

271